PENGUIN BOOKS

THE VOICE OF WAR

The Salamander Oasis Trust, a registered charity, was founded in 1976 by the editors and poets who participated in the original OASIS in the wartime Middle East. More than 17,000 poems and related documents – UK and Commonwealth – have been collected and donated to the Imperial War Museum to form a unique archive, a reference source for years ahead. 'A literary windfall' – *The Times*

Victor Selwyn, MBE, was born in London in the First World War and served as a foot soldier in the Second World War. He had graduated from the London School of Economics. On leave in Cairo in 1942 with David Burk, from the pre-war *Daily Mirror*, chasing the fate of his book on map reading and navigation (the subject he instructed), he met Denis Saunders – 'Almendro', the South African poet – and so launched OASIS, the anthology of poetry from the Middle East forces. His war ended in Italy, where he had his first reporting assignment for *La Gazzetta dello Sport*, Milan. Back home life was divided between research, using the Socratic method to get nearer the truth, and writing for newspapers ranging from the *Sunday Mirror* to economics features in the *Guardian*, and from research on containerization for *Rationeller Transport*, Frankfurt, to vetting scientific and medical stories. In 1976 he founded the Salamander Oasis Trust and co-edited five anthologies. In Brussels he produced the 'Guide to National Practices, Western Europe'. His hobby is reading.

D0048026

THE SALAMANDER OASIS TRUST

Fifty years after the end of the War in Europe – and fifty-two years after the original OASIS in wartime Middle East – we present this new collected edition of Second World War poetry. It comprises a considered selection from past anthologies, together with poems we have not previously been able to include, especially from the Commonwealth – from Canada, Australia and from the Uys Krige archive in South Africa.

As in our previous anthologies, this collection includes both the established poets one expects in a Second World War collection and the OASIS input – the poets, mostly unknown, we have discovered through appeals in the media and from so many kindly people who have volunteered information and sent us privately published editions and service magazines. The criteria for inclusion remain the same, i.e. poems written during the Second World War by those serving. (There are one or two exceptions where the poem must go in.) Poems written at the time enjoy an immediacy that later writing can only rarely recreate.

The Salamander Oasis Trust is a Registered Charity (274654) founded in 1976 by editors and poets who participated in the original OASIS. Over a decade and more, 14,000 poems have been collected and, published or not, lodged in the Imperial War Museum to form a unique archive, a reference source for years ahead. The Trust is also concerned with education and taking the poetry of the Second World War into schools. Lady Ryder of Warsaw is Trust Patron.

In contrast to other anthologies the OASIS anthologies are the work of a team – a team drawn from those who served in the Second World War and whose judgment is first-hand.

The Voice of War

POEMS OF THE SECOND WORLD WAR

The Oasis Collection

EDITOR-IN-CHIEF
Victor Selwyn

EDITORIAL ADVISERS
Denis Healey, Hamish Henderson, Robin Ivy,
Clifford Simmons, Jon Stallworthy

PENGUIN BOOKS

Published in Association With The Salamander Oasis Trust

PENGUIN BOOKS

Published by the Penguin Group
Penguin Books Ltd, 27 Wrights Lane, London w8 5tz
Penguin Books USA Inc., 375 Hudson Street, New York, New York 10014, USA
Penguin Books Australia Ltd, Ringwood, Victoria, Australia
Penguin Books Canada Ltd, 10 Alcorn Avenue, Toronto, Ontario, Canada m4v 3b2
Penguin Books (NZ) Ltd, 182–190 Wairau Road, Auckland 10, New Zealand

Penguin Books Ltd, Registered Offices: Harmondsworth, Middlesex, England

First published by Michael Joseph 1995
Published in Penguin Books 1996
1 3 5 7 9 10 8 6 4 2

Typeset in Monophoto Bembo
by Datix International Limited, Bungay, Suffolk
Printed in England by Clays Ltd, St Ives plc

In Memory

ALLISON, John Drummond: Lieutenant, East Surrey Regiment *Italy, 2 December 1943*

ALLWOOD, John Brian: Leading Aircraftman, RAFVR *Italy, 30 June 1944*

BOURNE, David: Pilot Officer, 43 Squadron RAFVR *United Kingdom, 5 September 1941*

BURT, William H.: Lieutenant, Highland Light Infantry *Germany, 10 April 1945*

CHAVE, O.C.: Flight Lieutenant, 15 Squadron RAF *Over Europe, 14 February 1943*

DOUGLAS, Keith C.: Captain, Derbyshire Yeomanry *Normandy, 9 June 1944* ★

GOLDSMITH, Anthony M.: Lieutenant, Royal Artillery *North Africa, 24 April 1943*

JARMAIN, William John F.: Major, Royal Artillery *Normandy, 26 June 1944*

KEYES, Sidney A.K.: Lieutenant, Royal West Kent Regiment *North Africa, 29 April 1943*

LEWIS, Alun: Lieutenant, South Wales Borderers *Burma, 5 March 1944*

LINMAR, E.: Sergeant Pilot, Royal Air Force *13 August 1940*

RICHARDSON, George Sydney: 36 (Torpedo Bomber) Squadron, Royal Air Force *26 January 1942*

SHARLAND, Malcolm N.: Lieutenant, Royal Engineers *Wounded Cassino 1944, died 19 July 1946*

SPENDER, Richard W.O.: Lieutenant, Parachute Regiment *North Africa, 28 March 1943*

STRICK, John Richard: Captain, Royal Ulster Rifles *Italy, 18 February 1944*

THOMPSON, William Frank: Major, Royal Artillery *Bulgaria, 10 June 1944*

WHITE, Alan V.H.: Lieutenant, Royal Artillery *Cassino Italy, 12 May 1944*

★ Served with Sherwood Rangers

Regiments and Units as listed by the War Graves Commission and War Office Records.

Dedication

From earliest times the poet has been war's reporter. In our anthology we have over one hundred named reporters, some with no names, who took part in war and saw and wrote with a poet's eye. They wrote mainly of people. For war is about people, those who survive and those who do not.

Many who did not return were the poets.

This, then, is also their memorial, to live on with their fellows, who returned speaking to generations to come of what men and women did, thought and felt in the War of Nineteen Thirty Nine to Forty Five.

Let it be the last!

V.S.

Contents

Note on the Arrangement of Poems

We have arranged the poems by six theatres of war, together with AIR and SEA and a final section THE WAR ENDS.

Generally within each area the poems are arranged alphabetically by names of the writers. However, in the 1939–40 section, clearly the poems about Norway and Dunkirk belong to the end. The POW poems appear in the theatres of war in which they were written. The Home Front poems cover the Blitz and the units serving at home from 1941 onwards. Most of the poems on the women's services will be in this group. Olivia Fitzroy's poems are included in the Naval section as the fliers were members of the Fleet Air Arm and she herself a Wren.

Finally, we have singled out two poems with which to 'frame' the entire anthology. Firstly, Dennis McHarrie's 'Luck' which, although written in the Desert Air Force, truly speaks for all who have served – any service, any war. It is timeless. The anthology concludes with Frank Thompson's moving memorial poem 'Polliciti Meliora'.

VICTOR SELWYN: Born Battersea, London. L.S.E. Co-founder OASIS, Middle East, 1942. Instructed Navigation and Map Reading Unit and wrote handbook. Served later in Italy. Post-war MBE., journalist and researcher. Joint founder of The Salamander Oasis Trust.

DENIS HEALEY: Born 1917. Served N. Africa and Italy, Beachmaster at Anzio. Major. Labour MP S.E. Leeds, 1952. Various government offices including Defence and Chancellor of the Exchequer. Baron Healey of Riddleston, 1992. Author of *My Secret Planet* and other works.

HAMISH HENDERSON: Born 1919, Blairgowrie, Perthshire. Dulwich College and Downing, Cambridge. Intelligence Officer 51st Highland Div. at Alamein. Mentioned in despatches. At Anzio liaison with Italian Partisans. Research Fellow, School of Scottish Studies, Edinburgh.

ROBIN IVY: Born 1919, Bedford. 1st Kensington Support Mg and Mortars, 78 Div. N. Africa, Italy and Austria. Read English at Cambridge. Teacher, now poet and artist.

CLIFFORD SIMMONS: Commissioned 6th Field Regt R.A. Liaison Officer 1st British Corps. Normandy D-Day. Mentioned in despatches. Staff Officer Germany and India. Director Alan Wingate (Publishers). Chairman Poetry Society 1981.

JON STALLWORTHY: Ox & Bucks Light Infantry 1953–5. Editor OUP 1959–71, Deputy Academic Publisher OUP 1972–4. Professor of English, Cornell University, Ithaca, NY. Visiting Fellow, All Souls, Oxford. Numerous awards including E.M. Forster Award 1976. Fellow, Royal Society of Literature.

INTRODUCTION
by Denis Healey

The last two world wars were unique in our history, not least for the cultural shock they inflicted on the whole of our society. Each of them took millions of young men and women away from their families and friends at the most sensitive stage in their lives. It put them into uniform to serve under strict discipline with total strangers in closed communities. It sent them abroad to kill other young men and women hundreds or thousands of miles away in cities, fields and mountains, in deserts and jungles. Finally, it subjected them to long periods of paralysing boredom, punctuated by short bursts of extreme excitement in which the prospect of death was always present.

For most of these men and women the war was the most intense experience they were ever to know. Thousands, who found the pressure almost too much to bear, turned to writing poetry as the only way of releasing it – for the first and often the last time in their lives. So both wars produced a cataract of poetry.

However, the poetry of the Second World War was very different from that of the first. Most of the poets we know of in the First World War were writing in the hope of publication. They were nearly all men, and men with university degrees, largely from public schools; Isaac Rosenberg was one of the few exceptions. The patriotic exaltation which led them to volunteer stumbled when they came face to face with the horrors of trench warfare. For the first time they began to ask how the war had come about. It was the old champion of the ordinary soldier, Rudyard Kipling, who gave them the answer: 'If any question why we died, Tell them, because our fathers lied.'

So the poems, plays and novels of the First World War expressed a mood of bitter contempt for the politicians and brasshats, together with a profound pity for their victims. The pacifism they engendered came to dominate the feelings of the next generation. In the middle nineteen thirties, the news of the concentration camps began to transform this pacifism into anti-fascism. By the time my generation had to face the Second World War we believed that we had no alternative but to fight the uncontestable evil of Nazism;

but we had no illusions about the fate which awaited us. Wilfred
Owen and Siegfried Sassoon had told us what to expect, though
the nature of our ordeal turned out to be rather different.

Except for Cassino, the Anzio beachhead and the last winter on
the Gothic Line in Italy, there was little trench warfare. Millions
served in the Middle and Far East and North-West Europe. The
Air Force was far larger, there were many more women in
uniform and the home front was subjected to heavy air raids. So
the poetry of the Second World War was far more diverse than
that of the First. Most of its poets came from ordinary homes, and
wrote their poems with no thought of publication. Some of the
best were from the Dominions, such as the South African Uys
Krige, the Australian infantryman J.E. Brookes and the New
Zealander Les Cleveland. A few of the Scots preferred to write in
Gaelic, making them even less acceptable to a literary establishment
based in London.

For all these reasons the poetry of the Second World War made
less impact on the peacetime public than that of the First. It offered
no equivalent to the intense concentration on the horrors of trench
warfare and it had no clear message, of hope or despair. As Dennis
McHarrie wrote:

> He died who loved to live,' they'll say,
> 'Unselfishly so we might have today!'
> Like hell! He fought because he had to fight;
> He died that's all. It was his unlucky night.

Some of the poets, such as Henry Reed, Sidney Keyes, Keith
Douglas and Gavin Ewart became well known at the time; others
were published later. But the great majority would have remained
unknown for ever but for the work of three young men serving in
Cairo in 1942, the most senior then a corporal. Victor Selwyn,
David Burk and the South African poet, Denis Saunders, appealed
to all serving men and women in the Middle East to submit poems
for inclusion in an anthology called *Oasis*. Within three months they
had collected 3,000 poems, selected 121 and persuaded another
group of enthusiasts in the Salamander Society to get them pub-
lished. The Society sold out the entire edition in Cairo in a matter
of months.

Nearly forty years later, the Salamander Trust, as it had become,
published *Return to Oasis* in London; this included the best of
another thousand wartime poems from the Middle East. There

followed *From Oasis into Italy*, which also covered the campaigns in North Africa and Italy. In 1985 Everyman's (Dent) Library published another Oasis selection, *Poems of the Second World War*. By then Victor Selwyn and his fellow-editors, Erik de Mauny and the late Professor Ian Fletcher, had collected more than 14,000 poems written on active service, from every phase and theatre of the war.

Their anthologies form an astonishing treasury, invaluable to historians no less than to all who love poetry. Commenting on some 'sad-coloured volumes' of history she had been given for review, Virginia Woolf wrote 'the machine they describe . . . but the heart of it they leave untouched. At any rate, we are left out, and history, in our opinion, lacks an eye.'

The Oasis collection gives history a thousand eyes, all with the sharp immediacy of a war photographer, but with a range and depth of insight which only poetry can provide. Besides men already known as poets, there are men who later became known for other reasons – Enoch Powell and Lord Hailsham, Spike Milligan and Dirk Bogarde, Kingsley Amis and Erik de Mauny, and above all Frank Thompson, whose death by firing squad in Bulgaria robbed the world of what might have been a great political leader as well as a major poet.

Some of the best poems, however, are by ordinary men and women who were moved to write only by the intensity of their feelings in the war. Anyone who served in the forces at that time will find poems which speak directly to them. It was a delight for me to find The D-Day Dodgers again, on the printed page. As a wartime beachmaster, I was particularly moved by Sean Jennet's trance-like apparition from an assault landing, Mahoney. I also felt for the first time what it was like to be a parachutist or a bomber pilot.

Most moving of all are some of the poems by young women, who describe not only the heartbreak of losing their loved ones but also the initial panic they felt at being thrown into barracks with other women from totally different backgrounds. Lisbeth David's lovely valedictory at the war's end must speak for thousands of other temporary women soldiers: 'But hey nonny the lark and the wren, I trow we shall never be meeting again.'

Very little class feeling could survive in the pressure cooker of the Second World War. The sense of common humanity overrode all else. Few fists were shaken at the politicians and the brasshats. The higher educational standards which made the poetry possible

affected the generals, too. In his foreword to the original *Oasis*,
General 'Jumbo' Wilson talked of those who found the war an
'aesthetic desert' – a phrase which would not have come so easily to
General Haig. Later collections owe much to spirited advice from
Field Marshal Lord Carver and General Sir John Hackett. The
former, as a young tank commander in the desert (GSo1 7th
Armoured), gave his General *Anna Karenina* to read before the
battle of Alamein.

Very few people who served in the last war will read the poems
in this book without pleasure and emotion. For those who did not
serve, they offer a unique understanding of what the last great
cataclysm meant for men and women like themselves. They demon-
strate the power of poetry to capture emotion, to calm the spirit
and to illuminate history. For those reasons no library and no
school should be without them.

FOREWORD
by General Sir John Hackett

The once widely-held conviction that while some fine poetry had come out of the First World War nothing of any value had emerged from the Second, has taken time to shake. This collection of poems from the Second World War, put together by the Salamander Oasis Trust, should do much to help ensure its final demolition. Those responsible for collecting and publishing the poems little knew what they were starting when some of them brought together verse originating in the wartime Middle East and published it under the title *Return to Oasis*, with an open request for more. Those people were pulling out a stopper, and, if they expected a trickle, could not fail to be surprised at what turned out to be a deluge. The compilers were the victims of their own huge success and the editorial burden was enormous. The BBC put on a presentation of this verse in an *Open Space* programme in July 1987. The Radio Four 'Not for Glory' programme, repeated twice, drew yet more manuscripts which have continued to come in for eventual deposit in the Imperial War Museum, where there are now more than 14,000 poems.

The question of what qualifies for inclusion in a collection such as this, chosen against what criteria, remains a lively one. The poems that have been chosen must have been written in time of war and offer clear evidence that they would have been written only under wartime pressure. Literary merit must occupy the highest place in our criteria *but not the only one*. It is the breathing of the human spirit that we have to hear, in all its many different modes. It has been so important to rescue and preserve what still remained of this wartime self-expression. Just as important, to me at any rate, is the need to fill out the human backdrop against which great events were played, by sketching in something of the character of those playing in them. I think of this collection in all its variety as a glimpse at part of the structure within which the 'history' was made, a sort of environmental archive without which all the factual chronicles of events and all the hardware on display have little meaning.

THE SECOND WORLD WAR: AN HISTORICAL REVIEW
by Field Marshal Lord Carver

The 1939–45 war was more truly a world war than the 1914–18 conflict, known as The Great War until the second one competed for the title. Both started as European conflicts, and were extended to regions beyond Europe and over all the oceans; but the entry of Japan, which was already at war with China, into the arena in 1941, directly involving the USA, which was already indirectly involved through Lend/Lease, made it truly a world war, affecting all continents and oceans. Neither Hitler, when he invaded Poland in September 1939, nor Britain and France, when they delivered an ultimatum to him to withdraw, imagined that it would spread to a global conflict. Both sides, as in 1914, thought that, although aerial operations might wreak horrific destruction on cities, hostilities on land and at sea were not likely to last long or to extend beyond Europe and the shores of the Mediterranean.

The origin of the war was the growing insistence of the British and French people that the extension of Germany's power by force over the smaller countries of Eastern Europe could no longer be tolerated. Austria had succumbed in 1938 and Czechoslovakia in 1939. Attempts to restrain Hitler's ambition by diplomatic means had failed ignominiously, and the situation had gravely turned for the worse when the Soviet-German non-aggression pact was signed on 23 August, 1939. The British Chiefs of Staff had warned the Prime Minister, Neville Chamberlain, that on no account should Britain be involved simultaneously in war with Germany, Italy and Japan, who since 1936 had been loosely allied in two separate pacts, one between Germany and Italy, the other between Germany and Japan. Germany invaded Poland on 1 September, 1939. When Germany refused to accept the British and French ultimatum to withdraw from Poland and war was declared on 3 September, neither Italy nor Japan joined in. Poland was speedily overrun and the bombing of Warsaw set a pattern for similar attacks in the world war that followed.

The so-called 'phoney war' that followed, in which there were no hostilities between the two sides, not even in the air, was broken when British and French intervention in Norway in April 1940 was forestalled by the German invasion of that country and Denmark. The result was disastrous for the British forces which took part in that ill-fated and ill-organized expedition. They had just succeeded in capturing Narvik when Germany launched its offensive in France and the Low Countries. The British army there saw little fighting before it was withdrawn from Dunkirk and Cherbourg in June, leaving all its equipment and nearly 40,000 prisoners of war behind.

Britain now stood alone, its people led by Winston Churchill, determined to resist. The German-planned invasion of Britain with the assembly of barges in Continental ports did not materialize, as the would-be invaders could not gain command of the skies. In the great air battles of September 1940, the RAF inflicted sufficient losses on the Luftwaffe to stop any moves across the Channel and North Sea. The Luftwaffe, however, continued its bombing of British cities whilst in return Britain's Bomber Command mounted a prolonged offensive against German towns and industry, to which Fighter Command made an essential contribution. While the 'few' of the RAF fought over South East England, Britain began its operation in the Middle East, the only place where its forces faced those of Mussolini's Italy. This campaign, which was to last until 1943, proved to be the last major campaign which Britain, with its Commonwealth partners, would direct on its own.

In December 1940 O'Connor attacked at Sidi Barrani and, in a brilliant campaign, routed the Italians, the remnants of whom were finally cut off and defeated south of Benghazi in February 1941. Meanwhile Wavell's forces had attacked the Italians in Ethiopia from north and south, defeated them and forced their surrender in May.

By that time the Germans had come to the rescue of their Italian ally in North Africa and in Greece, which Italy had invaded from Albania without consulting Hitler in October 1940. British forces had been sent to Greece in March 1941, weakening those in Libya facing the newly arrived Rommel, who drove them back to the Egyptian frontier, isolating the Australian garrison of Tobruk. The troops in Greece saw little fighting, being forced to retreat. The New Zealanders and many of the British were transferred to Crete, which fell to German airborne attack at the end of May. The whole course of the war was transformed by Germany's invasion of Russia in June 1941 and again by the entry of Japan into the lists in December 1941. Still at war with China, her forces occupied French Indo-China when France fell in 1940. On 8 December, 1941, as her naval aircraft struck at the American fleet in Pearl

Harbor, leading to the American declaration of war against her, her forces attacked Hong Kong and invaded Malaya. In Malaya the British forces, the army's divisions being Indian and Australian, were ill-prepared and badly deployed to face the battle-experienced Japanese. They were immediately forced to withdraw, as the RAF abandoned its airfields, the navy suffering a severe blow with the loss of the battleships *Prince of Wales* and *Repulse* to Japanese air attack. The culmination of this disastrous campaign was the fall of Singapore on 15 February, 1942, 130,000 British, Indian and Australian troops entering the grim compounds of Japanese prisoner-of-war camps. By then the Japanese had already invaded Burma.

The diversion of troops and aircraft from the Middle East had weakened Auchinleck's ability to withstand Rommel's counter-strokes in Libya. In February he had attacked and forced Ritchie's Eighth Army back to the Gazala Line, covering Tobruk. Rommel, after fierce tank battles round Tobruk, drove the Eighth Army all the way back to El Alamein, only fifty miles from Alexandria.

This was the low ebb of the war. But the tide was turning as the United States mobilized and deployed its strength, the first signs of this being seen in major naval battles against the Japanese in the Pacific. Montgomery's victory at El Alamein, coinciding with the Anglo-American landings under Eisenhower in French North Africa in November, the British contribution to which was Anderson's 1st Army, was followed by a massive Russian counter-offensive which encircled the German Sixth Army facing Stalingrad. From then on, the anti-Axis alliance, which styled itself The United Nations, of which Britain, the United States and the Soviet Union were the principal powers, was set on the path to victory. It was not to be an easy one and they were to see many setbacks, but progress towards victory was inexorable.

In May 1943 the German and Italian forces in North Africa surrendered at Tunis to the Anglo-American forces. The successful invasion of Sicily in July was followed by landings in Italy in September. But Hitler, who had originally decided to withdraw to the north, had second thoughts and decided to fight for every inch of Italy's rugged terrain. As a result the American, French and British forces were faced with fighting battles as fierce, and enduring hardships as great, as those experienced by their forbears in the First World War. The fiercest were those involved in trying to break into the Liri valley around Cassino, to which the landing at Anzio was intended to be a contribution, in the early months of 1944. The deadlock was broken in May, as Juin's French, in Mark Clark's US Fifth Army, broke through the Aurunci Mountains, and Anders's Poles, in Leese's British Eighth Army, at last cleared Monte Cassino.

Meanwhile, as Russia's huge armies struck blow after blow against the German armies and two days after Mark Clark's Fifth Army, under Alexander, entered Rome, Eisenhower's armies, under Montgomery, landed on the beaches of Normandy on 6 June 1944. But it was nearly a year later, on 8 May 1945, a week after British troops had joined hands with the Russians on the Baltic coast, before the German armies finally surrendered, those in Italy having done so three days earlier. In the Far East, Slim's Fourteenth Army had reconquered Burma and entered Rangoon on 2 May, 1945; but the war against Japan did not come to an end until after two atomic bombs had been dropped on Hiroshima and Nagasaki on 6 and 9 August. On 12 September the Japanese surrendered to Admiral Mountbatten at Singapore, and four days later to Admiral Harcourt at Hong Kong.

While these movements of armies and fleets had been taking place, two other campaigns of great significance had been in train: the Battle of the Atlantic, the anti-submarine war to keep the lifelines to Britain open, and the war in the air. The former, combined with escorting convoys of supplies to Russia, was the navy's principal campaign, in which RAF Coastal Command played a vital part.

The Second World War, like the First, saw the whole nation in arms. Civilians at home were at times as much in the front line as those in uniform, London and the South East being subjected to bombardment by V1 and V2 rockets until Montgomery's forces had cleared their launching sites in France and the Low Countries. The whole life of the nation was devoted to its war effort. As also in the First, the contribution of the British Commonwealth must not be forgotten, nor that of our allies. It was the war in Russia which bled the German armies to death. Without that, the British and Americans could not have prevailed on their own. The fact that it is now inconceivable that the nations of Western Europe could go to war against each other is proof that that effort was not in vain.

The cost of the war to its participants was high, although, in terms of human casualties, in Britain's case, much less than that of the First World War – 326,000 in uniform and 62,000 civilians dead, compared with 950,000 in the First.

Requiescant in Pace.

THE SOUND OF OASIS
by Martin Jarvis

I became aware of these extraordinary poems in 1980. My old mentor (and founder of the National Youth Theatre) Michael Croft asked me if I would read some of them at the publication-launch of the first collection, 'Return to Oasis'. 'What?' I thought. 'Poems of the *Second* World War? Surely he means the *First*. He must want me to read out some Wilfred Owen – or Rupert Brooke . . .'

I was wrong! Like most people, I had no knowledge of any poetry written between 1939 and 1945. I was to learn swiftly from Michael, and from Victor Selwyn, to whom we owe so much for the re-discovery of many of these remarkable poems, that an immense amount was written during the war. Much of it is very fine indeed, some of it aspires to greatness. All of it is heartfelt.

I don't think any of us who attended that first presentation were quite prepared for the shattering effect that the poems, when read aloud, would exert upon the audience. (Except perhaps Victor who, I think, had foreseen with what emotive force the poetry would be received.) It was amazing to witness tears in the eyes of hitherto hard-bitten news journalists, radio and television reporters, eminent military figures, as well as members of the public. Hard, too, for the actor – me – to read aloud without that tell-tale lump in the throat.

To hear a poem 'performed' in public is a different experience from reading it to oneself. The listener hears it once and has only a single opportunity to absorb its meaning, rhythms and nuances. When looking at the poem on the page the private reader has a chance to study the piece, to re-read it, to consider at length a particular word, line or stanza.

So what should the actor do, presented with this one opportunity, to communicate the poem? I have never been a subscriber to the 'declamatory' school of verse-speaking. I prefer to try to inhabit the mind and heart of the poet and, as it were, to 'place' the poem carefully and accessibly – without pushing for any external effects – for the listener to absorb.

Every poem demands a different approach. Each poet is unique,

too. The jagged, zig-zagging rhythms of Kenneth Wilson's 'Atlan-
tic Convoy', with its subliminal, sonic sound-effects, require deli-
cate handling. And a strong stomach. As a performer, if I can
achieve the right pitch and roll of delivery, I will, I hope, persuade
the audience almost to 'see' the ship's radar-screen, to *feel* the cold,
night-time tension and *hear* the boom of the depth-charges:

> Dropped astern, thrown to each quarter;
> brilliant flashes on the water . . .

Another tone is required for the extraordinary 'War Poet' by
Sidney Keyes – so powerful in its vision, in its expression of the
pity of war:

> I am the man who looked for peace and found
> My own eyes barbed.

I have to be careful, in speaking it, not to get in the way, not to
over-decorate it. It is, as it were, a perfect morsel – it needs no
garnish. I must, although projecting it forward to the listening ear,
allow it to speak for itself. 'Take care of the sense and the sounds
will take care of themselves,' the late Michael Croft used to say
when directing us in Shakespeare. He was right. And his own
evocative 'Leaving the Med' needs no vocal embellishment:

> We have raced periscopes
> Slanting for murder –
> From neat waves, seen water lap blood's blue serge
> From gun decks when ships screamed . . .

We can see the images in our minds. No acting required.

   The same with Sidney Keyes. If one can capture the poet's inner
tone of voice – which, I believe, will come from the actor's
understanding of the poet's intention – then the compact poem,
lobbed gently into the ether, explodes with blinding, prophetic
force on the ear.

   Another magnificent poem, 'Luck' by Dennis McHarrie, has a
devastating effect – particularly when read aloud. I have spoken this
poem on television, radio, in the theatre and in the hospitable
rooms of the Poetry Society itself. However I may vary my
interpretation, the effect of the final couplet is always the same: like
a cynically tossed grenade working its bitter havoc on an unsuspect-
ing audience.

   Each of these poems, like a solitary fragment of some vast

hologram, gives a particular angle of insight. Not only into the various theatres of war – Dunkirk, Africa, Europe; war in the air and at sea – but also the minutiae of life (and death) within those locations. How could a new generation better grasp, than from Peter Young's 'Recce in Bocage Country', what it actually felt like to be on that patrol in the wooded Normandy countryside, 'pinned down in the sunken lane'. Listening. Waiting – for death or survival. The tense, electric tempo and the unpredictable rhyming scheme keep us guessing, as in a thriller, to the last breathtaking moment.

This infinitely moving collection tells us what was really happening during the war – and what occurred in the minds of those who took part. In responding to these poems, in all their diversity of mood and event, we can almost see, hear and smell the war itself. We recognize its madness, its heartbreak and, importantly, its humour. We hear, from many points of view, the philosophy of war and the bitter questioning of its validity. We find ourselves experiencing, whether we read or listen, the courage – and the fear – at the front line. The desolation of the desert, the terror in the jungle. We understand too, some of us for the first time, the stoic heroism of those who waited at home. Through these words, through these inner voices, we view the sights of war. And the sounds.

Among these poets are some whose vision and humanity will, I think, extend for all time. John Jarmain – whose compelling, personalised memory of 'El Alamein' gives us an unforgettable perspective on 'That crazy sea of sand.' Sidney Keyes – whose 'War Poet' and 'Advice for a Journey' ensures his place in the front rank, along with Keith Douglas – who was killed in Normandy in 1944. The OASIS poets Denis McHarrie and John Brookes, whose poems are a pleasure and a challenge, and Peter Roberts, whose RAF poem 'Frayed End' commemorates a rare experience, a burial service for a bomber pilot in this country. There are so many voices in these poems of those who took part, but I end with perhaps the most moving, the voice of Frank Thomson – captured and shot in Bulgaria in 1944. In 'Pollitici Meliora' he sums up for a generation the pity, the heroism and the tragedy of war. Of all war:

> Write on the stones no words of sadness –
> Only the gladness due,
> That we, who asked the most of living,
> Knew how to give it too.

Try reading that aloud.

HOW I WROTE MY FIRST POEM
Spike Milligan

It was January, 1944, Italy. A small group of Gunners had come forward to a decimated wood outside the village of Lauro overlooking the Garigliano plain. We were to dig gun positions for our Battery to occupy (19 Bty 56 Heavy Artillery) for the forthcoming attack across the Garigliano river to coincide with the attack on Cassino, we being the left flank. Owing to our close proximity to the enemy, work had to be done (digging gun pits, command post etc) with great stealth – mostly at night, it was bitter cold weather – a mixture of icy rain and hoar frost in the mornings. One night when we had completed the work I was in my dug-out, it was a quiet night – occasional harassing fire – and sporadic small arms fire from various sentries – or patrols meeting in some area between the lines. I could hear digging – nearby – and thought it was a similar operation to ours – I remember saying to my trench-mate 'Thank Christ we've finished ours' – but the digging I could hear was a much grimmer affair. It was the London Scottish (or The Scabs Fuseliers) burying their dead. Suddenly to the sound of rain a lone piper struck up 'Over the Sea to Skye', the words of the song come to mind 'Carry the boy who's born to be king' – it was a haunting experience. Then 10 days later – by which time our guns had moved in – came a midnight disaster. A German gun found our range and a direct hit on Sgt. Wilson's gun position – the camouflage net caught fire – the charges started to explode – all were killed – or burnt to death except two. Next day we buried them – we had no piper – just the sound of the guns around us – I felt moved to write what was in fact my first poem. I offer it to Oasis for what it's worth.

THE WORLD OF THE POETS: A RETROSPECTIVE VIEW
by Victor Selwyn

'L'homme est l'instrument premier du combat'
Ardant du Picq, quoted by Viscount Wavell in 'The Good Soldier' (1945)

The wealth of poetry from the Second World War forms a unique genre in British and Commonwealth history. These poems were written by men and women from all services and ranks, in contrast to the narrow group of the First World War poets. Unlike them, so many leading poets did not return to continue writing and counter the myth that the Second World War produced little of note.

The IN MEMORY page of this anthology testifies to their dedication. We could add more. Many were leaders of their units undertaking tasks they could have delegated. But it was *their* war, they believed. It was an age of ideas and ideals, and from the destruction a better world would emerge. In half a century the world has changed but not in the way the compassionate generation of the Second World War envisaged or intended.

To help understand the men and women of that war and, above all, answer the question why so many wrote, let us begin with one man, as yet undistinguished, spending his twenty-first birthday, digging, not in the garden of the London home where he grew up, but with the Australian infantry at Thermopylae, Greece. It was 24 April 1941. By a strange chance the Aussies were awaiting a German attack on the same ground where Leonidas and his 300 Spartans had fought to the last man against the Persians over two millennia before. No plaque commemorated this piece of history, but the man digging, John Brookes, had read the Greek legends.

And there on his birthday surveying the Thermoylae Pass, John Brookes related the story of the Spartans to his Aussie Mate, Bluey – who was unimpressed. So left to his thoughts, John Brookes interweaved the legend of the past with the present fate of the Aussie infantry, in an epic poem which takes us through the twenty-four hours from the first alert.

Weeks later the poem – all 130 lines – was committed to paper in a POW camp at Salonika. Structured and polished it needed no revision. It was written with no thought of a publisher and stayed in a shoebox under the stairs of a Somerset home with other poems until an appeal in the *Daily Telegraph* nearly forty years later drew it from its resting place. The poem owes much to Homer and Banjo Patterson, whose Australian folk poems John Brookes heard at camp fires on the 800-mile walk from Broken Hill to Sydney to enlist in 1939. A year before, restless, he worked his way by boat from Liverpool to Australia, arriving with 2/6 (12½p). The two-month walk to enlist proved no hardship. Like most children John Brookes had walked to school, usually unaccompanied. He walked weekends with friends. Others cycled. All in safety. The houses where they lived left their doors open. They were a community.

In the days before home life centred round a television set or computer game, people participated. John Brookes played cricket and football. At home he read. The sisters played the piano. The family devised their own entertainment. *They talked*. Words, the raw material of the poet. Reluctantly the father allowed a wireless set into the house. John, his brothers and sisters all qualified at the age of eleven for grammar school – the route bright children took to university. Many of our poets took that route.

Judging from the letters from the poets and families, even many of those who had left school at fourteen seemed to have an ability to write English fluently, to set out their thoughts, with few problems of syntax or spelling. Letter-writing proves important in our story. For as one of our poets Norman Morris – post war a London headmaster – has observed, the writing of letters home in the services, especially from new scenes abroad, led to writing articles for unit wall newspapers, service magazines and poetry. The creative bug was born. The writing skill developed.

Our colleague Erik de Mauny has written of that world: 'The poets – from the Commonwealth and Britain – all shared a common cultural tradition which still derived from the durable inheritance of the Renaissance. They built on the best of the past, and created the new, but with learning, skill, talent and application. They were neither haunted by the fear of being labelled old-fash-ioned, nor obsessed by the belief that yesterday is already dated. True recognition did not depend on having an astute PR, or on a fleeting appearance on the "box". So those who made it were a little older, more mature and not so rich.'

One could add that those who made it did not need an amplifier, synthesiser or an industry to relieve the younger generation of their earnings. Study, skill and application were mandatory.

Significantly, of our poets, ordinary citizens before they enlisted, writers in the war, so many were to become professors, lecturers, headmasters, medical consultants, journalists and broadcasters, bringing with them that independence of thought, enquiring minds and, importantly, the intellectual discipline from their education and early years.

Culture does not grow in a vacuum. All ability and inspiration can run into the sand without the soil to grow in and the climate to make it thrive. The Second World War saw a coincidence of factors – cultural, political and economic – that meant freedom of thought for those taking part. The war encouraged the independently minded, the voluntary organisations, particularly the women's without which the home front could not have worked. They needed no direction.

This independence of mind owed much to the classics tradition in education, as well as Britain's island history. Consider this injunction in the Army Bureau of Current Affairs wartime handbook:

An intelligent instructor will avoid ramming his own views down the men's throats. It is a cardinal sin. Discussion is one of the best stimulants to thought. Nothing is so effective in making one formulate one's own thoughts and opinions on a subject as hearing what other people think, particularly if one disagrees with them.

Men had to arrive at conclusions through discussion. Socrates would have been proud. In any case troops would suspect an official handout, it could be counter-productive.

Contradictory as it may sound, this freedom went hand in hand with the planning and controls needed to win the war – raw materials, manpower, investment, permission to set up a factory, the disposal of profits, overseas investments and, of course, rationing. Short of a Gestapo, the plan could only work with the co-operation of the people, of trade unions, employers' organisations and joint works councils. Even more it depended on public attitudes. Here was a caring, uncommercial world. In 1944 the Army Directorate of Education published a handbook 'British Way and Purpose'. One quote sums up the attitude of the time. A. D. Lindsay, Master of Balliol poses the question:

Mr Churchill rallied the nation as it had never been rallied before by promising blood, toil, tears and sweat. Suppose he had said, 'Hold on and beat the Germans and you will have a world where everyone shall have a nice house, well fitted up, with a motor car and a refrigerator and a wireless, with a cinema just around the corner'?

The question needed no answer. No one would take this proposition seriously. It conflicted with the ethos of the time.

Men enlisted at two shillings (10 pence) a day and often sent a shilling of it home. At the end of the war Viscount Alanbrooke, Chief of the General Staff and Churchill's right hand, was obliged to sell his rare collection of books. The political thinking of the time was dominated by a determination not to go back to the nineteen thirties, to the depression and collapse of industries, throwing millions onto a meagre dole. The war ended that. But the concern with establishing a different Britain led to Beveridge and welfare, Butler and education, the subject of a Churchill speech which would certainly surprise today's world. Entitled 'A Four-Year Plan for a Post-War Britain', it looked ahead to state enterprise working with private enterprise. End the dole by having no unemployed. The speech was distributed to the troops. Our poets may have read it, as they did the plethora of service newspapers and magazines, in which mavericks had a field day. In this freedom poets wrote. Maybe it was an age of innocence. There was an essential belief in the goodness of people. People truly believed the world would be a better place. They could not envisage the technology and self interest that would transform the material expectations of life and change attitudes fundamentally, and the Empire too.

Who in 1944 could have envisaged technology with freedom from controls that can shift billions round the world in a split second, sink the currency of one country and make fortunes without feeding a soul? How far we have moved from counting the pennies!

Britain paid a very high price for the Second World War. In spite of forced savings the national debt rose by forty per cent, with a fifty per cent loss of overseas investments. The dollar would take over from the pound sterling.

But Hitler had to be stopped. For this, many gave their lives. As for the poets, they handed to posterity treasure from man's most wasteful occupation.

Luck

I suppose they'll say his last thoughts were of simple things,
Of April back at home, and the late sun on his wings;
Or that he murmured someone's name
As earth reclaimed him sheathed in flame.
Oh God! Let's have no more of empty words,
Lip service ornamenting death!
The worms don't spare the hero;
Nor can children feed upon resounding praises of his deed.
'He died who loved to live,' they'll say,
'Unselfishly so we might have today!'
Like hell! He fought because he had to fight;
He died that's all. It was his unlucky night.

DENNIS MCHARRIE

*OBE Wing Commander RAF, posted to 38 Bomber Squadron, Middle
East, 1942, as a Flight Lieutenant, moving to Barce near Benghazi.*

1939–40

Epitaph on a New Army

No drums they wished, whose thoughts were tied
To girls and jobs and mother,
Who rose and drilled and killed and died
Because they saw no other,

Who died without the hero's throb,
And if they trembled, hid it,
Who did not fancy much their job
But thought it best, and did it.

MICHAEL THWAITES

(Australia) *Royal Naval Volunteer Reserve 1939–45. Trawlers and corvettes. Atlantic and North Sea. Commanded corvette.*

Autumn, 1939

The beech boles whiten in the swollen stream;
Their red leaves, shaken from the creaking boughs,
Float down the flooded meadow, half in dream,
Seen in a mirror cracked by broken vows,

Water-logged, slower, deeper, swirling down
Between the indifferent hills who also saw
Old jaundiced knights jog listlessly to town
To fight for love in some unreal war.

Black leaves are piled against the roaring weir;
Dark closes round the manor and the hut;
The dead knight moulders on his rotting bier,
And one by one the warped old casements shut.

ALUN LEWIS

Wrote short stories of the war as well as poetry. Entered Army as Sapper in the Royal Engineers, commissioned in the infantry. India 1943. Killed 5 March 1944, on the Arakan front.

Ack Ack Said The Instructor

Ack Ack said the instructor
bofors tommy gun lewis gun
(which has 156 different parts –
EACH THE GRANDEST BRIGHTEST BESTEST
EACH THE ONLY GOD-DAMN THING
ON THE MARKET
GUARANTEED WARRANTEED MONEY BACK IF NOT SATISFIED
and this thing here's called the cruciform
(didn't any of you bastards
ever go to church?)
as you can see it's shaped like a cross

Yes said the instructor
blow his bloody brains out with
(our recognized brands the best that are made)
he's trying to blow your bloody brains out with
(OUR RECOGNIZED BRANDS THE BEST THAT ARE MADE).

BRIAN ALLWOOD

Joined RAF 1941, North Africa and Italy. Mentioned in despatches. Killed 30 June 1944 in a bridge collapse. Buried at Caserta, Italy.

The Colonel's Eye

Lampshades thinly veiled
In silver dust:
Rifles richly scaled
With ornate rust:
Respirators, modest and ascetic,
Free from Pickering's obscene cosmetic:
Bottles on some airy shelf bestowed
Which, till the previous midnight, flowed
With good McEwans Ale: the mystic grain
Of frosty foliage on the window pane.
All these I love. So why
Should they offend the Colonel's eye?

Beds and blankets ranged
In staggered lines,
And on them, forming strange
Surrealist designs,
Books, bayonets, button-sticks and soap;
Improper coils of black-out shutter rope:
Immaculate class officers arrayed
In far-from-regimental shoes of suede:
All these . . . and more . . .
I, but not Authority, adore.

Thank God that I
Have not the Colonel's eye.

O.C.T.U. Malta Barracks Aldershot

TOM BEAUMONT

Sapper Royal Engineers 1939. Commissioned, Indian Army in Sudan, India and Burma.

Armament Instructor

Drysouled, he mumbles names of working parts,
    watching the clock and book, scared lest he vary
system laid down. Never gay or merry,
    his words, like cherries, each have solid hearts,
and he spits them to the airmen, deft by habit,
    circumscribed by fear of losing tapes.
If any fidgets, or if another gapes,
    he pops with frightened temper like a rabbit.
Museumpiece himself, he grabs and snatches
    at information twisted, vague, uncommon,
and doles it at the men like mud, in patches.
    Sometimes, despite his fear, he's almost human,
and leaving guns, to human things he looks,
    and natters of glory and honour, both from books.

HERBERT CORBY

RAF Armourer in a bomber squadron. Foreign Service post-war.

Unseen Fire

This is a damned inhuman sort of war.
I have been fighting in a dressing-gown
Most of the night; I cannot see the guns,
The sweating gun-detachments or the planes;

I sweat down here before a symbol thrown
Upon a screen, sift facts, initiate
Swift calculations and swift orders; wait
For the precise split-second to order fire.

We chant our ritual words; beyond the phones
A ghost repeats the orders to the guns:
One Fire . . . Two Fire . . . ghosts answer: the guns roar
Abruptly; and an aircraft waging war
Inhumanly from nearly five miles height
Meets our bouquet of death – and turns sharp right.

This is a damned unnatural sort of war;
The pilot sits among the clouds, quite sure
About the values he is fighting for;
He cannot hear beyond his veil of sound,

He cannot see the people on the ground;
He only knows that on the sloping map
Of sea-fringed town and country people creep
Like ants – and who cares if ants laugh or weep?

To us he is no more than a machine
Shown on an instrument; what can he mean
In human terms? – a man, somebody's son,
Proud of his skill; compact of flesh and bone
Fragile as Icarus – and our desire
To see that damned machine come down on fire.

We've most of us seen aircraft crash in flame,
Seen how the cruel guardians of height,
Fire and the force of gravity, unite
To humanize the flying god and proclaim

His common clay; by hedge and field we came
Running through the darkness, tried to fight
The solid wall of heat. Only the white

Lilac of foam could get us near that frame –

That frame like a picked fish-bone; sprawled beneath –
Charred bodies, more like trunks of trees than men;
The ammunition began to go up then,
Another and more glittering type of spray;
We could not help them, six men burned to death –
I've had their burnt flesh in my lungs all day!

R.N. CURREY

(South Africa) *Royal Artillery and Army Educational Corps, posted to India 1943.*

Enlisting

How do you go to the wars? It's easy; you go to an office
Fill in a form, undress, submit to some interrogation,
Take an oath and a shilling or two, and you're in and it's over.
Afterwards walking away you pause to reflect on the price paid:
Never were human bonds so cheaply, so easily purchased,
Never was human soul so quickly, so easily bartered.
Now you must travel henceforth through life on a three-speed
    gear-box,
Knowing no possible states but duty, leave, or desertion.
And, what's more, you are not who you were, you are somebody
    else now:
Down between you and the world now drops the invisible curtain,
Fine, invisible, tougher than steel, more fluid than water,
(Element subtly refined from the gross regimental amalgam,
Blanco, barracks, and boots, kit, pay, drill, drink, and the
    NAAFI),
In between you and your friends and your house, between you and
    your clothes too
Sliding, sealing you off from all that is known and familiar.
There you have now no place, you move in another dimension.
Can it be thus that the dead may feel, in their first dissolution,
Loosed from the body, among yet barred from the body's
    surroundings,
Subject to new and mysterious laws, experience useless,

Shut from the world of sense in an incorporeal limbo,
Where no voice can sound, where speech and thought are
    confounded,
Fingers record no touch, eyes answer with no understanding?
Anyway that's how it is, and you'd better get used to it quickly.
Flatten your nose on the pane till it hurts – the toys are beyond
    reach.
Lightly touches you now the tip of the tyrant's finger;
Others have felt his fist and his heel, his spite and his fury,
Beating, burning, corrupting in absolute might and dominion;
Far you stand from the flames and the ruins; he touches you
    lightly;
But you must wear his chains before you learn how to break them.

R.H. ELLIS

*Enlisted British forces on St Crispin's Day 1939. Served as a subaltern
during the Second World War.*

The Bofors AA Gun

Such marvellous ways to kill a man!
An 'instrument of precision', a beauty,
The well-oiled shining marvel of our day
Points an accusing finger at the sky.
– But suddenly, traversing, elevating madly,
It plunges into action, more than eager
For the steel blood of those romantic birds
That threaten all the towns and roads.
O, that man's ingenuity, in this so subtle,
In such harmonious synchronization of parts,
Should against man be turned and he complaisant,
The pheasant-shooter be himself the pheasant!

GAVIN EWART

Officer RA, North Africa, Italy. Poet and critic.

All Day It Has Rained

All day it has rained, and we on the edge of the moors
Have sprawled in our bell-tents, moody and dull as boors,
Groundsheets and blankets spread on the muddy ground
And from the first grey wakening we have found
No refuge from the skirmishing fine rain
And the wind that made the canvas heave and flap
And the taut wet guy-ropes ravel out and snap.
All day the rain has glided, wave and mist and dream,
Drenching the gorse and heather, a gossamer stream
Too light to stir the acorns that suddenly
Snatched from their cups by the wild south-westerly
Pattered against the tent and our upturned dreaming faces.
And we stretched out, unbuttoning our braces,
Smoking a Woodbine, darning dirty socks,
Reading the Sunday papers – I saw a fox
And mentioned it in the note I scribbled home; –
And we talked of girls and dropping bombs on Rome,

And thought of the quiet dead and the loud celebrities
Exhorting us to slaughter, and the herded refugees;
– Yet thought softly, morosely of them, and as indifferently
As of ourselves or those whom we
For years have loved, and will again
Tomorrow maybe love; but now it is the rain
Possesses us entirely, the twilight and the rain.

And I can remember nothing dearer or more to my heart
Than the children I watched in the woods on Saturday
Shaking down burning chestnuts for the schoolyard's merry play,
Or the shaggy patient dog who followed me
By Sheet and Steep and up the wooded scree
To the Shoulder o' Mutton where Edward Thomas brooded long
On death and beauty – till a bullet stopped his song.

ALUN LEWIS

Wrote short stories of the war as well as poetry. Entered Army as Sapper in the Royal Engineers, commissioned in the infantry. India 1943. Killed 5 March 1944, on the Arakan front.

The Padre[1]

The Padre's got a cushy job, he roams about all day,
He doesn't work, he merely talks and wastes his time away.
He wears his collar back to front, and looks professional
But don't you let him take you in, he doesn't work at all.

It's War, boys, and we've got to fight, and that's our job for now;
The C.O. and the officers are here to tell us how,
The M.O's here to patch us up – we'll need him in this war –
But is there anybody who knows what a Padre's for?

The Army must be mechanised if we're to make a show
And every Fusilier admits we want an M.T.O.[2]
A Quartermaster there must be to superintend the store,
But only the Almighty knows just what the Padre's for.

And yet I've just been thinking, chaps, that surely he was sent
To do a job of some kind, for he's not an ornament;
I've heard it said by friends of mine who met a few in France
That Padres can come up to scratch if men give them a chance.

I get my problems and my thoughts, I get temptations, too,
And secret fears I'd like to share with someone, Bill, don't you?
We're not the only ones like that, there must be many more,
And so I've sometimes wondered if that's what Padre's for.

Mind you, I'm not afraid to die, and I don't ask for fuss,
But we've got girls or wives and kids who think the world of us
And if I get knocked out tonight and laid I don't know where,
Although I'm not a churchy chap I wouldn't mind a prayer.

Take that young fellow over there who's getting on so well –
If he gets shot his mother's heart is going to ache like hell;
If Padre wrote it couldn't bring him back, for nothing could,
And yet she'd be relieved to know that someone understood,

That someone understood, you know, someone who was nearby,
Who lived with him, and knew his name, perhaps who saw him
  die,
And every mother in the hour of bitterness and loss
Might like to know that someone tried to help the boy across.

I've asked you what a Padre's for: well now, I wonder, Bill
If he's been sent by Jesus Christ to help us up the hill?

He's not a saint and yet it's grand, tho' some might think it odd,
That we should have a fellow here to make us think of God.

1 Written when Padre with the Royal Welch Fusiliers, 1940
2 Mechanical Transport Officer

REV. K.W. PARKHURST

MBE, HCF *Army Chaplain. After Dunkirk 1st Bn Royal Welsh
Fusiliers and India and Burma with the 14th Army.*

Lessons of the War (To Alan Michell)

*Vixi duellis nuper idoneus
Et militavi non sine gloria*

I – Naming of Parts

Today we have naming of parts. Yesterday,
We had daily cleaning. And tomorrow morning,
We shall have what to do after firing. But today,
Today we have naming of parts. Japonica
Glistens like coral in all of the neighbouring gardens
     And today we have naming of parts.

This is the lower sling swivel. And this
Is the upper sling swivel, whose use you will see
When you are given your slings. And this is the piling swivel,
Which in your case you have not got. The branches
Hold in the gardens their silent, eloquent gestures,
     Which in our case we have not got.

This is the safety-catch, which is always released
With an easy flick of the thumb. And please do not let me
See anyone using his finger. You can do it quite easy
If you have any strength in your thumb. The blossoms
Are fragile and motionless, never letting anyone see
     Any of them using their finger.

And this you can see is the bolt. The purpose of this
Is to open the breech, as you see. We can slide it
Rapidly backwards and forwards; we call this

Easing the spring. And rapidly backwards and forwards
The early bees are assaulting and fumbling the flowers:
   They call it easing the Spring

They call it easing the Spring; it is perfectly easy
If you have any strength in your thumb: like the bolt,
And the breech, and the cocking-piece, and the point of balance,
Which in our case we have not got; and the almond-blossom
Silent in all of the gardens and the bees going backwards and
   forwards.
   For today we have naming of parts.

2 – Judging Distances

Not only how far away, but the way that you say it
Is very important. Perhaps you may never get
The knack of judging a distance, but at least you know
How to report on a landscape: the central sector,
The right of arc and that, which we had last Tuesday,
And at least you know

That maps are of time, not place, so far as the army
Happens to be concerned – the reason being,
Is one which need not delay us. Again, you know
There are three kinds of tree, three only, the fir and the poplar,
And those which have bushy tops to; and lastly
That things only seem to be things.

A barn is not called a barn, to put it more plainly,
Or a field in the distance, where sheep may be safely grazing.
You must never be over-sure. You must say, when reporting:
At five o'clock in the central sector is a dozen
Of what appear to be animals; whatever you do,
Don't call the bleeders *sheep*.

I am sure that's quite clear; and suppose, for the sake of example,
The one at the end, asleep, endeavours to tell us
What he sees over there to the west, and how far away,
After first having come to attention. There to the west,
On the fields of summer the sun and the shadows bestow
Vestments of purple and gold.

The still white dwellings are like a mirage in the heat,
And under the swaying elms a man and a woman
Lie gently together. Which is, perhaps, only to say
That there is a row of houses to the left of arc,
And that under some poplars a pair of what appear to be humans
Appear to be loving.

Well that, for an answer, is what we might rightly call
Moderately satisfactory only, the reason being,
Is that two things have been omitted, and those are important.
The human beings, now: in what direction are they,
And how far away, would you say? And do not forget
There may be dead ground in between.

There may be dead ground in between; and I may not have got
The knack of judging a distance; I will only venture
A guess that perhaps between me and the apparent lovers,
(Who, incidentally, appear by now to have finished,)
At seven o'clock from the houses, is roughly a distance
Of about one year and a half.

HENRY REED

*Called up in the Army, 1941, Royal Army Ordnance Corps, but released
to work at the Foreign Office. Radio writer after the war.*

War Song

A lesson that their children knew by heart
Where it lay stonily in that September.
Conscripted man, anonymous in hot
Brown or blue, intoned his rank and number.
The discs, strung from his neck, no amulet
Against the ache of loss, were worn in darkness
Under grave blankets in the narrow cot
After the bugle's skirmish with night's silence.
In trembling cities civil sleep was probed
By the wild sirens' blind and wounded howling;
White searchlights hosed the sky; black planets throbbed;
All night all buildings put on total mourning.

And when dawn yawned, the washed skies were afloat
With silver saveloys whose idle motion
And conference with puffed clouds appeared to mock
Bereaving night and morning's lamentation.
And then, down country lanes, the crop-haired sons
And nephews of the skeletons of Flanders
Made séance of their march, as, on their tongues,
The old ghosts sang again of Tipperary,
Packing kit-bags, getting back to Blighty,
But soon, bewildered, sank back to their graves
When other songs were bawled – a jaunty music
With false, bragging words: The Siegfried Line
Transformed with comic washing hanging from it,

Sergeants and Corporals were blessed, the barrel rolled;
But behind the grinning words and steady tramping
The Sergeant of the dark was taking names
And marking time to that lugubrious singing.
We're saying goodbye to them all: and, far away
From gunpit, barrack-square and trench, the mother
Sewed the dark garments for tomorrow's mourning.

VERNON SCANNELL

*Gordon Highlanders. 51st Highland Division from Alamein to Tunis,
Sicily and Normandy. Poet, novelist and critic.*

Before the first Parachute Descent

All my world has suddenly gone quiet
Like a railway carriage as it draws into a station;
Conversation fails, laughter dies,
And the turning of pages and the striking of matches cease.
All life is lapsed into nervous consciousness,
Frozen, like blades of grass in blocks of ice,
Except where one small persistent voice in the corner
Compares with the questioning silence –
With the situation of an electric present –
With self-opinions, pride and confidence of an untried past.

The Officer Cadet (Extract)

My life jerks,
Like an unwanted casing
Pushed in the back by an ungrateful ejector,
To a pile of stale blankets and damp kit-bags,
Where everything smells of metal and of metal polish,
And where one's world,
Suddenly so remote from anything rational,
Revolves round boot polish and a brighter shine.

I cannot understand why
To fight for a few simple things
Necessitates polishing the toes of one's boots
'Until you can see your face in them.'
I have no wish to see my face;
And there are mirrors.
Neither do I see the cause nor wisdom
Of teaching supple bodies to behave like crank-shafts
And walk about like the most stupid
And self-opinioned wood pigeon in that little spinney
Where I once fell off the old white pony.
But that was in the days when
A bright wit and a clean neck
Were more important than polished buttons and shiny badges.

I have learnt wisdom here.
One can learn to love through opposites.
Sometimes I have unquenchable longings to lie
On the warm grass, perhaps by Binton Woods,
And watch the timid primrose smiling from her bed.
I love most the primrose
When I am surrounded by her opposites;
I can find nothing more unlike
A primrose
Than a Coldstream Guard Sergeant-Major.

RICHARD SPENDER

Enlisted London Irish Regiment 1940. Officer, the Parachute Regiment.
Killed 28 March 1943 leading troops near Bizerta, Tunisia.

'We're gonna set fire to the sea'[1]

I heard through the office window
The usual rider from Div –
A glib knowall with the sideboards
Of a typical cartoon spiv –
I heard him say in a casual way 'Sarr'nt Major!'
As he slurped a mug of our tea,
'I kid you not, Top Secret, we're gonna set fire to the sea'.

I was called to C.O.'s orders in a hush-hush sort of way;
'No notes, gentlemen, just listen! and what I've got to say
Is frightfully, frightfully secret,' he said, 'There are plans' –
and paused for effect, I suppose –
'With oil and gadgets and pipes and hose,
It all seems quite crazy to me,
Yes plans, to set fire, yes fire, to this our sector of sea.'

I called in at 'The Trip to Jerusalem' –
I'd noticed the brewers' dray;
The landlord was a friend of ours, a Home Guard Corporal he;
I drank my pints and chatted, and then he slipped to me,
Wrapped up, two bottles of whisky in a hush-hush sort of way.
'For God's sake keep these quiet,' he whispered – pause – 'Do we,
Like most of my customers say,
Have plans, daft plans, to burn up
Our stretch of the wet North Sea?'

Somewhere in Essex, 1940

1 This anti-invasion plan was more advanced on the South Coast. The 'leak'
was partly due to the fact the local council workers had to be involved so that
the sewage outfall pipes could be used. The 'black' propaganda people used
this when it became almost public knowledge.

DOUGLAS STREET

*Commissioned 1/7 Middlesex, MMG (Medium Machine Gun) TA
British Expeditionary Force, 3rd Division Dunkirk. Chief instructor
Intelligence Staff Course. Liaison with General Leclerc, Free French,
GSO 1 Intelligence 8th Army. SOE Yugoslavia and Greece, liaison in
Trieste. Commanded Allied Information Services under the then General
Sir John Harding.*

The Tarn

'We'd better split now. Keep behind the trees
Down to the tarn's edge. If there's a plane, come back
And meet me here: don't fire, they'll have MGs.
– We'll need to get as close as we can get.'
I heard the silky rustle of the skis
And stood stock-still, listening till it had gone.
I threaded one stick through the ring and strap
Of the other, and held them so in my left hand.
I cocked my tommy-gun – so loud, so loud
That little click! Zigzag from tree to tree,
Straining for any other sound beyond
The swishing of my skis, I ran to the tarn.
Between the black, still branches of a spruce
I looked across the ice: only the wind
Had made black random furrows in the snow.

Norway 1940

JOHN BUXTON

*No. 1 Independent Company. A pre-war poet, taken prisoner in Norway,
1940, interned in Oflag VII.*

Refugees
(Road to La Rochelle, 1940)

The aspens shiver as the Summer breeze
Drifts softly through the avenue of trees.
It ruffles plodding peasant women's skirts,
Plays over chests, and under open shirts,
And tousles bobbing curls that frame the child,
Who lolls at ease among the chattels piled.
The creaking farm cart trundles through the dust,
Wheels raising clouds, that settle like a crust
On sweating brow, and horse's steaming flank.
None see on high, the glint, the sudden bank,
Or hear the roar, the rattling coughing spit. –
Shocked silence; – then, as fiends from the Pit,

The wailing screams of souls, doomed, damned and lost,
Where crumpled dolls lie sprawling, careless tossed,
With skirts awry, and shirts mere bloody rags;
Yet still the horse plods on, the cart still drags,
The sun still shines; dust hangs still in the air,
And still, among the chattels, I see where
The curly head still lolls, with eyes that gaze
Unseeing at the aspen-filtered rays.

L.D. DEAL

Dunkirk (Extract)

All through the night, and in the next day's light
The endless columns came. Here was Defeat.
The men marched doggedly, and kept their arms,
But sleep weighed on their backs so that they reeled,
Staggering as they passed. Their force was spent.
Only, like old Horatius, each man saw
Far off his home, and seeing, plodded on.
At last they ceased. The sun shone down, and we
Were left to watch along a dusty road.

That night we blew our guns. We placed a shell
Fuse downwards in each muzzle. Then we put
Another in the breech, secured a wire
Fast to the firing lever, crouched, and pulled.
It sounded like a cry of agony,
The crash and clang of splitting, tempered steel.
Thus did our guns, our treasured colours, pass;
And we were left bewildered, weaponless;
And rose and marched, our faces to the sea.

We formed in line beside the water's edge.
The little waves made oddly home-like sounds,
Breaking in half-seen surf upon the strand.
The night was full of noise; the whistling thud
The shells made in the sand, and pattering stones;
The cries cut short, the shouts of units' names;
The crack of distant shots, and bren gun fire;

The sudden clattering crash of masonry.
Steadily, all the time, the marching tramp
Of feet passed by along the shell-torn road,
Under the growling thunder of the guns.

The major said 'The boats cannot get in,
There is no depth of water. Follow me.'
And so we followed, wading in our ranks
Into the blackness of the sea. And there,
Lit by the burning oil across the swell,
We stood and waited for the unseen boats.

Oars in the darkness, rowlocks, shadowy shapes
Of boats that searched. We heard a seaman's hail.
Then we swam out, and struggled with our gear,
Clutching the looming gunwales. Strong hands pulled,
And we were in and heaving with the rest,
Until at last they turned. The dark oars dipped,
The laden craft crept slowly out to sea,
To where in silence lay the English ships.

B.G. BONALLACK

*Engineer. Honourable Artillery Company 92nd Field Regiment Royal
Artillery. British Expeditionary Force (Rear-guard Dunkirk). Sicily. D-
Day. Italy. Germany. 'Dunkirk' was begun in France 1940 and completed
on the Anzio beachhead three years later.*

THE MIDDLE EAST

OASIS and Middle East Poetry

OASIS could only have originated in the Middle East. Three months by boat round the Cape, away from the War Office, it enjoyed a freedom for which no parallel is known, a paradise for the independent and eccentric. The army wrote its own rule book.

A character named Popski ran a private army whilst the Long Range Desert Group roamed behind enemy lines – both directed by General Sir John Hackett, then Lt. Col. G1 Raiding Forces Middle East. The War Office in its wisdom posted writers and academics to staff the myraid of intelligence agencies in Cairo, who in turn ran literary magazines and promoted the Middle East as the cultural centre of the war outside Britain.

OASIS, 'The Middle East Anthology of Poetry from the Forces' came from a question posed by three servicemen meeting by chance on leave in November 1942, in 'Music For All' run by Lady Russell Pasha, wife of the Cairo Police Chief. The three: Denis Saunders, of the South African Air Force, who wrote poetry under the name 'Almendro', David Burk, pre-war journalist and Victor Selwyn.

The question was asked: *The War of 1914–1918 produced the most moving poetry. Was poetry being written in this war?* If that question had not been asked there would have been no OASIS or four post-war anthologies and now this new collection.

The senior rank between the three then was corporal – true war substantive – but they had their appeal for poetry on civilian radio, forces radio, in army newspapers and the civilian press. This was the Middle East. They had a friend at GHQ, Johnny Walker, Randolph Churchill's staff sergeant, founder of the Buckshee Wheelers – a story in itself. Denis Healey, in his appraisal, tells of three thousand poems coming in from eight hundred would-be contributors. Few were established poets. The flood came from the grass roots; highly literate people who had obviously read poetry, from Palgrave's *Golden Treasury* to Auden and Elliott. It was a grass-roots war.

Night Preceding Battle

Spoamy,
Slashing at the shore,
Salt skimmering in the moonlight,
And always that roar
Like a family quarrel. Tonight
I look across the disarranged sea,
Undulating unaltered, only I,
Different and detached, divining Me
Formulated as a breathing question-mark
Crivelling in lust-pregnated casing,
Like bee seducing pollened virgin,
Questions 'Why?'

Why dust-born society advancing dust's decay,
Cradled in metal-moulded rhetoric, insane
Distortion of armed arbitration?
With this 'Why?' pounding, thumping in my brain
I demand God end His holiday
And influence the situation.

Yesterday I embraced my plough with masochistic pleasure,
Worrying if my economic seeds would be enough
To feed the hungry. Soil and work were the measure
Of my education.

Today I killed a man. God forgive me!
Tomorrow I shall sow another political corpse,
Or be dead myself. And strangely
I am satisfied to be applauded killer.
Holy Mary plead my dutied sin's legality.
Is there no end, reason, answer? Damn the sea!

Spoamy,
Slashing at the shore,
Salt skimmering in the moonlight,
And always that roar

Like a family quarrel. Tonight
They are rolling up the guns for tomorrow's battle.
I must not be late to hear Death rattle
In my enemy's throat.

The flame of Hell pythoning
Around my trigger finger insinuates coercion,
And feeling body's blooded-reeds contracting,
Dispose of humanity's humiliated feelings
And know that I am ready.

Christ, it's cold tonight!

'ALMENDRO'

(South Africa) *'Almendro' was the name used by Denis Saunders, South African Air Force, poet and joint founder of Oasis in Cairo, 1942. Served later in Italy.*

Chez-Nous
(Tobruk)

In my cave lives a solitary rat,
(A celibate rat,
I can vouch for that);
He hasn't a mate for miles around
And he lives on what he can find on the ground,
Though the country's such
That that's not much.
I don't like he
And he can't stand me
But we need the roof so there we be.

In my cave lives a type of flea,
(A scurrilous flea
Believe you me);
And though he's such a tiny thing
His bite is worse than a scorpion's sting.
He lives on Rat,
But worse than that
He lives on me
This scurrilous flea
With all his numerous progeny.

Near my cave lives the octave bird,
(The queerest bird
You've ever heard);

He sings eight notes as he climbs the scale
Though the topmost note is known to fail.
He's very small,
Just like us all.
So in we fit
Though we're cramped a bit –
Old Rat
And Flea
And Bird
And Me.

A.G. AUSTIN

(Australia) *Served with A.I.F. in Middle East, New Guinea, 1940–45;
M.C. at Alamein, 1942. Senior lecturer, University of Melbourne.*

Landscape Near Tobruk

This land was made for War. As glass
Resists the bite of vitriol, so this hard
And calcined earth rejects
The battle's hot, corrosive impact. Here
Is no nubile, girlish land, no green
And virginal countryside for War
To violate. This land is hard,
Inviolable, the battle's aftermath
Presents no ravaged and emotive scene,
No landscape à la Goya. Here are no trees
Uprooted, gutted farms; the unsalvaged scrap,
The scattered petrol-cans, the upturned
And abandoned truck, the fallen Heinkel; all
The rusted and angular detritus
Of war, seem scarcely to impinge
Upon the hard, resistant surface of
This lunar land: ephemeral
As trippers' leavings, paper-bags and orange-peel
Upon Ben Nevis. Sun and sand
Inhibit here the mind's habitual
And easy gestures; hand and eye

Perform their functions with a robot-cunning –
The sly and casual movements of
The shadowed thief. The soldiers camped
In the rock-strewn wadi merge
Like lizard or jerboa in the brown
And neutral ambient: stripped at gunsite,
Or splashing like glad beasts at sundown in
The brackish pool, their smooth
And lion-coloured bodies seem
The indigenous fauna of an unexplored,
Unspoiled country: harmless, easy to trap,
And tender-fleshed – a hunter's prize.

JOCELYN BROOKE

Royal Army Medical Corps North Africa and Italy. Died 1966.

Stane Jock[1]

*For the glory of the Highland Division
on the night of 23 October 1942*

Atween the mune an' the yird[2]
    There is quick steel:
Atween the steel and the yird
    There is quick stane!

The man-trap field is fu' o' men
    Walking saftly.
The man-eating mandrakes scream
    As they bite.

The stane Jock o' Beaumont Hamel
    Is fa'en doon.
There's nae mair pipes in France –
    Nae mair sweet croon.

But this nicht stane Jock,
    Walks in the sand!
This nicht I hear the pipes,
    I hear the band!

There's nane deid but his dead e'en
    Glower at the west.
There's nane living but stepping hard
    Towards the west.

For the stane fa'n in France
    Here rises a living stane –
For the mindin' o' men killed
    Here rises a killing stane!

Yon pinke'ed craw, the mune,
    Sees a field o' strange plants –
Fire and sand fused glassily
    Into flowers on a wall.

An' the wa' is o' stane,
    An' the wa' walks
Covered wi' red flowers –
    A stane striding to destiny!

Gallus laddies a'l
    Stanes o' destiny!
Stane Jock in the mantrap field
    Walking saftly.

1 Name of the stone memorial on the Western Front of the
first World War
2 Earth

W.H. BURT

*Lieutenant in 51st Highland Reconnaissance Regiment. Killed in Germany
shortly before the end of the War.*

Heartbreak Camp

To Major S.C. Mason of the Nigerian Regiment

Red as the guardroom lamp
The moon inspects the trees:
High over Heartbreak Camp,
Orion stands at ease:

With buttons lit, for Sentry,
He challenges who's there
Acceding all the entry
Whose passport is Despair.

All joys are privates there
Who seldom go on leave
And only sorrows wear
Three chevrons on their sleeve:

But boredom wears three pips,
A fiend of monstrous size,
With curses on his lips
And circles round his eyes.

All round, for league on league
And labouring up the hills,
The clouds are on fatigue,
Collecting damps and chills.

Sir Dysentery Malaria,
A famous brigadier,
Commands the whole sub-area,
And stalking in his rear,

A more ferocious colonel
Lord Tremens (of the Drunks)
To whose commands infernal
We tremble in our bunks.

Here, till the pale aurora
Dismiss the stars from drill,
I dream of my Señora
Behind the guardroom grille.

In the outcry of crickets
And the silence of guitars,
I watch the lonely pickets
And the slow patrol of stars.

Our vineyard and the terrace
By the Tagus, they recall,
With the Rose of the Sierras,
Whom I love the best of all!

My heart was once her campfire
And burned for her alone,
Fed with the thyme and samphire
That azure days had grown.

My thoughts for their safari
Have scarcely taken wings
Through spaces wide and starry
To hear her stroke the strings:

But ere one word be spoken
A fiend my elbow jogs,
The reverie is broken
By the tomtom of the wogs:

And, all illusions killing,
Upon the stillness jars
A far hyaena drilling
His company of stars.

Snapshot of Nairobi

With orange-peel the streets are strown
And pips, beyond computing
On every shoulder save my own,
That's fractured with saluting.

May 1943

ROY CAMPBELL

(South Africa) *North and East Africa as Sergeant, King's African Rifles,
until invalided 1944. Died in motor accident 1957.*

Bisearta

Chi mi rè geàrd na h–oidhche
dreòs air chrith 'na fhroidhneas thall air faire,
a' clapail le a sgiathaibh,
a' sgapadh 's a' ciaradh rionnagan na h–àird'ud.

Shaoileadh tu gun cluinnte,
ge cian, o'bhuillsgein ochanaich no caoineadh,
ràn corruich no gàir fuatha,
comhart chon cuthaich uaidh no ulfhairt fhaolchon,
gun ruigeadh drannd an fhòirneirt
o'n fhùirneis òmair iomall fhéin an t-saoghail;
ach sud a' dol an leud e
ri oir an speur an tosdachd olc is aognaidh.

C' ainm nochd a th' orra,
na sràidean bochda anns an sgeith gach uinneag
a lasraichean 's a deatach,
a sradagan is sgreadail a luchd thuinidh,
is taigh air thaigh 'ga reubadh
am broinn a chéile am brùchdadh toit a' tuiteam?
Is có an nochd tha 'g atach
am Bàs a theachd gu grad 'nan cainntibh uile,
no a' spàirn measg chlach is shailthean
air bhàinidh a' gairm air cobhair, is nach cluinnear?
Cò an nochd a phàidheas
sean chìs àbhaisteach na fala cumant?

Uair dearg mar lod na h-àraich,
uair bàn mar ghile thràighte an eagail éitigh,
a' dìreadh 's uair a' teànadh,
a' sìneadh le sitheadh àrd 's a' call a mheudachd,
'a fannachadh car aitil
's ag at mar anail dhiabhail air dhéinead,
an t-Olc 'na chridhe 's 'na chuisle,
chì mi 'na bhuillean a' sìoladh 's a' leum e.
Tha 'n dreos 'na oillt air fàire,
'na fhàinne ròis is òir am bun nan speuran,
a' breugnachadh 's ag àicheadh
le shoillse sèimhe àrsaidh àrd nan reultan.

Bizerta

I see during the night guard
a blaze flickering, fringing the skyline over yonder,
beating with its wings
and scattering and dimming the stars of that airt.

You would think that there would be heard
from its midst, though far away, wailing and lamentation,
the roar of rage and the yell of hate,
the barking of the dogs from it or the howling of wolves,
that the snarl of violence would reach
from yon amber furnace the very edge of the world;
but younder it spreads
along the rim of the sky in evil ghastly silence.

What is their name tonight,
the poor streets where every window spews
its flame and smoke,
its sparks and the screaming of its inmates,
while house upon house is rent
and collapses in a gust of smoke?
And who tonight are beseeching
Death to come quickly in all their tongues,
or are struggling among stones and beams,
crying in frenzy for help, and are not heard?
Who tonight is paying
the old accustomed tax of common blood?

Now red like a battlefield puddle,
now pale like the drained whiteness of foul fear,
climbing and sinking,
reaching and darting up and shrinking in size,
growing faint for a moment
and swelling like the breath of a devil in intensity,
I see Evil as a pulse
and a heart declining and leaping in throbs.
The blaze, a horror on the skyline,
a ring of rose and gold at the foot of the sky,
belies and denies
with its light the ancient high tranquillity of the stars.

DEORSA CAIMBEUL HAY
GEORGE CAMPBELL HAY

Served in Middle East. Wrote poetry in several languages but chiefly in
Scots Gaelic (acquired in childhood).

Alternative

The question rises almost daily
In the gunpit, grimly, gaily –
Is it the shelling you prefer
Or the bombing? – All the air
Crouching in silence, tensely waiting –
The distant thud – the daily hating –
The whining scream – the crashing roar,
Forever nearer – ever more
Intimately:

Then are the strong weak and the brave
Lie flattened low in their sandy grave,
Counting the leaden seconds dropping
Heavy as heart-beats, slowly – stopping –
Knowing each moment, dearer, clearer –
Death creeps methodically nearer –

Or shall we stand, hands to our eyes
And watch the foeman in the skies,
Knowing the peril but unheeding
For the sheer beauty of the speeding
Planes that dive and, turning, mount again –
Light of their silver load – count again
The known numbers, note foreseen effect,
The chaos, sand and limestone wrecked
Into a halo round the sun
A cloud about our friendly gun?

I'd rather look death in the face
Born by a bomber's speed and grace –
Swinging down its rainbow arc
Like a falcon to its mark –
Than grovel like a nerveless slave
With nothing but his skin to save,
Crouching beneath the ugly Hell
Made by the calculated shell.

LOUIS CHALLONER

Western Desert, 'Knightsbridge', Alamein (twice), Tobruk to Tunis.
Head teacher, Newham Primary School. Died 1993.

Beyond the Wire

Beyond the wire
An awkward shadow dims the sand,
A twisted body,
Fallen with outstretched hand.

The last patrol
Returned, churning the night's quiet dust,
Leaving on the wire
A stain of blood to rust.

Six men went out
In search of new enemy mines;
Only five returned;
The sixth had found new lines.

As he crouched,
Dark in the pale light of the moon,
A sentry saw him,
Ready, alas, too soon.

The silent night
Leapt with the shock of rifle fire –
Now his body lies
Alone, beyond the wire.

JOHN CROMER BRAUN

OBE *Major, Served Middle East. Co-founder of the Salamander Society.
Secretary, Advertising Standards Authority. EC Consumer Protection.*

Dead German Youth

He lay there, mutilated and forlorn,
Save that his face was woundless, and his hair
Drooped forward and caressed his boyish brow.
He looked so tired, as if his life had been
Too full of pain and anguish to endure,
And like a weary child who tires of play
He lay there, waiting for decay.

I feel no anger towards you, German boy,
Whom war has driven down the path of pain.
Would God we could have met in peace
And laughed and talked with tankards full of beer,
For I would rather hear your youthful mirth
At stories which I often loved to tell
Than stand here looking down at you
So terrible, so quiet and so still.

C.P.S. DENHOLM-YOUNG

OBE, FCIS *Commanded the Signal Regt of the 51st Highland Division.*

Grave near Sirte

No poppies bleed above his blood.
His diary closed before last spring.
Upon his cross there greens no second bud.
He feels no more the sandstorm's sting.

The sweating dew upon his helmet's steel
Dries through each day to rust.
Caressing sand he cannot feel
Has blanketed his lust.

Eyes look no longer to the sea
His hope had often crossed.
Rocks shade his bones, and no dark tree,
No thaw for this death's frost.

Not British and not German now he's dead,
He breeds no grasses from his rot.
The coast road and the Arab pass his bed
And waste no musing on his lot.

December 1942

Elegy

No water ever in this wadi's bed.
Its ripples are the wind's, and sand.
The long dawn shadow's silent tread
Darkens no wet grasses and no joyous land.
Only the winds are mirthful in this sand.

A beefbox cross: 'Italian dead.'
'Serves the buggers right. Waste of bloody wood.
Aussies should know better,'
We coldly said.

This at the wadi's end. The late wind sang
Through the rocks. Our long shadows fast
Followed minds elsewhere, as the last boot rang.

Yet the mind that wakes in this night's bed
Broods on that wadi where the wind and sand
Mock the tethered shadow's cross-bound tread,
The cross marking time in that sombre land,
The dupes who were men and now are sand.

Libya, December 1942

Libyan Epitaph

The snake is dead. The lethal life
Is broken free. The hypodermic teeth
Still hold uninjected death. The knife
So keen-edged rusts by its sandy sheath.

Under the minute scales how fine the bone.
How delicate the spectrum of his spinal bloom.
How rippled his last shudder. How alone
He lies upon his grave, the ancient womb.

Symbol of subtle sin, he has sin's wage,
Who knew no myths of why old Adam died.
His foe was always knowable. His rage
Reached little past his supple, lovely pride.

More deadly I, though clumsier my art.
I fight for causes, less innocent my heart.

8 December 1942

DAN DAVIN

(New Zealand) CBE *Commander 23rd NZ Battalion Greece. Wounded Crete. Official NZ historian. Served at Cassino. Novelist. OUP former Trust Chairman. Died 1990.*

How to Kill

Under the parabola of a ball,
a child turning into a man,
I looked into the air too long.
The ball fell in my hand, it sang
in the closed fist: *Open, open
Behold a gift designed to kill.*

Now in my dial of glass appears
the soldier who is going to die.
He smiles, and moves about in ways
his mother knows, habits of his.
The wires touch his face; I cry
NOW. Death, like a familiar, hears

and look, has made a man of dust
of a man of flesh. This sorcery
I do. Being damned, I am amused
to see the centre of love diffused
and the waves of love travel into vacancy.
How easy it is to make a ghost.

The weightless mosquito touches
her tiny shadow on the stone,
and with how like, how infinite
a likeness, man and shadow meet.
They fuse. A shadow is a man
when the mosquito death approaches.

Tunisia-Cairo, 1943

'I think I am Becoming a God'

The noble horse with courage in his eye
clean in the bone, looks up at a shellburst.
Away fly the images of the shires
but he puts the pipe back in his mouth.

Peter was unfortunately killed by an 88:
it took his leg away – he died in the ambulance.
When I saw him crawling he said:
'It's most unfair – they've shot my foot off.'

How can I live among this gentle
Obsolescent breed of heroes, and not weep?
Unicorns, almost,
for they are fading into two legends
in which their stupidity and chivalry
are celebrated. Each, fool and hero, will be an immortal.

These plains were their cricket pitch
and in the mountains the tremendous drop fences
brought down some of the runners. Here
under the stones and earth they dispose themselves
in famous attitudes of unconcern.

Enfidaville, 1943

Elegy for an 88 Gunner

(Published elsewhere under the title 'Vergissmeinicht')

Three weeks gone and the combatants gone,
returning over the nightmare ground
we found the place again and found
the soldier sprawling in the sun.

The frowning barrel of his gun
overshadows him. As we came on
that day, he hit my tank with one
like the entry of a demon.

And smiling in the gunpit spoil
is a picture of his girl
who has written: *Steffi, Vergissmeinicht.*
in a copybook Gothic script.

We see him almost with content,
abased and seeming to have paid,
mocked by his durable equipment
that's hard and good when he's decayed.

But she would weep to see today
how on his skin the swart flies move,
the dust upon the paper eye
and the burst stomach like a cave.

For here the lover and the killer are mingled
who had one body and one heart;
and Death, who had the soldier singled
has done the lover mortal hurt.

Homs, Tripolitania, 1943

On a Return From Egypt

To stand here in the wings of Europe
disheartened, I have come away
from the sick land where in the sun lay
the gentle sloe-eyed murderers
of themselves, exquisites under a curse;
here to exercise my depleted fury.

For the heart is a coal, growing colder
when jewelled cerulean seas change
into grey rocks, grey water-fringe
sea and sky altering like a cloth
till colour and sheen are gone both:
cold is an opiate of the soldier.

And all my endeavours are unlucky explorers
come back, abandoning the expedition;
the specimens, the lilies of ambition
still spring in their climate, still unpicked:
but time, time is all I lacked
to find them, as the great collectors before me.

The next month, then, is a window
and with a crash I'll split the glass.
Behind it stands one I must kiss,
person of love or death
a person or a wraith,
I fear what I shall find.

Egypt–England, 1943–44

KEITH DOUGLAS

Captain, Royal Armoured Corps. Professional soldier and poet, independent-minded, he disobeyed orders to take his tank into action at El Alamein, wounded; made final revision of his poems before leaving for Normandy, June 1944, where he was killed on 9 June 1944. The poems were handed by him to Tambimuttu, Editions Poetry London, from whom the Trust has taken the poet's version in contrast to others who revised the poetry years later.

Soldiers at the Base

Among lupine faces on the rabid posters
'V.D. is dangerous to the Family' and
'Buy National Savings Now', in their blunt postures,
Ranked, numbered, moved, removed, the squaddies stand.

Those who past polemical terrain
Bumbled by tank and lorry to the front
But hazard if their day may bloom again
In quiet-keyed living, the menial stunt.

Others in flycapped kitchens, office and hutment, band,
Dressing the sick sweet altars of the Latrine;
Outflanked by boredom, sliverings of sand;
Sensed, the high rigours of the lost campaign.

So I, raw poet, notionally quite least
Of such uncompassed travellers, come
By war, all langour, on this middling east
And jeopard in survival's trivium.

A carrier, standing for its convoy;
I talk to a serious trooper. All these ends.

O Predellas, Aumbries, Archlutes, arcs of joy;
Over there, up the Blue, is freedom, death and friends.

Base, all base, in our off-coloured dreams,
Clawed not those waxed infantas, dimly kind;
But divas in frot velvet, whose bare screams
Skewed us like shot. *We have fallen too far behind.*

Geneifa, January 1944

IAN FLETCHER

Served in Middle East, including Sudan. Poetry includes: Orisons, Picaresque & Metaphysical Motets *and* Twenty One Poems. *Shortly before he died in 1988, he selected for the Trust the poems from his friend from the Middle East, Frank Thompson, sent to him by his brother, the historian E. P. Thompson, who had held them for 45 years.*

Egypt

Who knows the lights at last, who knows the cities
And the unloving hands upon the thighs
Would yet return to seek his home-town pretties
For the shy finger-tips and sidelong eyes.

Who knows the world, the flesh, the compromises
Would go back to the theory in the book:
Who knows the place the poster advertises
Back to the poster for another look.

But nets the fellah spreads beside the river
Where the green waters criss-cross in the sun
End certain migratory hopes for ever;
In that white light, all shadows are undone.

The desert slays. But safe from Allah's justice
Where the broad river of His Mercy lies,
Where ground for labour, or where scope for lust is,
The crooked and tall and cunning cities rise.

The green Nile irrigates a barren region,
All the coarse palms are ankle-deep in sand;

No love roots deep, though easy loves are legion:
The heart's as hot and hungry as the hand.

In airless evenings, at the café table,
The soldier sips his thick sweet coffee up:
The dry grounds, like the moral to my fable,
Are bitter at the bottom of the cup.

Christmas Letter Home

To my sister in Aberdeen.

Drifting and innocent and sad like snow,
Now memories tease me wherever I go.
And I think of the glitter of granite and distances
And against the blue sky the lovely and bare trees,
And slippery pavements spangled with delight
Under the needles of a Winter's night,
And I remember the dances with scarf and cane,
Strolling home in the cold with the silly refrain
Of a tune by Cole Porter or Irving Berlin
Warming a naughty memory up like gin,
And Bunny and Stella and Joyce and Rosemary
Chattering on sofas or preparing tea,
With their delicate voices and their small white hands
This is the sorrow everyone understands.
More than Rostov's artillery, more than the planes
Skirting the cyclonic islands, this remains,
The little, lovely taste of youth we had;
The guns and not our silliness were mad.
All the unloved and ugly seeking power
Were mad, and not our trivial evening hour
Of swirling taffetas and muslin girls,
Oh, not their hands, their profiles or their curls,
Oh, not the evenings of coffee and sherry and snow,
Oh, not the music. Let us rise and go –
But then the months and oceans lie between,
And once again the dust of Spring, the green
Bright peaks of buds upon the poplar trees,

And summer's strawberries and autumn's ease,
And all the marble gestures of the dead,
Before my eyes caress again your head,
Your tiny strawberry mouth, your bell of hair,
Your blue eyes with their deep and shallow stare,
Before your hand upon my arm can still
The nerves that everything but home makes ill:
In this historic poster-world I move,
Noise, movement, emptiness, but never love.
Yet all this grief we had to have my dear,
And most who grieve have never known, I fear,
The lucky streak for which we die and live
And to the luckless must the lucky give
All trust; all energy, whatever lies
Under the anger of democracies:
Whatever strikes the towering torturer down,
Whatever can outface the bully's frown,
Talk to the stammerer, spare a cigarette
For tramps at midnight . . . oh, defend it yet!
Some Christmas I shall meet you. Oh and then
Though all the boys you used to like are men,
Though all my girls are married, though my verse
Has pretty steadily been growing worse,
We shall be happy; we shall smile and say,
'These years, it only seems like yesterday
I saw you sitting in that very chair.'
'You have not changed the way you do your hair.'
'These years were painful then?' 'I hardly know.
Something lies gently over them, like snow,
A sort of numbing white forgetfulness.'

And so good night, this Christmas, and God Bless!

The Fallen

When they fall, men grasp at feathers,
Cheat the knowledge of their doom
With hot hopes, and see all weathers
Fine, not overhung with gloom.

They have failed, and there's no falling
Further. Uncrowned heads are light.
Ambition no more is calling.
Restlessness has passed with fright.

None but fools offer their pity
To the fallen who at last,
Driven from their tyrant city,
Into freedom have been cast.

G.S. FRASER

Warrant Officer Class 2, Army Middle East, Ministry of Information. Lectured in Japan and at Leicester University. Helped found The Salamander Oasis Trust.

Mechanization

Only seven months have passed but what a change they've made.
Remember how it used to be when troops got on parade?
'See those bits are fitted right!
See those girths are tight!
Mind you shake the blankets out before you put 'em on!'
How the nose-bands caught the light, how the steel-work shone!

All that's very different now. We dress like garage hands;
Gone now the clink of bit and spur; no trumpets now, no bands.
'Petrol, oil and water right?
All the wheel-nuts tight?
Did you check the levels up before you got aboard?'
No more, alas, the head-tossed foam, the fretful foot that pawed:
Oh glory that was Tetrarch's might, oh drabness that is Ford!

E.F. GOSLING

Lieutenant Colonel, Yeomanry Regiment, Middle East.

FIRST ELEGY[1]
End of a Campaign

There are many dead in the brutish desert,
        who lie uneasy
among the scrub in this landscape of half-wit
stunted ill-will. For the dead land is insatiate
and necrophilous. The sand is blowing about still.
Many who for various reasons, or because
        of mere unanswerable compulsion, came here
and fought among the clutching gravestones,
        shivered and sweated,
cried out, suffered thirst, were stoically silent, cursed
the spittering machine-guns, were homesick for Europe
and fast embedded in quicksand of Africa
        agonized and died.
And sleep now. Sleep here the sleep of the dust.

There were our own, there were the others.
Their deaths were like their lives, human and animal.
There were no gods and precious few heroes.
What they regretted when they died had nothing to do with
        race and leader, realm indivisible,
laboured Augustan speeches or vague imperial heritage.
(They saw through that guff before the axe fell.)
        Their longing turned to
the lost world glimpsed in the memory of letters:
an evening at the pictures in the friendly dark,
two knowing conspirators smiling and whispering secrets; or else
a family gathering in the homely kitchen
with Mum so proud of her boys in uniform:
        their thoughts trembled
between moments of estrangement, and ecstatic moments
of reconciliation: and their desire
crucified itself against the unutterable shadow of someone
whose photo was in their wallets.
Then death made his incision.

There were our own, there were the others.
Therefore, minding the great word of Glencoe's
son, that we should not disfigure ourselves

with villainy of hatred; and seeing that all
have gone down like curs into anonymous silence,
I will bear witness for I knew the others.
Seeing that littoral and interior are alike indifferent
and the birds are drawn again to our welcoming north
why should I not sing *them*, the dead, the innocent?

1 This and the next two poems are from *Elegies for the Dead in Cyrenaica*

SECOND ELEGY
Halfaya

(For Luigi Castigliano)

At dawn, under the concise razor-edge
of the escarpment, the laager sleeps. No petrol fires yet
blow flame for brew-up. Up on the pass a sentry
inhales his Nazionale. Horse-shoe curve of the bay
grows visible beneath him. He smokes and yawns.
Ooo-augh,
            and the limitless
shabby lion-pelt of the desert completes and rounds
his limitless ennui.

At dawn, in the gathering impetus of day, the laager sleeps.
Some restless princes dream: first light denies them
the luxury of nothing. But others their mates more lucky
drown in the lightless grottoes. (Companionable death
has lent them his ease for a moment.)
            The dreamers remember
a departure like a migration. They recall a landscape
associated with warmth and veils and a pantomime
but never focused exactly. The flopping curtain
reveals scene-shifters running with freshly painted
incongruous sets. Here childhood's prairie garden
looms like a pampas, where grown-ups stalk (gross outlaws)
on legs of tree trunk: recedes: and the strepitant jungle
 dwindles to scruff of shrubs on a docile common,
 all but real for a moment, then gone.

          The sleepers turn
gone but still no nothing laves them.
O misery, desire, desire, tautening cords of the bedrack!
Eros, in the teeth of Yahveh and his tight-lipped sect
confound the deniers of their youth! Let war lie wounded!
Eros, grant forgiveness and release
and return – against which they erect it,
the cairn of patience. *No dear, won't be long now
keep fingers crossed, chin up, keep smiling darling
be seeing you soon.*

On the horizon fires fluff now,
further than they seem.

          Sollum and Halfaya
a while yet before we leave you in quiet
and our needle swings north.

          The sleepers toss
and turn before waking: they feel through their blankets
the cold of the malevolent bomb-thumped desert,
impartial
hostile to both.

The laager is one.
Friends and enemies, haters and lovers
both sleep and dream.

So Long

*(Recrossing the Sollum Frontier from Libya into Egypt, 22 May 1943, in a
lorry carrying captured enemy equipment)*

To the war in Africa that's over – goodnight.
   To thousands of assorted vehicles, in every stage of decomposition,
   littering the desert from here to Tunis – goodnight.
To thousands of guns and armoured fighting vehicles
   brewed up, blackened and charred
   from Alamein to here, from here to Tunis – goodnight.

To thousands of crosses of every shape and pattern,
  alone or in little huddles, under which the unlucky bastards lie—
    goodnight

                 Horse-shoe curve of the bay,
              clean razor-edge of the escarpment,
           tonight it's the sunset only that's blooding you.

Halfaya and Sollum: I think that at long last
  we can promise you a little quiet.

So long. I hope I won't be seeing you.

To the sodding desert – you know what you can do with yourself.

To the African deadland – God help you – and goodnight.

HAMISH HENDERSON

*Intelligence Officer, Alamein. 51st Highland Div., Libya, Tunisia and
Sicily. Mentioned in despatches. At Anzio. Liaison with Italian partisans.
Research Fellow in School of Scottish Studies.*

Night Patrol

        Muttered the sea, the hill
        And silent wadis lay
        Black in the moon, when we to kill
        Went on our silent way.

        Whispers of listless wind
        Hissed in the drifting sand
        And ancient names gaunt bushes signed
        In a forgotten hand.

        Menacing ill the wrack
        Of last year's battle frowned
        Grim in the dark, most like the mark
        Of Cain upon the ground.

        Silent, we came, we killed.
        One blow, and quiet he lay.

One cry, and all was stilled:
Then silent we crept away.

QUINTIN HOGG

*(Viscount Hailsham of St Marylebone, CH, FRS), Rifle Brigade,
Middle East. Later Lord Chancellor.*

War Poet

I am the man who looked for peace and found
My own eyes barbed.
I am the man who groped for words and found
An arrow in my hand.
I am the builder whose firm walls surround
A slipping land.
When I grow sick or mad
Mock me not nor chain me;
When I reach for the wind
Cast me not down
Though my face is a burnt book
And a wasted town.

March 1942

Advice for a Journey

The drums mutter for war, and soon we must begin
To seek the country where they say that joy
Springs flowerlike among the rocks, to win
The fabulous golden mountain of our peace.

O my friends, we are too young
To be explorers, have no skill nor compass,
Nor even that iron certitude which swung
Our fathers at their self-fulfilling North

So take no rations, remember not your homes –
Only the blind and stubborn hope to track

This wilderness. The thoughtful leave their bones
In windy foodless meadows of despair.

Never look back, nor too far forward search
For the white Everest of your desire;
The screes roll underfoot, and you will never reach
Those brittle peaks which only clouds may walk.

Others have come before you, and immortal
Live like reflections. Their still faces
Will give you courage to ignore the subtle
Sneer of the gentian and the ice-worn pebble.

The fifes cry death and the sharp winds call;
Set your face to the rock; go on, go out
Into the bad lands of battle, the cloud-wall
Of the future, my friends, and leave your fear.

Go forth, my friends, the raven is no sibyl
Break the clouds' anger with your unchanged faces.
You'll find, maybe, the dream under the hill –
But never Canaan, nor any golden mountain.

SIDNEY KEYES

*Lieutenant in Queens Own West Kent. Captured on patrol in N. Africa
and died 19 April, 1943.*

Sand

We have seen sand frothing like the sea
About our wheels and in our wake,
Clouds rolling yellow and opaque,
Thick-smoking from the ground;
Wrapped in the dust from sun and sky
Without a mark to guide them by
Men drove along unseeing in the cloud,
Peering to find a track, to find a way,
With eyes stung red, clown-faces coated grey.
Then with sore lips we cursed the sand,
Cursed this sullen gritty land
– Cursed and dragged on our blind and clogging way.

We have felt the fevered Khamsin blow
Which whips the desert into sting and spite
Of dry-sand driving rain (the only rain
The parched and dusty sand-lands know,
The hot dry driven sand), the desert floor
Whipped by the wind drives needles in the air
Which pricked our eyelids blind; and in a night,
Sifting the drifted sandhills grain by grain,
Covers our shallow tracks, our laboured road,
Makes false the maps we made with such slow care.

And we have seen wonders, spinning towers of sand
– Moving pillars of cloud by day –
Which passed and twitched our tents away;
Lakes where no water was, and in the sky
Grey shimmering palms. We have learned the sun and stars
And new simplicities, living by our cars
In wastes without one tree or living thing,
Where the flat horizon's level ring
Is equal everywhere without a change.

Yet sand has been kind for us to lie at ease,
Its soft dug walls have sheltered and made a shield
From fear and danger, and the chilly night.
And as we quit this bare unlovely land,
Strangely again see houses, hills and trees,
We will remember older things than these,
Indigo skies pricked out with brilliant light,
The smooth unshadowed candour of the sand.

Buerat-el-Hsun, January 1943

At a War Grave

No grave is rich, the dust that herein lies
Beneath this white cross mixing with the sand
Was vital once, with skill of eye and hand
And speed of brain. These will not re-arise
These riches, nor will they be replaced;

They are lost and nothing now, and here is left
Only a worthless corpse of sense bereft,
Symbol of death, and sacrifice and waste.

El Alamein, 30 October 1942

El Alamein

There are flowers now, they say, at Alamein;
Yes, flowers in the minefields now.
So those that come to view that vacant scene,
Where death remains and agony has been
Will find the lilies grow –
Flowers, and nothing that we know.

So they rang the bells for us and Alamein,
Bells which we could not hear.
And to those that heard the bells what could it mean,
The name of loss and pride, El Alamein?
– Not the murk and harm of war.
But their hope, their own warm prayer.

It will become a staid historic name,
That crazy sea of sand!
Like Troy or Agincourt its single fame
Will be the garland for our brow, our claim,
On us a fleck of glory to the end;
And there our dead will keep their holy ground.

But this is not the place that we recall,
The crowded desert crossed with foaming tracks,
The one blotched building, lacking half a wall,
The grey-faced men, sand-powdered over all;
The tanks, the guns, the trucks,
The black, dark-smoking wrecks.

So be it; none but us has known that land;
El Alamein will still be only ours
And those ten days of chaos in the sand.
Others will come who cannot understand,

Will halt beside the rusty minefield wires
and find there, flowers.

JOHN JARMAIN

*Captain 51st Highland Division, anti-tank unit. Chiefly Western Desert,
but killed in Normandy, 26 June 1944. The night before he worked
through the records of his unit, assessing each man. Like Keith Douglas,
he foresaw his own end. Against advice he went on a recce into St
Honorine la Chardonnerette, to be killed by a German mortar bomb.*

The Taking of the Koppie

No, it was only a touch of dysentery, he said. He was doing fine
    now thank you . . . What the hell were the chaps grousing
    about anyhow?

He was sitting on the edge of his hospital cot clad only in a slip
    with both his feet on the floor,
his strong young body straight and graceful as a tree, golden as
    any pomegranate but only firmer,
its smooth surface uncracked, gashed with no fissure by the
    burning blazing sun of war;
and with his muscles rippling lightly
like a vlei's shallows by the reeds touched by the first breath of
    the wind of dawn,
as he swung his one leg over onto the other.

He was telling us about the death of the colonel and the major
    whom all the men, especially the younger ones, worshipped.
'The colonel copped it from a stray bullet. It must have been a
    sniper . . .
just a neat little hole in the middle of his forehead, no bigger than
    a tickey, and he dropped dead in his tracks.
The major was leading us over some rough open ground
    between the gully and the far koppie
when a burst of machine gun bullets smacked from the kloof,
    tearing him open;
he was a long way ahead of us all and as he fell he shouted:
"Stop! Stay where you are! Don't come near me! Look out for

those machine guns! There's one in the antheap and one on the
   ledge . . .
   Bring up the mortars! The rest take cover!"
Then he rolled over on his back, blood streaming all over his
   body, and with a dabble of blood on his lips he died – Christ,
   what a man he was!'

The boy reached for a match box, then lighting a cigarette, he
   continued:
'We came on them about ten minutes later, three Ities curled up
   on some straw in a sort of dugout
– as snug as a bug on a rug – and they were sleeping . . .
The two on the outside were young, I noticed. They were all
   unshaven. The bloke in the middle had a dirty grey stubble of
   beard – and that's all I noticed . . .'

As the boy stopped talking he moved, his hair falling in thick
   yellow curls over his forehead, his eyes.
And as I caught the soft gleam of blue behind the strands of gold
I was suddenly reminded of quiet pools of water after rain
among the golden gorse that mantle in early summer
the browning hills of Provence.

'Then I put my bayonet through each of them in turn, just in the
   right place, and they did not even grunt or murmur . . .'

There was no sadism in his voice, no savagery, no brutal pride
   or perverse eagerness to impress,
no joy, no exultation.
He spoke as if he were telling of a rugby match
in which he wasn't much interested
and in which he took no sides.

And as I looked at his eyes again
I was struck with wonderment
at their bigness, their blueness, their clarity
and how young they were, how innocent.

Before Sidi Rezegh

'– When
will the offensive start?
This time
we won't shove the horse before the cart,

will we?'
'– Not on your life! . . .'

Here
marooned among the sands,
lost for ever it seems

in these grey wastes (haunted by the wind, made spectral by the
    driving dust), dim now, dimmer than dreams,
where no sun shines, nothing gleams,
not even the truck's small squat mirror (still exposed contrary to
    the brigade major's express commands);
in the dead heart of this deadest of dead lands
where nothing, nothing stands
fast or fixed, erect in a horizontal world,
only the sand lifts,
only the sand drifts, shifts,
twirled
by the wind, swirled
by the wild wind's spasmodic eddies, hurled
forward ceaselessly
as over a bone-dry beach the powder of a myriad shells lashed by a
    gale sprung screaming from the sea;

here
in this desertland of wind, sand and dust and a great tank battle
    impending;
in whose vast vacant depths one hears at dawn under the falling
    dew, under a brilliant blood-red sky, no song of lark ascending;
and whose sole song – o soon, too soon! – will be the blast of the
    barrage, a blending
of the dive-bomber's swelling drone, its sudden screech as it swoops
    down, with the thunder of cannon: the crackle
of rapid rifle-fire with the Bofors' steady pounding, slow and deep,
    deliberate: the crazy cackle
of machine-guns spitting their spraying, splaying bullets with the
    reverberate never-ending
roar of the sixty-pounders, shrill whistle of shells, the whine, the
    scream, the crump of bombs descending;
here

somewhere,
nowhere
as in a limbo lost
where till today no human tracks have ever crossed,
the long convoy stands in the late afternoon, has somehow got stuck
– only the conversation never flags, back of the truck.
Do you hear? Benghazi or bust,
Benghazi or bust . . .'

Is it the wind's monologue,
muffled, mournful?
Or the sands' patter
falling flatter, flatter
to a low halftone
insistent as the dry scraping of bone upon bone?
Or merely the men's idle chatter
as they stumble about the truck searching for bullybeef, groping
    among the boxes, tins, dixies with a dull clatter?

Who speaks?
What voices are these
rising above the wind's moan,
rising above the truckflaps' jerky drumming, the sands' dull drone
that have as monotonous, as wearied a sound as the slow drip-drop
    of water on worn stone?
'– *Kry end, man, kry end! Skei uit!*' '– Yes, turn it up . . .'
    '– Piet's right, you're getting rattled, Ken . . .
What's biting you? The thought of death? But then death will
    come, *must* come, like measles to all men.
And once it's over and done with, well, you're damn dead and
    there's no more dying then!'
'– Bill, wait, wait! We'll go together! Bill, Bill . . .'

Is it the wind's monologue,
muffled, mournful?
Or the sands' patter
falling flatter, flatter
to a low halftone
insistent as the dry scraping of bone upon bone?
Or merely the men's idle chatter

as they stumble about the truck searching for bullybeef, groping
   among the boxes tins, dixies with a dull clatter?

Who calls?
Who speaks?
Who in this half light stumbles
incessantly, again and again
as over rough broken ground? Who fumbles
with clumsy hands as under a leaden, sagging sky daylong the
   tentative rain?
Who in this dim drowned world of sense and thought mumbles
brokenly, back of my brain?

'– So man your gun and fight like fun and let the world go hang,
my son, and let the world go hang, go hang!

'– Pull finger, Piet! Pass me the jam . . . Thanks, that's wizard . . .'
'Damm! There's grit even in the jam tin . . .'
   '– Just listen to it! It's no blasted wind that, but a blizzard . . .'

Slowly, cumbersomely the long convoy stirs, wakes
to life again and like a sluggish monster that has been a long time
   sleeping, shakes
itself along its entire length, jerks, jolts once, twice, then churning
   up sand takes
to the main track, goes skeetering down the escarpment's
   crumbling slope with a grinding, screeching of brakes.

Now the voices die . . .
Now only the wind and the sand and the slipping, sliding wheels
   reply
and the heart
echoing this one cry
– the dumb, desiccated heart
sunk into its own silences, apart,
without pity, without pain,
drained even of its own despair –
rising to a single spate of sound
as the wheels grip, slip faster over the hard firm ground,
again and again, again:
When will the offensive start?
When will the offensive start?

WHEN
WILL
THE OFFENSIVE
START?

On the Libyan Border, November 1941

Hospital Ship *(Abridged)*
(Translated from Afrikaans by the poet)

Day by day
a thick sticky sea:
a single slab
of greyish blue treacle
unfolding itself
in a solitary furrow
slowly, turgidly
from the stern
of the S.S. Amra.

Day by day
against the vague horizon,
upon the ragged fringes of the earth,
the dull blunted edges of the world,
scarcely higher than the grey sea's surface,
and yet greyer
equally barren
equally forsaken
equally forsaken desert;

at times heaving itself up
above its flat dead levels
into a chain of mountains
with every cliff, every cape, every crest
rigid and gaunt and naked,
and whose sharp-pointed peaks
while they cut into sight
rasp the horizon's rim,
bite like the teeth of a saw
deep into the hard heavens,
devouring the sky

Day by day
this torrid tropical heat
that drips from the armpits,
streams from the pallid foreheads
of the sick and wounded,
deadens the sparkle
on the surgeon's silver and nickel instruments
into a glassy glitter,
glazes the glistening panels, copper and bronze work,
slips a thin moist film
over the shining rails, balustrades, door-knobs, handles,
and sweats itself out in a muggy ooze
against the white walls
of every cabin, every ward
even here on the topmost deck.

And now
softly,
almost imperceptible
— like a slow, stealing in on the senses —
the rain,
the rain,
the rippling rain
come from beyond the sea's limit,
the sky's stark circle, the earth's jagged frontiers,
the rain
whispering from far and near
over the waters

The rain
calm as an old man
who with quiet gestures,
quiet demeanour,
comes trolling,
lost in thought,
across the fields;
and who leaning on his staff,
wanders where the flowers
show white among the grass.

Now the rain whispers.
The sea, as sibilant, whispers with it.

while the S.S. Arma,
slender and slim and snow-white,
with its only sound
a soft seething of spume about its bows,
its only motion
a slight tremor through its entire body,
slips silent as a shadow
through the rain
whispering over the waters.

Suddenly
here in the ward
on the top deck
we sense the rain,
we feel, hear, smell it,
we see the rain!
Some of the wounded
sit bolt upright in their beds
with their mouths half open
– and joy
like floodwaters
long dammed up
bursts its bonds,
lifts us out of ourselves,
rears us upon its toppling crests
and then sweeps on
eddying away . . .
while the rain
whispers over the sea
and the sea
whispers under the rain.

Gulf of Aden, 17 May, 1941

UYS KRIGE

(South Africa) *War correspondent Egypt and Abyssinia. South Africa's
leading Second World War poet. POW Camp No. 78, Italy.*

Poem

I have remained in the café
Long since the sour red wine
Sank to black dregs in my glass
And think if the chair next to mine
Will again be tenanted, who will come in
Before the café's beetle dark begins.

You, coming first with crinkled eyes
Into the yellow shout of light
And the stale smell, suddenly
From the unreceptive night's
Old fingers which our own new war unties
To blind in blackout streets the cars' weak eyes;

Sitting at my table, pretending
That no one watches you,
Hesitant, beginning politely to speak
How empty the time, having nothing to do;
Why were you quick-eyed frightened,
So that at each newcomer your throat muscles tightened?

Later the woman with a sloppy mouth,
Humped in the chair next to mine,
Not very hopeful amateur tart
Whose cheap hot smell spoilt the taste of wine;
Why were your meaty hands not still,
Not for a moment still?

I do not want your body
Or your soul, or your creed,
You have no glance, nor grace
Nor love that I need;
Though from the eyes the soul is fever ill
And the hands are never still.

Being nothing to me these are brethren,
Sloppy mouth, moth hands and loose eyes
These are the friends I have and will hold
In our hate and sentimental lies;
We are the ancient easy game, we are yet cheap
For power and slaughter; these are the friends I will keep.

Because I hate and want no reason,
No more of words or scientific logic,
No more the regretful, relentless
Equation of the economic;
These are my friends, whose eyes were put out
By those they do not know to hate.

Military Hospital

The Matron, red-caped, terrible,
Inspects the ward; incredible
How tall she is – six foot – how stare
Those brown, protuberant eyes – beware,
Beware lest looming by your bed
It enter into her great head –
So huge she is, so weak you are –
To order you an enema.

L.K. LAWLER

In Middle East and Palestine. BBC.

Glac a' Bhais

*Thubhairt Nàsach air choreigin gun tug am Furair air ais do fhir na Gearmailte
'a' chòir agus an sonas bàs fhaotainn anns an àraich'.*

'Na shuidhe marbh an 'Glaic a' Bhàis'
fo Dhruim Ruidhìseit,
gill' òg 's a logan sìos m' a ghruaïdh
's a thuar grìsionn.

Smaoinich mi air a' chòir's an àgh
a fhuair e bho Fhurair,
bhith tuiteam ann an raon an àir
gun éirigh tuilleadh;

air a' ghreadhnachas 's air a' chliù
nach d' fhuair e' na aonar,
ged b' esan bu bhrònaiche snuadh
ann an glaic air laomadh

le cuileagan mu chuirp ghlas'
air gainmhich lachduinn
's i'salach–bhuidhe 's làn de raip
's de sprùidhlich catha.

An robh an gille air an dream
a mhàb na h-Iùdhaich
's na Comunnaich, no air an dream
bu mhotha, dhiùbh–san

a threòoaicheadh bho thoiseach àl
gun deòin gu buaireadh
agus bruaillean cuthaich gach blàir
air sgàth uachdaran?

Ge b'e a dheòin-san no a chàs,
a neoichiontas no mhìorun,
cha do nochd e toileachadh 'na bhàs
fo Dhruim Ruidhìseit.

Death Valley

*Some Nazi or other has said that the Fuehrer had restored to German manhood
the 'right and joy of dying in battle'*

Sitting dead in 'Death Valley'
below the Ruweisat Ridge
a boy with his forelock down about his cheek
and his face slate-grey;

I thought of the right and the joy
that he got from his Fuehrer,
of falling in the field of slaughter
to rise no more;

of the pomp and the fame
that he had, not alone,
though he was the most piteous to see
in a valley gone to seed

with flies about grey corpses
on a dun sand
dirty yellow and full of the rubbish
and fragments of battle.

Was the boy of the band
who abused the Jews
and Communists, or of the greater
band of those

led, from the beginning of generations,
unwillingly to the trial
and mad delirium of every war
for the sake of rulers?

Whatever his desire or mishap,
his innocence or malignity,
he showed no pleasure in his death
below the Ruweisat Ridge.

Latha Foghair

'S mi air an t-slios ud
latha foghair,
na sligean a'sianail mu m' chluasan
agus sianar marbh ri mo ghualainn,
rag-mharbh – is reòta mur b'e 'n teas –
mar gum b' ann a' fuireach ri fios.

Nuair thàinig an sgriach
a mach as a' ghréin,
á buille 's bualadh do-fhaicsinn,
leum an lasair agus streap an ceathach
agus bhàrc e gacha rathad:
dalladh nan sùl, sgoltadh claistinn.

'S 'na dhéidh, an sianar marbh,
fad an latha;
am miosg nan sligean 'san t-strannraich
anns a' mhadainn,
agus a rithist aig meadhon-latha
agus 'san fheasgar.

Ris a' ghréin 's i cho coma,
cho geal cràiteach;
air a' ghainmhich 's i cho tìorail

socair bàidheil;
agus fo reultan Africa,
's iad leugach àlainn.

Ghabh aon Taghadh iadsan
's cha d' ghabh e mise,
gun fhoighneachd dhinn
có b' fheàrr no bu mhiosa:
ar liom, cho diabhlaidh coma
ris na sligean.

Sianar marbh ri mo ghualainn
latha foghair.

An Autumn Day

On that slope
on an autumn day,
the shells soughing about my ears
and six dead men at my shoulder,
dead and stiff — and frozen were it not for the heat
as if they were waiting for a message.

When the screech came
out of the sun,
out of an invisible throbbing;
the flame leaped and the smoke climbed
and surged every way:
blinding of eyes, splitting of hearing.

And after it, the six men dead
the whole day:
among the shells snoring
in the morning,
and again at midday
and in the evening.

In the sun, which was so indifferent,
so white and painful;
on the sand which was so comfortable
easy and kindly;
and under the stars of Africa,
jewelled and beautiful.

One Election took them
and did not take me,
without asking us
which was better or worse:
it seemed as devilishly indifferent
as the shells.

Six men dead at my shoulder
on an Autumn day.

SOMHAIRLE MACGILL-EAIN
SORLEY MACLEAN

Signals Corps in the Desert, wounded at Alamein.

El-Alamein

'Se nochd oidhche bhatail mhóir,
'S tha gach aon againn air dòigh,
Le 'rifle' 's biodag thruis nar dòrn
Air bruachan ciùin El-Alamein.

Tha'n t-anmoch nis ri tarraing dlùth,
Tha ghealach togail ceann 's na neuil,
'S tha balaich chalma ri cur cùrs
Air tulaich àrd El-Alamein.

'S beag mo chàil bhith 'n so an dràsd;
'S mór gum b'àill leam à bhith tàmh
An Eilean Leódhais le mo ghràdh
Fo sgàil Fir Bhréige Chalanais.

Ach sud am 'Fifty-first' an sàs,
Seòid na b'fheàrr cha deach gu blàr,
Na Siphorts, 's Camronaich 's Earr-Ghaidheal
Cur smùid ast' le'n cuid bhiodagan.

Tha nise seachdain agus còrr
Bho chuir mi na rainn-s' air dòigh,
'S tha Rommel le chuid Africa Corp
Air ruaig air falbh bho Alamein.

Cha robh buaidh bha sud gun phrìs,
Phàigh sinn oirr' le fuil ar crìdh;
Tha sinn fàgail mìltean sìnt'
San uaigh an ùir El-Alamein.

Chan eil an so ach dùthaich thruagh,
Chan eil deoch innte na biadh;
'Bully Beef' is brioscaid chruaidh,
'Se sud am biadh tha againne.

Bu shuarach leam bhith greis gun bhiadh,
Greis gun thàmh is greis gun dìon,
Ach tart ro-mhór thug bhuam mo chiall
'S a dh'fhàg mi 'n diugh ri fannachadh.

Is ged tha teas na fàsaich mhóir
Ga mo phianadh 's ga mo leòn,
Na faighinn-s' innte làn mo bheòil
De dh'uisge fuar cha ghearaininn.

Nan robh agam 'n so an dràsd
Cothrom air an Tobair Bhàin
Chan fhàgainn i gum biodh i tràight'
Ged bhiodh innt' na gallanan.

El-Alamein

Tonight is the night of the battle
And each one of us is in good order,
With a rifle and bayonet gripped in our hands
On the line of El Alamein.

Evening is now drawing near;
The moon raises her head in the clouds,
And strong resolute men are setting a course
To the high mounds of Alamein.

Little my appetite to be here;
Now would I were resting
With my love in the Isle of Lewis
Underneath the shade of the Callanish Standing Stones.

But there's the 51st[1] into action,
Better lads never went into battle:
The Seaforths, Camerons and Argylls
Dashing them to pieces with their bayonets.

There is now a week and more
Since I put these verses together,
And Rommel with his Africa Corps
Is in flight from Alamein

That victory was not without price
Paid with the blood of our hearts;
We are leaving thousands prostrate
In graves in the dust of Alamein.

This is but poor country
Without food or drink of its own;
'Bully beef' and hard biscuit,
That is the food we carry.

I am indifferent a while to being without food,
A while without rest or without shelter,
But the great thirst has taken my sense away,
Leaving me feebly fatigued.

And though the heat of the wide desert
Pain is wounding to me,
If I could only get a mouthful
Of cold water I would not complain.

But if I had here
One chance to get at the White Well[2]
I wouldn't leave her until she was dry
Though there are gallons upon gallons within her.

1 51st Highland Division.
2 The well at home.

ORAIN Á BRADHAGAIR, Á CALANAIS, 'S ÁS AN RUBHA LE CALUM
MACLEÒID NO CALUM CUDDY Á CALANAIS
MALCOLM MACLEOD

Served with The Seaforth Highlanders, 51st Highland Division, in North
Africa.

Desert Conflict

Written by Sgt Calvin Makabo 1946 Coy. A.A.P.C. (Basuto), on the occasion of King George VI's visit to the Western Desert in 1943 after the defeat of Rommel. Sgt Makabo was drowned west of Tripoli later in 1943. Translation by Sgt Alexander Qoboshane.

Cast your eyes and look over to the ocean and see ships.
It is far, you cannot see with your naked eyes.
Had it not been so, you could see the track of a big sea snake.
It is dusty, it is where the sea dogs play.
Raise the waves and hide yourselves, for you see the country has
    changed.
England and Berlin are in confliction.
It is where we saw bulls in a rage,
Each one being proud of its equipment.

A woman left the baby and ran away,
The women up north are crying,
They cry facing towards the east,
And say 'There our husbands have disappeared'.
Keep silent and listen to the war affairs.
Year before last in September,
There were great flashes towards the west.
It is there the enemy were troublesome.
The Resident Commissioner heard from home,
He heard about great deeds done by Africans,
He heard they were victorious.
Rommel neglected his duties.
The son of Makabo has taken part in those deeds.
The Chiefs at home heard – Chiefs Theko, Litingoana, Seele Tane
    and Mahabe

You always deceive us and say that
His Majesty King George VI is not seen.
A telegraphic message was sent from England to Tripoli.
It was received in the morning,

And delivered to the companies on Saturday, 21st June.
All Companies according to their race and colour
Coming to cheer the King.
There were those with three stars on their shoulder,

And those who had a crown in their hands.

The General Lyon[1] went down by the main road being silent.
There was wireless round his motor car,
And cannons guarding him on all sides;
Then the soldiers cheered the King as he passed and shouted
  HURRAH!

1 'General Lyon' was the code name for the King.

CALVIN MAKABO

The Captured

Barrage silk cast shadows where we sat
on kit bags gas mask and tin hat embedded in a crusted sand.
We sat swatting Egypt's flies with a peaked hat.
Our R.T.O.[1] was having someone on the mat,
still we sat, watching rusted prows of
sunken ships – grim reminder this was war,
a harbour bombed a little while before –
now Tewfik slumbered, as we reclined
uncomfortably on an alien shore.

Marching four abreast in column array
Hitler's beaten army halted for transport in the Bay,
tired features creased by particles of desert dust
shabby uniforms infested by its all embracing crust,
dust – entrenched itself in ridges on head gear sadly worn,
irritated sweated forelocks closely shorn.
Down-at-heel boots made no imprint in sand
fringing polluted land – ugly born.

Bleak eyes had this sullen band
arrogant in their shifting sideways stare,
eyes that had witnessed swift victory in other lands –
then reluctant surrender chill despair
a valedictory to high hopes
to triumph that was never really there.
Where shifting dunes shimmer under Libya's molten sky
vultures cast shadows flying high

over rock cairned graves where comrades lie.
'Neath windswept desert's rim barb wire had hemmed them in;
between reaching fingers of twisted wire
threadbare prisoners huddled as cattle in a byre
their hearts racked with questioning doubt,
minds seared from barb's reality.
Beings filled with but one desire
to throw twigs on a home hearth fire.
Sentry go on sentry beat made mockery of a dream complete –
they scrambled for the 'cigs' we threw –
then cursed us 'cause there were so few.

Egypt, 1941

1 Railway Transport Officer

WILLIAM E. MORRIS

(New Zealand) NZEF in Western Desert and Italy. NCO on railway lines to run military stock in Desert Construction Unit, June 1940 (12th Railway Survey Company).

It's Always Mealtime

Oh, they're queueing up for breakfast, they have rattled on the
    gong;
Hear the mess tins jingle-jangle. Let us go and join the throng.
There is porridge made from biscuits. There's a Soya for the fry.
There is tea that tastes of onions; there is bread that's rather dry;
And the cooks are looking browned off as they pass the grub
    along.
Oh, that look they get from cookhouses and drinking tea too
    strong.

Oh, it must be time for tiffin. What d'you think it is today?
Well, there's fish and meat and pickle mixed in some peculiar way.
There is yellow cheese as usual, and marg., and that's the lot –
Oh, help yourself to biscuits, 'cos the weather's ——— hot.
And the cooks are looking browned off as a dollop each one deals.
The look they get from arguing and never eating meals.

You can tell it's time for dinner by the fidgets of the queue,
And it's world-without-end bully meat mocked up as pie or stew,
And if you're mighty lucky, there'll be flour in the 'duff,'
But the chances are it's rice again, and rice is . . . rough.
So the cooks are looking browned off, slightly woebegone and
    worn.
The look that comes from cards all night, and lighting fires at
    dawn.

N.T. MORRIS

*Enlisted September 1940, 50th Royal Tank Regt., Western Desert,
Sicily, Italy and Greece.*

Halt for Lunch

A light wind whips the flame to furnace heat.
'It's on the boil, throw out the milk and tea,'
Says Atkins, 'what we going to have to eat?'
Somebody stirs the petrol-sodden sand;
The dixie-lid spurts steam.
                    'There's M and V'
I say, 'as good as anything. And canned
Pineapple.'
            They agree. The cans are stood
In water on the fire-tin. Mercifully
The dust storm has died down.
                    'There is some wood
Somewhere inside the truck' says Cpl Dean.
The air is very still. A smell of bully,
And chips and onions fried in margarine
Comes from a truck a hundred yards from ours.
The sky would match a Suffolk sky at home,
Pale blue and cloudless. Small sweet-scented flowers
Make sweet pretence of Spring. The burnt-out husk
Of a wild idea conceived in distant Rome
Stands near at hand, where desert scrub and musk
Have given place to strange, hewn wooden plants,
Whose harvest has been plucked, and whose rough branches

Are done with Spring forever.
　　　　　　　　Two spidery ants
With triply bulbous bodies come and go
In aimless haste.
　　　　　　　Some men are digging trenches
Unhurriedly. McCartney tries to sew
A button on his trousers at the back,
And turns round like a corkscrew.
　　　　　　　　　　'Take 'em off'
Says Atkins.
　　　　　　'What, in front of you?' says Mac,
And tries to blush. He does not find that easy,
Being older than us all in years and love,
Three times in jail, and twelve years in the Army.
I lean against the wheel and close my eyes,
The water in the tin is bubbling softly.
Two amorous and persistent desert flies
Whine in my ears. Small sounds can sometimes quell
The roaring of great silences.
　　　　　　　　Then faintly
A new sound strikes the air, a surge and swell
Like angry breakers on grim distant shores –
A sullen hateful sound, evil, portentous,
That grows in wrath and volume, till it roars
Its hatred and defiance overhead.
From half a score fierce throats.
　　　　　　　　'Look out, they're Stukas!'
'Where's my tin hat?'
　　　　　　　Ghent has already fled.
We jump into a trench. The mighty throbbing
Is changing key. Two of us have a Bren
And one a rifle. Ghent is almost sobbing,
From breathlessness and panic. It is the first.
The planes turn round into the sun, and then:
A sudden pause.
　　　　　　　These moments are the worst.
Five dreadful seconds, five eternities,
Five bars of trembling silence.
　　　　　　　　Nothing stirs.
Breathless and tense we listen. Here it is:
A throb, a hum, a deep full-throated roar,

The whistling of rushing air, and now our ears
Are helpless in the turmoil and furore
Of impact and explosion. As they land,
Bursting and crashing to a wild crescendo,
The bombs send up great founts of smoke and sand.
Wandering shrapnel whistles through the air,
Uttering a long-drawn sigh, as if in sorrow
At finding no soft mark or target there.
The planes are past us now. The last bombs fall,
The roaring dies away; and it is over.
We clamber up and dust ourselves. 'That's all,'
Says Atkins, 'that's our lot. Cups up for tea.'
And when the smoke has lifted we discover
One truck ablaze; one torch for Liberty.

G.C. NORMAN

Territorial Army 1939 and served in France, Egypt, North Africa and Italy.

Shite-Hawk Over the Desert

Part red, part brown, black-barred, and with a head
Of greyish-white, he builds his nest with sticks.
For these and other scraps, where men have bled
In desert-lands, and saints accepted kicks,
He soars beneath the blue, above the red
Of day's hot sand. The weary camel licks
Thick mud. The kite flies by the dead
Of battle, hardly hears the clicks
Of bayonet-fixing, or of metal tread
Of tank, or safety-catch. He knows our tricks
Too well. With summer's dried up river-bed
As our last refuge, in our desperate fix,
We watch him hover, scorning noon's bright sun,
And wonder if our time is nearly done.

K. PARKER

Eighth Army.

The Net

The net like a white vault, hung overhead
Dewy and glistening in the full moon's light,
Which cast a shadow-pattern of the thread
Over our face and arms, laid still and white
Like polished ivories on the dark bed.
The truck's low side concealed from us the sight
Of tents and bivouacs and track-torn sand
That lay without; only a distant sound
Of gunfire sometimes or, more close at hand,
A bomb, with dull concussion of the ground,
Pressed in upon our world, where, all else banned,
Our lonely souls eddied like echoing sound
Under the white cathedral of the net,
And like a skylark in captivity
Hung fluttering in the meshes of our fate,
With death at hand and, round, eternity.

ENOCH POWELL

MBE. *Rose from Private to Brigadier. GHQ, MEF.*

Soldiers Bathing

The sea at evening moves across the sand.
Under a reddening sky I watch the freedom of a band
Of soldiers who belong to me. Stripped bare
For bathing in the sea, they shout and run in the warm air;
Their flesh, worn by the trade of war, revives
And my mind towards the meaning of it strives.
All's pathos now. The body that was gross,
Rank, ravenous, disgusting in the act or in repose,
All fever, filth and sweat, its bestial strength
And bestial decay, by pain and labour grows at length
Fragile and luminous. 'Poor bare forked animal,'
Conscious of his desires and needs and flesh that rise and fall,
Stands in the soft air, tasting after toil
The sweetness of his nakedness: letting the sea-waves coil

Their frothy tongues about his feet, forgets
His hatred of the war, its terrible pressure that begets
A machinery of death and slavery,
Each being a slave and making slaves of others: finds that he
Remembers his old freedom in a game
Mocking himself, and comically mimics fear and shame.

He plays with death and animality;
And reading in the shadows of his pallid flesh, I see
The idea of Michelangelo's cartoon
Of soldiers bathing, breaking off before they were half done
At some sortie of the enemy, an episode
Of the Pisan wars with Florence. I remember how he showed
Their muscular limbs that clamber from the water,
And heads that turn across the shoulder, eager for the slaughter,
Forgetful of their bodies that are bare,
And hot to buckle on and use the weapons lying there.
– And I think too of the theme another found
When, shadowing men's bodies on a sinister red ground,
Another Florentine, Pollaiuolo,
Painted a naked battle: warriors, straddled, hacked the foe,
Dug their bare toes into the ground and slew
The brother-naked man who lay between their feet and drew
His lips back from his teeth in a grimace.

They were Italians who knew war's sorrow and disgrace
And showed the thing suspended, stripped: a theme
Born out of the experience of war's horrible extreme
Beneath a sky where even the air flows
With lacrimae Christi. For that rage, that bitterness, those blows,
That hatred of the slain, what could they be
But indirectly or directly a commentary
On the Crucifixion? And the picture burns
With indignation and pity and despair by turns,
Because it is the obverse of the scene
Where Christ hangs murdered, stripped, upon the Cross. I mean,
That is the explanation of its rage.

And we too have our bitterness and pity that engage
Blood, spirit, in this war. But night begins,
Night of the mind: who nowadays is conscious of our sins?
Though every human deed concerns our blood,

And even we must know, what nobody had understood,
That some great love is over all we do,
And that is what has driven us to this fury, for so few
Can suffer all the terror of that love:
The terror of that love has set us spinning in this groove
Greased with our blood.

      These dry themselves and dress,
Combing their hair, forget the fear and shame of nakedness.
Because to love is frightening we prefer
The freedom of our crimes. Yet, as I drink the dusky air,
I feel a strange delight that fills me full,
Strange gratitude, as if evil itself were beautiful,
And kiss the wound in thought, while in the west
I watch a streak of red that might have issued from Christ's breast.

F.T. PRINCE

Captain, Intelligence Corps MEF. Professor of English at Southampton University.

Landscape: Western Desert

    Winds carve this land
    And velvet whorls of sand
    Annul footprint and grave
    Of lover, fool, and knave.
    Briefly the vetches bloom
    In the blind desert room
    When humble, bright and brave
    Met common doom.

    Their gear and shift
    Smother in soft sand-drift,
    Less perishable, less
    Soon in rottenness.
    Their war-spent tools of trade
    In the huge space parade;
    And with this last distress,
    All scores are paid.

And who will see,
In such last anarchy
Of loveless lapse and loss
Which the blind sands now gloss,
The common heart which meant
Such good in its intent;
Such noble common dross
Suddenly spent.

JOHN PUDNEY

RAF Squadron Leader, 1940–5. RAF Poet of the War.

Danse Grotesque

The Devil played the drums when Peter died
An overture of bombs and crashing sound
    A whirling slip of splinter caught his side
    And deftly set his body spinning round

Alas! He missed his final curtain calls
A khaki Harlequin in 'Danse Grotesque'
    With just a single vulture in the stalls
    To witness so superb an arabesque.

God of the Flies

Mundy, McCall, and Browne, and Saul,
Mulholland, Geer, and Snoddie,
Porton, Horton, and Heptonstall
Are dying in the wadi.

Charlie and Fred are already dead,
And Sergeant Crisp is sleeping
His final sleep beside the jeep . . .
His wife will soon be weeping.

But tell our wives that *Life* survives,
For God is mighty clever.

While He supplies eternal flies
The desert lives for ever.

Yes, tell our wives that *Life* survives.
A clever fellow, God is,
For He supplies eternal flies
To populate the wadis.

JOHN RIMINGTON

*Royal Army Service Corps. Drove tank transporter. Whilst briefly
captured lost many manuscripts. Helped set up Salamander Oasis Trust.*

You Mustn't Drop Your Aitches at G.H.Q.

You mustn't drop your aitches at G.H.Q.,
There are lots of things you really mustn't do.
There isn't any chance of our ever being beaten
If the D.A.Q.M.G. has been to Eton.

You mustn't utter jokes about G.H.Q.,
It's only helping Hitler if you do.
For certain things are sacred, and you mustn't ever laugh
At the educated efforts of the Staff.

Don't think we never work,
Don't think we mean to shirk
If the enemy advances any nearer
With our colours flying high
We will fight and we will die
In a fortified position in Gezira.

So if you have ambitions to retire to gilded bliss,
With mornings spent dictating to a blonde Semira-miss,
Your manners must be perfect, or your marks are very few;
You mustn't drop your aitches at G.H.Q.

You mustn't drop your aitches at G.H.Q.,
There are lots of things you really mustn't do.
You mustn't be a fusspot wanting action on the 'phone,
Just pass the file and leave the thing alone.

You mustn't reach the office at unfashionable hours.
You mustn't sign the bumph that comes in such depressing showers,
For hustle is a thing to which no officer will stoop
As a member of the short-range desert group.

> If you're desert-worn and hardy
> From a sojourn out at Maadi,
> And you want to go to Shepheard's on the spree,
> If a comely AT you know,
> It is strictly comme il faut
> To get your clerk to vet her pedigree.

You mustn't miss your Friday night's immersion in Amami,
You mustn't speak to boot-blacks, or to members of EIGHTH Army,
Your tunic must be spotless though your duties may be few,
You mustn't drop your aitches at G.H.Q.

JOHN ROPES

OBE. *Served in Western Desert. Brigadier at GHQ Cairo; put on entertainments for the troops.*

Epigram

The proprietor of a brothel in Benghazi was decorated by the Germans and the Italians, during the summer of 1942, for devotion to duty

> Benghazi, to its worthy pimp's delight,
> Becomes the City of the Dreadful Knight:
> And Axis chivalry records his name
> Forever in its bawdy house of fame:
> As for the ladies, it must be deplored
> That lack of virtue is its own reward.

F.G.H. SALUSBURY

Daily Herald War Correspondent.

Tripoli

I've a mouth like a parrot's cage
And a roaring thirst inside,
My liver's a swollen, sullen rage –
Last night I was blind to the wide.

Canned as an owl, last night,
Drunk as a fiddler's bitch,
Oiled and stewed and pissed and tight,
Sewn-up, asleep in a ditch.

I can't remember much
And I wouldn't remember more
For vino gave me the golden touch
And a wit like Bernard Shaw's.

I'm rather weak at the knee
And not too strong in the head
But last night angels sang to me
And the world was a rosy red!

NOTE: Military historians are agreed that Eighth Army took Tripoli at its last gasp – we were out of food, cigarettes, tea and almost out of petrol – though it came as a surprise to us to be greeted as 'Liberators'. What historians have tactfully ignored is the sudden introduction of wine in unlimited quantities to men who existed for months on an inadequate ration of brackish water. The result was the most glorious binge enjoyed by every man from Trooper to Brass Hat, excepting only Monty himself who was wise enough to look the other way.

PETER A. SANDERS

Captain Royal Army Ordnance Corps, Inspecting Officer Western Desert 1941.

Askari Song: Airdrop[1]

Amai[2]

Amai,
The great Brown Bird on high:
Amai,
Amai,
Amai watu.[3]

Cruel the Zungus[4] and weird their ways –
But for their Brown Bird we have only praise,
Dropping white flowers of food from high,
A trail of stars along an empty sky.

We have known hunger, starvation in peace, till
Now, in war, near death, our bellies fill

Amai, let the Bird be very close at hand
When we are back in our Nyasaland.

Amai,
Amai,
The great Brown Bird on high:
Amai,
Amai,
Amai watu.

1 Nyasaland African soldiers sang about everything – even about
Dakotas supplying the forces in Burma with food.
2 Mother (Nyanja language).
3 Our mother.
4 White men.

GEORGE SHEPPERSON

*Commissioned Northamptonshire Regt. Seconded King's African Rifles,
East Africa. Professor of Commonwealth and American History,
Edinburgh.*

Beach Burial

Softly and humbly to the Gulf of Arabs
The convoys of dead sailors come;
At night they sway and wander in the waters far under,
But morning rolls them in the foam.

Between the sob and clubbing of the gunfire
Someone, it seems, has time for this,
To pluck them from the shallows and bury them in burrows
And tread the sand upon their nakedness;

And each cross, the driven stake of tidewood,
Bears the last signature of men,

Written with such perplexity, with such bewildered pity,
The words choke as they begin –

'Unknown seaman' – the ghostly pencil
Wavers and fades, the purple drips,
The breath of the wet season has washed their inscriptions
As blue as drowned men's lips,

Dead seamen, gone in search of the same landfall,
Whether as enemies they fought,
Or fought with us, or neither; the sand joins them together,
Enlisted on the other front.

El Alamein, 1962

KENNETH SLESSOR

(Australia) *Official Australian war correspondent, Second World War;
Greece, Middle East and New Guinea. Edited various literary journals.
Poems published in* One Hundred Poems *1944.*

Day's Journey

Starting at early light from the old fort
Across the dry flaked mud, you remember,
We left the well on our right and the crosses,
Drove west all day through the camel-scrub,
Tossing in convoy like a mobile orchard,
An olive-yard on wheels, irregular,
Spaced over miles: were bombed: were bombed again,
Until the air was dust: drove on due west
Past the sheikh's tomb of stones, past the dry spring,
Until at dust from the escarpment
Rumbled and boomed the guns' resentment,
Impersonal, the protest of a Titan
Impartially disgusted, while the sun
Signed off in angry flames.
                    We halted,
Quietly, in the close leaguer, half ashamed.

Hospital

Long corridor, white beds, red crosses,
Repair-shop for men: half-hearted light
From bosses in the ceiling fails to reach
The tedious tiled floor: without much feeling
They group in dressing-gowns around the doors
Eat pomegranates in a messy way,
Compare their gifts – 'Look at this camel, Bill –
Cost me three-hundred mils – real cedar-wood –
Bought it for Sue – wiv "Nazareth" on its back' –
Swop thumb-smudged photographs – 'A Russian girl
– Met her in Tel Aviv – very nice too!' –
Mingle approval with sound criticism.
The boy who has lost a hand hangs on the wireless,
Shuffles his feet to music, gropes for rhythm.

Two interruptions – when a sister passes,
Her smooth gray calves like magnets quickly covered
With hungry glances and when laughter breaks
Light and uncertain from that room,
Where the officer with a bullet in his skull
Has lain for months, and is said to have recovered.

8 October 1941

FRANK THOMPSON

Volunteered although under-age. Commissioned Royal Artillery 1940. GHQ liaison regiment, Libya, Persia, Iran and Sicilian landings. Dropped in Yugoslavia; ambushed in May 1944 with a group of Bulgarian partisans near Sofia. Notwithstanding wearing the King's uniform, treated as a rebel. 'Tried' at Litakovo defending himself in fluent Bulgarian condemning Fascism. Shot 10 June 1944. Had working knowledge of nine European languages. Poetry compares with the best of the First World War.

Lecturing To Troops

They sit like shrubs among the cans and desert
thistles
in the tree's broken shade and the sea-glare:

strange violent men, with dirty unfamiliar muscles,
sweating down the brown breast, wanting girls and
     beer.
The branches shake down sand along a crawling air,
    and drinks are miles towards the sun
    and Molly and Polly and Pam are gone.

Waiting for my announcement, I feel neat and shy,
   foreign before their curious helplessness,
innocence bought by action, like the sea's amnesty:
all my clean cleverness is tiny, is a loss;
and it is useless to be friendly and precise
     – thin as a hornet in a dome
     against the cries of death and home.

How can they be so tolerant – they who have lost
   the kiss of tolerance – and patient to endure
calm unnecessity? They have walked horror's coast,
loosened the flesh in flame, slept with naked war:
while I come taut and scatheless with a virgin air,
     diffident as a looking-glass,
     with the fat lexicon of peace.

The strangeness holds them: a new planet's uniform,
   grasped like the frilly pin-ups in their tent
– something without the urgency of hate and harm,
something forgotten.
       But that is not what I meant:
I should have been the miles that made them
     innocent,
    and something natural as the sun
    from the beginning to everyone
    though Harry and Larry and Len are gone.

Coastal Battery, Tripolitania

TERENCE TILLER

Lecturer in English History, Fuad 1 University, Cairo 1939–46. Post-war, radio writer and producer, BBC.

Lament of a Desert Rat

I've learnt to wash in petrol tins, and shave myself in tea
Whilst balancing the fragments of a mirror on my knee
I've learnt to dodge the eighty-eights, and flying lumps of lead
And to keep a foot of sand between a Stuka and my head
I've learnt to keep my ration bag crammed full of buckshee food
And to take my Army ration, and to pinch what else I could
I've learnt to cook my bully-beef with candle-ends and string
In an empty petrol can, or any other thing
I've learnt to use my jack-knife for anything I please
A bread-knife, or a chopper, or a prong for toasting cheese
I've learnt to gather souvenirs, that home I hoped to send
And hump them round for months and months, and dump them
  in the end
But one day when this blooming war is just a memory
I'll laugh at all these troubles, when I'm drifting o'er the sea
But until that longed-for day arrives, I'll have to be content
With bully-beef and rice and prunes, and sleeping in a tent.

N.J. TRAPNELL

Eighth Army.

The Ghosts

Daylight is a hoverer and diamond
A poor jewel for you. The brightness of eyes
Is what we remember, and the gay laugh
With which you left. The careless passionate glances
Over the shoulder, bravery for girls.

Magic made mazes where you walked
And it was Sunday and the weather fine
Walking that hill. And you said:
'Thoughts will last for ever.' And I replied:
'Like ghosts these moments will haunt.'

But nightfall came and wrapped us close
In each other's arms, On the soft couch
It was two children playing at love

On the first bright evening of the world.
Remembering that, I often embrace a ghost.

The moonlight shone across the room
As you left; and as you passed
The beam caught your face and held your hair
In a kind of fire. Then with a smile
The door closed. I heard your step on the stairs.

And next day the armies sailed;
I watched from a window the banners waving
And felt inside me the noise and the cheering
I could not hear. From that moment I was left
With memories of ghosts and ghosts of memories.

JOHN WALLER

Middle East 1941–6, RASC, Captain. Ministry of Information, Athens.

'La Belle Indifference'

I hate that which is changing me
to treat all my past friends
with cold, impersonal disinterest
Perhaps War makes inevitable
that false, local loyalty, only
to the immediate companions
of your own small circle.
One grows armoured like a lobster
against loss – can grow new limbs, claws.
Survival inhibits any feeling, save the joy
of survival. Your own miserable hide . . .
To hell with the Rest, England Home and Duty.

Take Terry, Company Clerk.
At Qassassin we shared spartan end of Coy. Office
shared Leave to Cairo, every darn thing
until I asked for a transfer to a fighting platoon.

A thousand miles later, up in the snows
of Florina Pass, just after the action

against the 'Adolf Hitler Leibstandarte' SS
the Coy. Commander comes over with, 'Your friend,
Lance Corporal Spears, has been wounded.
Took a Bren into the Railway Tunnel
so that you blighters could get out . . .
Caught it by blast. Both eyes.
Not likely to see again.'
                    I say nothing.
Betray no reaction. Cannot feel. Terry BLIND!
I cannot even breathe, 'Poor bastard.'
Now heading south in complete dark
only able to finger head bandages
in a stinking Red Crossed camion
on that bumping, rotten road.
Either I have a character defect
or else my loyalties froze hard up there.
We eye what's pitifully left of 'A' Coy.
Shrug. Crowd round the steaming brew.
Only the Section counts.

VICTOR WEST

*Lance Corporal 1st Rangers KRRC, Greece and Crete 1941. POW 4
years, escaped off-line march, 17 April 1945; in débâcle of Third Reich took
control of German village, Brunn, Bavaria.*

Leave, Compassionate, Children, Production, for the use of

*At the end of the war Sir James Grigg, Minister of War, authorized leave for
fathering children*

In distant lands the stalwart bands of would-be fathers wait,
Certificates to join their mates upon affairs of State,
For para 3 (appendix B) will authorize a chap,
to reproduce, for scheduled use, the species homo sap.

When good Sir James takes down their names in files, to procreate,
This caveat the unborn brat must circumnavigate:
'All who have wives (past thirty-five) and children unbegot
And certified that they have tried, are able, and have not

'May stake a claim. But if their aim is not, or has succeeded,
we can't allow that here and now their services are needed.'
All who apply must certify that they can understand
What lies behind the subtle mind of the Middle East Command.

The Middle East has now released a gallant group of men,
Of future Dads, like Galahads, who have the strength of ten,
And every dame must be the same, for it is infra dig,
That they should dare a child to bear uncertified by Grigg.

1945

ANONYMOUS

Lilli Marlene

Copyright 1940 by Apollo Verlag, Paul Lincke, Berlin, and E.M.I. with permission

Music by Norbert Schultze

Lilli Marlene, sung by the Germans, sung by the British, a hit too in occupied Europe, became the song of World War Two – much to the disgust of the German Propaganda Minister, Dr Josef Goebbels. It was not martial enough – just a sentimental lyric by Hans Leip, a German Infantryman in World War One, set to music by Norbert Schultze in 1938 and recorded by Lale Andersen, daughter of a Bremerhaven sailor, in March 1938.

At first it did not catch on. Then in late spring of 1941 Radio Belgrade – then under German occupation and transmitting to Rommel's forces in the Western Desert – asked for records to be sent from Vienna. Lilli Marlene was one of them.

The armies of the Desert – on both sides – adopted it. Not only was Dr Goebbels apprehensive but the British authorities, fearing the song's popularity might demoralise the troops, commissioned Tommy Connor to write an English version, published in 1942 and recorded by Anne Shelton and the Ambrose Orchestra, and by Marlene Dietrich in the USA. The song enjoyed many parodies, including the 'D–Day Dodgers'.

Lili Marleen
(Hans Leip)

1

Vor der Kaserne
vor dem großen Tor
stand eine Laterne,
und steht sie noch davor,
so wolln sir uns da wiedersehn,
bei der Laterne wolln wir stehn
wie einst, Lili Marleen.

2

Unsre beiden Schatten
sahn wie einer aus;
daß wir so lieb uns hatten,
das sah man gleich daraus.
Und alle Leute solln es sehn,
wenn wir bei der Laterne stehn
wie einst, Lili Marleen.

3

Schon rief der Posten:
Sie blasen Zapfenstreich;
es kann drei Tage kosten! –
Kam'rad, ich komm ja gleich.
Da sagten wir auf Wiedersehn.
Wie gerne wollt ich mit dir gehn,
mit dir, Lili Marleen!

4

Deine Schritte kennt sie,
deinen zieren Gang,

alle Abend brennt sie,
mich vergaß sie lang.
Und sollte mir ein Leids geschehn,
wer wird bei der Laterne stehn
mit dir, Lili Marleen?

5

Aus dem stillen Raume,
aus der Erde Grund
hebt mich wie im Traume
dein verliebter Mund.
Wenn sich die späten Nebel drehn,
werd ich bei der Laterne stehn
wie einst, Lili Marleen.

Lily Marlène
(Henry-Lemarchand)

1

Devant la caserne
Quand le jour s'enfuit
La vieille lanterne
Soudain s'allume et luit.
C'est dans ce coin là que le soir
On s'attendait remplis d'espoir
Tous deux Lily Marlène
Tous deux Lily Marlène

2

Et dans la nuit sombre
Nos corps enlacés
Ne faisaient qu'une ombre
Lorsque je t'embrassais
Nous échangions ingénûment
Joue contre joue bien des serments
Tous deux, Lily Marlène.
Tous deux, Lily Marlène.

3
Le temps passe vite
Lorsque l'on est deux
Hélas! on se quitte
Voici le couvre-feu . . .
Te souviens–tu de nos regrets
Lorsqu'il fallait nous séparer?
Dis–moi, Lily Marlène?
Dis–moi, Lily Marlène?

4
La vieille lanterne
S'allume toujours
Devant la caserne
Lorsque finit le jour.
Mais tout me paraît étranger
Aurais-je donc beaucoup changé?
Dis–moi, Lily Marlène
Dis–moi, Lily Marlène.

5
Cette tendre histoire
De nos chers vingt ans
Chante, en ma mémoire
Malgré les jours, les ans
Il me semble entendre ton pas
Et je te serre entre mes bras
Lily . . . Lily Marlène.
Lily . . . Lily Marlène.

Lilli Marlene
(Tommy Connor)

1
Underneath the lantern
By the barrack gate,
Darling I remember
The way you used to wait:
'Twas there that you whispered tenderly,

That you lov'd me,
You'd always be
My Lilli of the lamplight,
My own LILLI MARLENE.

2
Time would come for roll call,
Time for us to part,
Darling I'd caress you;
And press you to my heart;
And there 'neath that far off lantern light,
I'd hold you tight,
We'd kiss 'Good-night',
My Lilli of the lamplight,
My own LILLI MARLENE.

3
Orders came for sailing
Somewhere over there,
All confined to barracks
Was more than I could bear;
I knew you were waiting in the street,
I heard your feet,
But could not meet:
My Lilli of the lamplight
My own LILLI MARLENE.

4
Resting in a billet
Just behind the line,
Even tho' we're parted
Your lips are close to mine;
You wait where that lantern softly gleams,
Your sweet face seems,
To haunt my dreams
My Lilli of the lamplight,
My own LILLI MARLENE.

NOTE: *These three poems and the music were collected by Dr rer pol Christoph Seidelmann from Berlin archive.*

THE HOME FRONT

Reason for Refusal

Busy old lady, charitable tray
Of social emblems: poppies, people's blood –
I must refuse, make you flush pink
Perplexed by abrupt No-thank-you.
Yearly I keep up this small priggishness,
Would wince worse if I wore one.
Make me feel better, fetch a white feather, do.

Everyone has list of dead in war,
Regrets most of them, e.g.

Uncle Cyril; small boy in lace and velvet
With pushing sisters muscling all around him,
And lofty brothers, whiskers and stiff collars;
The youngest was the one who copped it.
My mother showed him to me,
Neat letters high up on the cenotaph
That wedding-caked it up above the park,
And shadowed birds on Isaac Watts' white shoulders.

And father's friends, like Sandy Vincent;
Brushed sandy hair, moustache, and staring eyes.
Kitchener claimed him, but the Southern Railway
Held back my father, made him guilty.
I hated the khaki photograph,
It left a patch on the wallpaper after I took it down.

Others I knew stick in the mind,
And Tony Lister often –
Eyes like holes in foolscap, suffered from piles,
Day after day went sick with constipation
Until they told him he could drive a truck –

Blown up with Second Troop in Greece:
We sang all night once when we were on guard.

And Ken Gee, our lance-corporal, Christian Scientist –
Everyone liked him, knew that he was good –
Had leg and arm blown off, then died.

Not all were good. Gross Corporal Rowlandson
Fell in the canal, the corrupt Sweet-water,
And rolled there like a log, drunk and drowned.

And I've always been glad of the death of Dick Benjamin,
A foxy urgent dainty ball-room dancer –
Found a new role in military necessity
As R.S.M. He waltzed out on parade
To make himself hated. Really hated, not an act.
He was a proper little porcelain sergeant-major –
The earliest bomb made smithereens;
Coincidence only, several have assured me.

In the school hall was pretty glass
Where prissy light shone through St George –
The highest holiest manhood, he!
And underneath were slain Old Boys
In tasteful lettering on whited slab –
And, each November, Ferdy the Headmaster
Reared himself squat and rolled his eyeballs upward,
Rolled the whole roll-call off an oily tongue,
Remorselessly from A to Z.

Of all the squirmers, Roger Frampton's lips
Most elegantly curled, showed most disgust.
He was a pattern of accomplishments,
And joined the Party first, and left it first,
At OCTU won a prize belt, most improbable,
Was desert-killed in '40, much too soon.

His name should burn right through that monument.

No poppy, thank you.

MARTIN BELL

*Royal Engineers. Gregory Fellow at Leeds University from 1967 to 1969
and later Department of Fine Art at Leeds Polytechnic. Died 1978.*

Steel Cathedrals

It seems to me, I spend my life in stations.
Going, coming, standing, waiting.
Paddington, Darlington, Shrewsbury, York.
I know them all most bitterly.

Dawn stations, with a steel light, and waxen figures.
Dust, stone, and clanking sounds, hiss of weary steam.
Night stations, shaded light, fading pools of colour.
Shadows and the shuffling of a million feet.

Khaki, blue, and bulky kitbags, rifles gleaming dull.
Metal sound of army boots, and smoker's coughs.
Titter of harlots in their silver foxes.
Cases, casks, and coffins, clanging of the trolleys.
Tea urns tarnished, and the greasy white of cups.
Dry buns, Woodbines, Picture Post and Penguins;
and the blaze of magazines.
Grinding sound of trains, and rattle of the platform gates.
Running feet and sudden shouts, clink of glasses from the buffet.
Smell of drains, tar, fish and chips and sweaty scent, honk of
    taxis;
and the gleam of cigarettes.
Iron pillars, cupolas of glass, girders messed by pigeons;
the lazy singing of a drunk.
Sailors going to Chatham, soldiers going to Crewe.
Aching bulk of kit and packs, tin hats swinging.
The station clock with staggering hands and callous face,
says twenty-five-to-nine.
A cigarette, a cup of tea, a bun,
and my train goes at ten.

1943

D. VAN DEN BOGAERDE

*Queens Royal Regiment. Served in Europe and in the Far East. Better
known as film actor Dirk Bogarde.*

Salvage Song (or: The Housewife's Dream)

My saucepans have all been surrendered,
The teapot is gone from the hob,
The colander's leaving the cabbage
For a very much different job.
So now, when I hear on the wireless

Of Hurricanes showing their mettle,
I see, in a vision before me,
A Dornier chased by my kettle.

ELSIE CAWSER

Dairy Laboratory worker in war and in voluntary organizations. Lives in Doveridge, Derbyshire.

First Night in Barracks

Don't cry, young woman,
In your badly made bed;
Pull the grey blanket
Over your head.

Your mother cries, too,
On your first night from home,
Fearing your safety
Now you're on your own.

Take comfort, young woman.
If only you knew
Most of the others
Are crying, too.

Guildford, 1944

I Didn't Believe It . . .

Two weeks in uniform
Strangers now friends.
Rosa teaching us to polish shoes;
Senga, the expert, pressing skirts.
Every morning
Jacky rushes to help me make my bed:
Three biscuits, neatly stacked.
On top, sheets and pillows wrapped
In one big grey blanket.

Two weeks confined to barracks
Then let free.
Best-dressed, checked in the guardroom,
Then off to town.
Self-conscious, shy,
We glanced in darkened windows
At our familiar faces in unfamiliar clothes,
Straightening our hats and shoulders,
Laughing when caught.
We shared chocolate, fish and chips,
And returned sober and properly dressed
In good time.

But three girls stayed out.
They'd been seen in a pub
With some Americans.
'They're fast,' someone whispered.
I couldn't believe it.
Seemed nice and friendly.

They were brought back by M.P.s
At lunchtime next day.
Dirty, untidy, defiant;
One wearing a U.S. army jacket.
They collected their things and left.
Never saw them again.

Someone shocked me saying,
'They boasted they'd each had thirty men.'
I didn't think it possible
So I didn't believe it, *then*.

Guildford, 1944

Morse Lesson

A cold, cold room with cold, cold girls
In buttoned greatcoats, scarves and mitts;
Frozen fingers try to write
The letters for the dah-dah-dits.

'Faster, faster,' says the sergeant;
Slower, slower work our brains.
Feet are numb, our blood is frozen,
Every movement causing pains.

Yet – four of us swam in the sea
Just last week, on Christmas Day,
Through frosty foam and fringe of ice,
Warmer than we are today.

Isle of Man, 1945

JOY CORFIELD

Joined ATS 1944 at Guildford. Special Wireless Operator, then driver in Germany.

Portsmouth Cypher School

i think this is hell
i'll say it again
    and make my point well
i think this is hell
no doubt you can tell
not prone to complain
i think this is hell
i'll say it again.

Kings Cross to Liverpool

Clinging to small essentials, cup and comb,
We have entrained, half-knowing what we did;
Now we have slept our last long night at home,
Stuck 'CABIN' on our lives and closed the lid.
How many months before we savour rightly
This gentle land that now we leave so lightly?

LISBETH DAVID

WRNS 1942, W/T Operator – commissioned Third Officer WRNS

1943, Cypher Office on staff of NCSO Belfast, C-in-C Portsmouth (Fort Southwick) and C-in-C East Indies (Colombo).

Sonnet: To Albert in a Pub on New Year's Eve

'I would not have her second-hand,' he said,
As gaze to gaze we drained a glass of beer.
I paused, and could not get it from my head –
What bitterness to drink to the New Year.
The thought came slow that this was sacrilege:
Love, like a worn-out garment handed down,
Love, which is bounded by no bond or pledge,
Patterned to this man's form – that woman's gown.
Ah no, if you have kissed beneath the stars
And felt the spirit striving through the clay
Remember that eternity was yours ·
Though love but lasted for a single day:
What matter if she loved a thousand more
Yet gave you love alone in that one hour.

Cheadle, January 1942

MADGE DONALD

LACW RAF Intelligence.

The End of a Leave

Out of the damp black light,
The noise of locomotives,
A thousand whispering,
Sharp-nailed, sinewed, slight,
I meet that alien thing
Your hand, with all its motives.

Far from the roof of night
And iron these encounter;
In the gigantic hall

As the severing light
Menaces, human, small,
These hands exchange their counters.

Suddenly our relation
Is terrifyingly simple
Against our wretched times,
Like a hand which mimes
Love in this anguished station
Against a whole world's pull.

ROY FULLER

Ordinary Seaman 1941. 'Service discipline made my verse more precise.' 1942 East Africa. 1943 Fleet Air Arm. Professor of Poetry 1968–73, Oxford University. Governor of the BBC 1972/3–80. Awarded Queen's Gold Medal for poetry.

Promotion

In Room Four-Five Staff Captain X
received a file 're fireproof flex'.
He took a piece of paper and
began, as usual, 'Yours to hand . . .'
and ended up in mild reproof,
'This office deals with flex, rainproof.
In course of time your file will be
forwarded to FFP.
Meanwhile, for information and
attention, passed to Flexes, Land.'
Thus, ah thus, it all commenced.
Each office, in a form condensed,
added remarks and chits and quotes,
and half a hundred knowing notes,
until the file, now leather-bound,
chock full of 'seen' and 'no trace found'
and 'passed to you' and 'acked with thanks',
and 'flex, suggested use in tanks',
'not known' and 'see my urgent tel.'
and 'vide flex, electric bell',
is five years old and come to rest

with him who understands it best.
In Room Four-Five now Colonel X
has opened up a 'Part Two, Flex'.

London, July 1945

GEORGE T. GILLESPIE

(Canada) Commissioned into the Border Regiment 1940. Service in France, Canada, Belgium and South-East Asia. Twice wounded and mentioned in despatches. Captain. September 1945–6 interpreter officer POW Camp, Brough-on-Sands. Professor of German.

Doodlebugs

A bomb, last night, fell close by Radlett.
The pulsing engine stopped right overhead.
Four minutes to the crash. Slowly we counted;
One girl cried 'Oh God! Dear God!'
The tension grew to bursting point; the blast
Shattered the windows. We breathed again.
Always the bombs come over in early evening
Just before we go on shift. We talk of rush-hour traffic
But underneath the fear remains. Death can come
From so many angles. Tomorrow, next week, next month
It may not pass us by.

Shenley, Herts, 1944

GRACE GRIFFITHS

Joined ATS (Royal Signals, Special Y Section) 1942. Stationed at Shenley, Herts and Harrogate.

Reveille – 1943

The day calls coldly, and the billet stirs
To habit-grafted routine; yawning men
Tousle their hair, stretching like sleepy curs
Roused by the boot of duty from their den

Of frowsy, warm and timeless luxury,
S... light cigarettes, cough, and scratch,
... nt their penury;
... n to catch
... heir morning dreams —
... han they've known
... red moorland streams,
... ewter, and the sown
...ds, cheeky music-halls,
... the peace that's found
...ng evening sound;
...dren laughing . . . to his own
back . . . go back. No good.
A coarse roar batters on the hood
...ge; the squirrel cage
...; and Now begins.

Conscript

...m worlds of good', they said,
...e was — a puny chap
he used to be, ... emember — always at books and that,
but since he joined
he's broadened out. They've made a man of him;
You wouldn't know him now'.

Deep-sunk in rain-soaked ditch, with weeds and filth
stopping his mouth, the soldier lies;
swollen and black, his face turns to the skies
in blank, unquestioning stare, his body, tight
and big as flood-drowned pig, lurches and sways,
to wind and water. Yes, he's broadened out —
he's twice the man he was; a pity, though,
his life should run, like bright oil down a gutter,
to implement some politician's brag.

His world went out
through that neat hole in temple, quickly and easily
as words from windy mouths. And loves unknown,

and skies unseen, and books unread,
forever lost, he's dead.

You wouldn't know him now.

December 1940

F.A. HORN

Royal Army Ordnance Corps. Typography specialist.

Alien Country

Coming on leave,
while the world goes up in flames,
is to come, not home,
but to an alien and mysterious country,
where the language and pre-occupations
are remote from one's own
and difficult to interpret.

Family talk is all of food.
'This is short, that is shorter.
We're supposed to get offal
but I never see any.
Expect the butcher gives it to his fancy woman.
They say we'll get a bit more cheese next week.
That'll please your father
but I'll believe it when I see it.
But, even if we get more cheese,
we'll get less of something else
so it'll be all the same in the long run.'

In Brewer Street, just after the rowdy and dangerous Soho pubs,
where I'd been drinking, closed for the night,
a shabby old man in a fawn mackintosh
and a battered trilby hat
materialised out of the darkness,
whispered a furtive invitation.
Not to see a dirty film-show.
Not to an orgy.
Not to enjoy two women simultaneously

or even one on her own.
'Fancy a nice juicy steak, guv, the real thing,' he muttered.
'Rump or fillet. As much as you can eat.
Chips and peas as well.
Not far from 'ere. Just a few minutes' walk,' he wheedled.
'You only got to follow me. But, if you see a copper,
just pretend you ain't nothing to do with me.'

Clearly, the fate of western civilisation depends
upon tins of Spam and packets of dried egg
and draconian measures to ensure that the butchers
do not reserve their offal for their fancy women.

The talk of my friends is guarded.
I come and go on leave and (as they see it)
am uncommitted, disinterested, uninvolved, transient,
a tourist, circumspectly welcomed
temporarily among them but not, now, one of them,
not, now, one of the natives of the place.

When, Barbara, I was last on leave,
Peter (still in his reserved occupation)
had moved in with you
and, over the quart bottles filled with draught bitter
brought from The Flask just before closing time,
there was talk about books and there were the latest issues
of Horizon and Poetry London to discuss.
This time, perhaps, your husband, the Mad Major,
will have returned and, as once before,
will talk a lot of balls to me
about battle training with the Bren gun,
while you, Barbara, having earlier made sure
that all copies of Horizon and Poetry London
and all other evidence of Peter's recent occupation
have been removed, will look on, warily and uneasily,
in case, in some forgetful, unguarded or, even,
treacherous moment, I let slip a reference
to previous visits and the conversations
over the bottles of draught bitter.

And, Sylvia, this time you have offered
no invitations to your loud and vulgar parties
in your house in The Grove,
nor any hint that any such ever occurred.

Something, obviously, has happened to curb your goings-on
but, native Sylvia, you clearly do not intend
to confide in a mere tourist about such matters.

And, Brenda, will you be asking me back, as before,
to lie with you beneath the shiny eiderdown,
to make love while Geraldo plays on the wireless
on your bedside table?
Or, on the other hand, when I meet you in the pub,
will you, by a casual gesture, a dismissive glance,
indicate that someone else has replaced me
under the shiny eiderdown and that Geraldo no longer plays for me
on your wireless.

I venture with trepidation into this alien country
with its ambiguous landscape, obscure pre-occupations
and shifting relationships.

JIM HOVELL

*Air Ministry for two years before joining 61st Training Regiment, Royal
Armoured Corps in March, 1942. Commissioned 155 RAC and Yorkshire
Hussars, North-west Europe 1944, Liaison officer with HQ33 Independent
Armoured Brigade.*

Air-Raid Casualties: Ashridge Hospital (Extract)

On Sundays friends arrive with kindly words
To peer at those whom war has crushed;
They bring the roar of health into these hushed
And solemn wards –
The summer wind blows through the doors and cools
The sweating forehead; it revives
Memories of other lives
Spent lying in the fields, or by sea-pools;
And ears that can discern
Only the whistling of a bomb it soothes
With tales of water splashing into smooth
Deep rivers fringed with ferns.
Nurses with level eyes, and chaste

In long starched dresses, move
Amongst the maimed, giving love
To strengthen bodies gone to waste.
The convalescents have been wheeled outside,
The sunshine strikes their cheeks and idle fingers,
Bringing to each a sensuous languor
And sentimental sorrow for the dead.

PATRICIA LEDWARD

Driver with AA Unit, ATS. Edited Poems of This War *with Colin Strang (1942).*

The Shirkers' Brigade

In trouble free towns set well in the West
Away from the rigours of war
Live a small class of people – a positive pest
Who idle and slack as before.
The men of the Shirkers' Brigade.

A select little army of well-to-do folks
With money to spend as they will
In similar patterns of black evening cloaks
They gorge and guzzle their fill.
For theirs is a life of laughter and fun
The peace and contentment it brings
Away from the dangers of airplane or gun
Away from the struggle – away from the Hun
The men of the Shirkers' Brigade.

Though battles be lost and countries laid low
For want of the weapons of war
The Shirkers' Brigade to their pleasures still go
The order is 'play – as before'
Not theirs is the toil of a good fighting man
In factory or airplane or tank
When the fighting began they scuttled and ran
Now they're lounging and scrounging as hard as they can
The men of the Shirkers' Brigade.
                                        By what mystic right

The 'Shirkers' Brigade' is allowed.
'To each is accorded only his worth'
Should be our maxim today.

1941, Palace Hotel, Torquay

DEREK MARTIN

Wing Commander, OBE. Flew Sunderland flying boats over the Bay of Biscay. March 1941 crashed in bad weather and became a founder-member of the Guinea Pig Club. (Crash survivors — so-called as they became guinea pigs for surgeons.) 1944 India Chief of Staff joint-service force Cocos Islands off Java. Far East Air Force Headquarters in Singapore, staff officer. Badly injured serving with NATO in Norway.

Aubade 1940

Low behind Battersea power-station the dawn sags,
Dipping shafts of madder in a pearl pool.
Across the roofs a dogtail of smoke scampers and wags.

A sentry at the barracks renovates his nail
With bayonet-point, stamps hard to thaw his legs,
Wanting relief, and breakfast, and the mail.

Up from the shelters a new day returns.
Past crestfallen houses and bomb-shuffled slates
Workers kick shrapnel off the paving-stones.

And the whole city opens with a shout.
Hatred's more fierce the fiercer London burns.
The fires their last night's bombing lit are out.
In Bermondsey and Bow the fires are out; the water
That hissed with melted sugar, has been calmed.
And Peace sits spinning like Pohjola's daughter

Virginal on a rainbow. Suspended above doom
On stalks of hope, the barrage-balloons shine bright
Like a hundred shuttles waiting in the loom.

GEOFFREY MATTHEWS

Royal Signals, Middle East. Lectured at Leeds and Reading Universities.

Week-end Leave (Extract)

To waken slowly in this strange high-ceilinged room!
Cool wet winds lift the curtain's skirt;
Trees across the street nod to a sleep-eyed cloud,
Their foreheads glistening in the rain.
To-day I shall have time to live,
To stop and watch people in streets, pigeons on roofs,
Children at play in parks, wheelbarrows and men digging,
Carthorses, the sheen of plough furrows like smooth hair, ponds,
Sparrows carrying crumbs, the art of well-laid hedges.

An old tweed jacket hangs behind the door
Smelling of heather, tobacco, and burnt wood;
Coloured ties fall sprawled across the broad mirror,
And grey trousers loll in the deep arm-chair.

From down the hill where soiled shirt-sleeves
Take down the chalked-on black-out blinds,
Puff in and out their shops with shutters,
Where cold, red hands and smeared print aprons
Put vegetables in rows before their shops,
Down there in the world
(Like a bugle-call shaking me by the shoulder as I lie in bed)
Come the advancing chimes of city bells.
I can doze, and watch the clock tick round
Long past reveille, past the first parade,
And on and on, dragging
Shiny boots along the circle of an army day.

We'll have tea at an old inn
Standing beckoning at the roadside –
A kindly old lady, in a shawl, smiling at a gate,
With wood fires and small square windows, bright curtains,
And flowers in pots on window-sills.

One more night in the careless freedom of that room.
Perhaps we will not wake up . . .
They have big warm farms in Warwickshire
And sloping lawns,
Gardens full of thick trees, lying stretched out
With their green legs dabbling in the Avon.
Perhaps next week we can go on the river,

Or lie all night
Amongst the clover in some Midland barn.

O God! To-morrow I go back.

January 1942

RICHARD SPENDER

Enlisted London Irish Regiment 1940. Officer, the Parachute Regiment. Killed 28 March 1943 leading troops against German machine-gun positions near Bizerta, Tunisia.

Brief Sanctuary

You from the guns
and I from tending
made love at an inn;
deep-dusked
in a narrow room
were freed from war,
from fear of our fear,
made of our smooth limbs
our sweet love
sanctuary
each for the other.

In the empty saloon
drank then cool wine
and sang as you
strummed the piano.
When time moved from us
and we must go,
we drew our glasses close
on the bare table,
their shadows one.
Look, we said,
they will stand here
together
when we have gone,
images of ourselves,

witnesses to our love.
As we left
you smiled at me
lifting the latch,
then the bombs came . . .

Behind the Screens

Meticulously
I dress your wound
knowing you cannot live.
In ten swift rivers
from my finger-tips
compassion runs
into your pale body
that is so hurt
it is no more
than the keeper
of your being.
Behind these screens,
soldier,
we two are steeped
in a peace deeper
than life gives,
you with closed eyes
and I moving quietly
as though you could wake,
all my senses aware
that your other self
is here,
waiting to begin
life without end.

JO WESTREN

RAMC nursing member, attached anti-aircraft command; Colchester Military Hospital.

Messes

The Officers' mess at St. Sulpice Barracks
(coolly verandahed for summer drinking
overlooking a grassy yard and trees)
is Out-of-Bounds for Other Ranks:

we're confined to canteens,
ablution rooms and nit parades,
kit inspections,
double-deckers, barrack boxes, food from
chipped enamel pans on trestle tables
where each day the Duty Officer comes inquiring
'Any complaints?'

Meltzer's eaten her own
sardines
five times this week because of pork
Hebert doesn't like herrings
O'Rourke thinks the macaroni disgusting
and Tremblay's found
a cockroach
baked into a pie

Evenings
we sit beside the canteen's
small open window
hearing clinking glasses, voices, laughter
from the officers' verandah
and we gossip about their romances –
with married Captain this and Major that

And our Company Commander
living out a fantasy we've all had
takes unauthorized leave to go to Halifax
with her departing lover –
and is replaced

Summer 1944

Recruit

We're waiting
to go to Kitchener for Basic Training

and at St. Sulpice Barracks of the C.W.A.C.
the Montreal Star
takes pictures of us
skiing down a mountain slope
just three feet high
to show that Cwacs have
outdoor exercise and
fun and
the friend I joined up with
laughs out from the poster on the
recruiting station wall
from under a tin hat –
released from scrubbing floors for
publicity shots
and even if her blonde curls are
too long and touch her
battledress collar
it's permitted for the good cause of
recruiting

Company night we're all C.B.ed for
movies
about V.D. and 'Desert Victory' –

and then a film about
Service Women
having their hair styled
and uniforms fitted –
experimenting with discreet makeup.

Some of us
carry flags for Victory Loan
and are rewarded with
a ride around the city in an open truck
on a Saturday afternoon
from which I see
another friend in white bridal satin
the groom in khaki

on the steps of the fraternity house
where once I went
dancing

June 1943

50 Coy. C.W.A.C. – 96 Addison Road, London, W8

We share the street
with the Pioneer Corps
ditch-diggers of the British Army
who whistle at us as we walk
down Addison Road to work.

We sleep under the bomb-cracked ceiling
of a Canadian diplomat's
former town house
and we've strung an outside clothes line
for our panties, slips and bras

At night
the Pioneer Corps
conducts manoeuvres
in our garden

steals our silky underwear
for their rationed
girlfriends.

March 1945

Addison Road, Kensingon – 50 Company CWAC

Addison Road
in winter blackout
seven a.m. and dawn
struggling through misty chimneys

we shuffle in the street
stretch out stiff arms in 'Right dress'
to touch the next girl's sleeve

with its yellow maple leaf on brown –
'fried egg' badge of service overseas

then walk down Addison Road
past high walls lacking their iron gates
to Holland Park

Up the dark stairs to the office
where the sergeant-major gives us
the night's casualty cards
and we type cables
with particulars of wounds
sometimes imagining delivery of the news
to mothers, wives

more often thinking of getting off early
to the NAAFI at Notting Hill Gate
where Elizabeth Arden cosmetics
sell cheap to Canadian
service women

until it comes at last
the casualty card
for a friend

January 1945

PATIENCE WHEATLEY

(Canada) *Served in the Canadian Women's Army Corps from June 1943
to June 1946, at the Canadian forces' record office in Acton, London.*

Winter in Nissenland

Hastily now skies empty their whiteness
powdering the surface of the week-old snow
the wind has sullied.
And in tubular huts men crouch over fires
telling of their ways with women
turn eagerly to argue
recalling the plague in the cattle
their strike in the docks

the fish catch and furnace heat
the time when . . .

And hands dealing cards falter
coins cease clinking
razor pauses on the jerking bristles
the arm scratching in the armpit is withdrawn
cuckold suspends his reprimanding letter which must ignore
the price he paid was seven stouts for a forgetful whore;
thrown back mouth incanting vapid details
of the last-night joke
hangs inanely before it can compress
to the movement of these sticks which grope
for paths in the argument.
Only the prone body on the bed
with open mouth and feet together
lies still
as though it had been whipped.

But rockface is soon reached
and forward faces lower
events master the restive mind
barbéd wire of the present,
frontier between desire and reality
distraction and action,
and over it, the forbidding guard –
Future.
They challenge him:

And the snow falls
silent, hasty.

1942

PETER YOUNG

*1941–46 trooper Westminster Dragoons, RAC Sergeant Army Education
Corps. Has written over thirty books for schools. Joint Editor of Open
University Children With Special Needs series.*

THE MEDITERRANEAN,
NORTH AFRICA, ITALY AND
THE BALKANS

Verity

In memory of Captain Hedley Verity, injured in Sicily. Taken POW, buried at Caserta. Pre-war, Yorkshire and England slow left arm bowler

The ruth and truth you taught have come full circle
On that fell island all whose history lies,
Far now from Bramhall Lane and far from Scarborough
You recollect how foolish are the wise.

On this great ground more marvellous than Lord's
– Time takes more spin than nineteen thirty four –
You face at last that vast that Bradman-shaming
Batsman whose cuts obey no natural law.

Run up again, as gravely smile as ever,
Veer without fear your left unlucky arm
In His so dark direction, but no length
However lovely can disturb the harm
That is His style, defer the winning drive
Or shake the crowd from their uproarious calm.

DRUMMOND ALLISON

East Surrey Regiment. North Africa and Italy. Killed in action on the Garigliano, Italy, 2 December 1943.

Scorn

I laugh at death, accuse her whore,
for she seduced, while in the mirth
of life, my comrades, when she tore
their fragile plants from out the earth.
So, if her finger beckons me,
enticing, luring me to go
in meekness to her skirts, and be
enfolded in their pleats, I know
my parting will be well-content,
since neither rot, nor all decay,
erases those few moments lent

by many years to one who spent
his life compiling just one perfect day.

'ALMENDRO'

(South Africa) *'Almendro' was the name used by Denis Saunders, South African Air Force, poet and joint founder of Oasis in Cairo, 1942. Served later in Italy.*

Dalmatian Islanders

These were peaceful people, and the hills, their world,
hedged in by changing seas, to rocky breasts
took prints of intimacy with gentle feet.
These rocks, white-piled a million gleaming cairns,
or walled around with meagre fields they hid,
saw silent fortitude reach dogged mastery,
and grimly watched, amazed, a people grow.
These waters, savaging the stranger craft,
conspiring with the rocks to spoil their keels,
took fathers to their death, and saw the sons
tight-lipped at dawn confront their rage anew.
Through centuries the thirsty sun beat down on them,
parching their vineyards; from their hard-hewn wells
spirited off the precious hoarded drops
of water. Yet they'll say they loved the sun.
For these were peaceful people. In their hearts
no bitterness that Nature was so harsh,
no whined complaint to Heaven in need they raised.
Man had not harmed them; therefore friends of Man,
and all men friends, their life was hard but glad.
And Man has struck them, vilely, from behind,
thinking to bend them, beaten, to his will.

These are quiet people, but their eyes are hard,
and sounds we know can number none to tear
and chill the heart as when their women mourn.

ROBIN BENN

Counter-Battery Fire

The sun is gone, the convent bells bring
their dolorous single ringing in the dales.
Subalterns flick their frequencies in gin
and gunners wash themselves in canvas pails.
The voices in the olive groves grow still;
silence and sadness with the dark descend,
drawing the moon up from the shadow hill
into a realm of stars that has no end.

Sleep folds us tranquil through the changing night
under the turning of the watchful Plough,
in army blankets, out of mind and sight.
The thinning darkness shatters. 'What's the row?'
'Getting it heavy over on the right.'
Telephone chinks: 'Bombard H.20. Now!'

J. BEVAN

Royal Artillery – commissioned 1943. Action in Italy.

Spring Offensive, 1941

In where the smoke runs black against the snow,
And bullets drum against the rocks, he went,
And saw men die, with childish wonderment! –
Where bayonets glitter in the sudden glow,
And sleek shells scream, and mortars cough below:
There tanks lurch up, and shudder to a halt
Before the superb anger of the guns:
Then flares go up – the rattle of a bolt –
Rifles stutter – and voices curse the Huns. . . .
And then, he jerked and toppled to the ground,
His ears too full of noise, his eyes of light;
His scattered cartridge clips glint brassy-bright;
A Vickers cackles madly from a mound . . .

Oh, where the red anemone brims over
To swarm in brambled riot down a rise,

There we will lay him, lay your widow'd lover,
And wipe the poor burnt face, and gently cover
The look of startled wonder in the eyes . . .
Let Beauty come, let her alone
Bemoan those broken lips with kisses from her own.

Greece, April 1941

MAURICE BIGGS

(Australia) *Second AIF Middle East, Greece, Crete, New Guinea, where
wounded. Published 'Poems of War and Peace' (1945).*

Burial Party

The stairs were shot away so someone fetched
a ladder, up we went and found him stretched
out on the balcony. His eyes were closed,
his face serene. You might have diagnosed
it simply as malingering except
that when we turned him over . . . thus we kept
him face up which enabled him to show
his medal ribbons to advantage. So
we took down the Italian flag that flew
forlornly from the flagstaff which we knew
would come in handy as his winding sheet
and tied the rope's end to his booted feet.
He offered no objections so we laid
him uncomplaining on the balustrade,
made a sign of the Cross to please the Pope,
prepared to take the strain upon the rope –
and pushed him off. The trouble was a ledge
projected from the cornice and its edge
lent him a foothold. Hanging by the toes
head down he must have looked like one of those
high-wire trapezists when we hold our breath
below while watching them perform their death
defying feats; indeed a passing troop
of soldiery had gathered in a group
to see the fun. However hard we tried

to work him off the ledge he just defied
the laws of gravity. We hauled him back
a little way and tried creating slack
by jerking hard but this brave officer,
completely 'hors de combat' as it were,
upstaged us and performed on it instead
a 'danse macabre' standing on his head,
and those below, accustomed to a much
more solemn undertaking, seeing such
an unexpected 'tour de force' appeared
to find it entertaining for they cheered
him to the echo. Then the flagstaff broke
and that was that. A funny sort of joke!
Our hero did not take a curtain call,
there was no safety-net to break his fall.
He caught his head a very nasty crack
on his parade ground like we'd dropped a sack
of water melons on it. Someone said
'That's cheating mate, he was already dead!'
War kills of course, but furthermore it warps
men's sense of humour – laughing at a corpse!

Thermopylae 1941

A private soldier doubtless suffers less
from his privations than from ignorance
of what is going on; in terms of chess,
he is a pawn. But the significance
of our deployment on the forward slopes
of this position was not lost on us.
No purpose served consulting horoscopes
at Delphi; students of Herodotus
would know withdrawal to Thermopylae
and putting up barbed wire could only mean
fighting a rearguard action Q.E.D,
as Euclid would have put it. We had been
deposited into the warlike lap
of ancient deities. I said to Blue,
my Aussie mate, 'There was this famous chap
Leonidas, he was the Spartan who

defended it with just 300 men
against an army.' Bluey took a draw
upon his cigarette. 'Well stuff'im then!'
a pungent comment on the art of war.
Foreboding we looked back across the plain
which we had crossed, towards Lamia, towards
the north just as the Spartans must have lain
with spear and sword and watched the Persian hordes
amassing for the battle long ago.
It was deserted, a proscenium
where once Leonidas heard trumpets blow,
a theatre whose auditorium,
the home of gods, was mountains, and whose stage
was lapped by Homer's wine-dark seas as blue
as lapis lazuli, where in a rage
Poseidon wrecked Odysseus and his crew
and siren voices tempted. In the wings
of history we waited for a roll
of other drums and strident trumpetings
to usher in the gods of war. The soul
of Sparta stirred, could but the brave
Leonidas renew his mortal span
instead of merely turning in his grave,
and all his hoplites, perished to a man,
but resurrect themselves . . . I said 'They wore
long hair, the Spartans, a visible proof
that they were free, not helots, and before
the battle they would gravely sit aloof
and garland it with flowers.' Bluey spat.
Continuing to watch the empty road
across the plain he took off his tin-hat
(a proof that he was bald) and said 'A load
of bloody poufdahs!' Thus he laid the ghost
of brave Leonidas. Herodotus
informs us Xerxes, leader of the host,
when told was equally incredulous,
though whether from a soldier's point of view
of army discipline or on the grounds
of social prejudice like my mate Blue,
was not elaborated. With the sounds
of planes we kept our heads down. After dark

we dug slit-trenches neath the April moon
in silence broken only by the bark
of some Greek shepherd's dog while our platoon
commander and the sergeant walked about
discussing fields of fire. We lit a smoke,
which made the section corporal shout 'Put out
that bloody light!' It was the Colonel broke
the news, like some deus ex machina
descending from above. THEY SHALL NOT PASS . . .
THE LAST LINE OF DEFENCE etcetera,
all sentiments of which Leonidas
would have approved, and as he disappeared
into the moonlight, with a martial air,
a crown and two pips, everybody cheered
instead of putting flowers in their hair,
but muted just in case the Germans were
in earshot and from feeling (for myself
at any rate) that we should much prefer
that history did not repeat itself.
And later with our cigarettes concealed
behind cupped hands we peered into the night
across the darkened plain and it revealed
first one and then another point of light,
and then a hundred of them, moving down
the distant backcloth, shining off and on
like tiny jewels sparkling on a crown
of moonlit mountains, a phenomenon
caused by the winding path of their descent
round hair-pin bends cascading from the heights
beyond Lamia, our first presentiment
of evil genius – they were the lights
of Hitler's war machines! So fate had cast
us in the role of heroes in the same
arena where the heroes of the past
had closed their ranks and perished in the name
of freedom. Was there one of those among
the Spartans who, at the eleventh hour
upon the eve of battle, while he hung
his hair with many a patient-wreathed flower,
prayed that some unpredictable event
like Xerxes dropping dead, some miracle,

might even yet occur and thus prevent
the battle being joined the oracle
at Delphi notwithstanding? 'Time to pick
the flowers, Blue, that bloom upon the steep
hillside' I said 'make daisy-chains and stick
the buggers in our hair!' He was asleep.
So all night long I watched and when the skies
had lightened with the dawn (doubtless the last
that I should ever see with mortal eyes
before we joined those heroes of the past
in the Elysian fields) and bold day broke
across the misted plain on mythic banks
of white and yellow asphodel he woke
and heard combustion engines. German tanks?

I said a private soldier suffers less
from his privations than from ignorance
of what is going on, but we could guess
that some extraordinary circumstance
had made the sergeant, full pack, rifle slung,
rise up before us blotting out the sun.
Phoebus Apollo? Götterdämmerung
more likely! GREEKS CAPITULATED . . . HUN
MIGHT CUT US OFF . . . NO PANIC . . . GET
EMBUSSED . . .
YES 3-TON TRUCKS HAVE JUST ARRIVED . . . . I thanked
Pallas Athene, meanwhile Bluey cussed
and our lance-corporal said he'd been outflanked
at Passchendaele and got away with it.
As Bluey put it 'if some bloody mug
brasshat had only warned us, used a bit
of common sense we never need have dug
that something something slit-trench!' (Stuff 'im then?)
But as we drove away I must confess
it felt like a desertion. Those few men
with flowers in their hair were heroes! Yes!

JOHN BROOKES

*Private with 2/5 Bn Australian Infantry Force (AIF). Worked his passage
from Liverpool to Australia pre-war, landing with 2/6. On outbreak of war
walked from Broken Hill to Melbourne to enlist.*

Castiglione dei Pepoli

The last field slips between the chestnut stems.
   Far down below, the railway bridge's wreck,
Black gunpits, transport random-parked,
   Thin files of soldiers on a contour track:
Far up, beyond the woods, the summit's skull
   Seizing the sky with its ragged fangs of rock.

Raw is the rock, uncut by chisels: nude
   Trackless snow speaks no evangel.
The only movement in the earth and sky
   Is a silver fighter, splendid, single,
Whose shadow, leaping the hillsides hints
   The only too familiar angel.

A deep sea-silence presses on my ears:
   Sunlight, like a wind that beats the skin.
And clearer than my shadow on the snow,
   Harder than these ragged teeth of stone
In me lies faith a scattered skeleton,
   Christ's cross burning, Bethlehem in ruin.

Italy 1944

GUY BUTLER

(South Africa) *Served Middle East and Italy with South African forces.*

Cassino (Extract)

At the face of the smoking crag
a horde of screeching machines
labour at this season's assignment:
spurts of furious dust rise and fall,
curtaining flesh ripped and thwacked
by fanged rods of shrapnel:
Engines howl full throttle
and claw at wreckage of sandbags,
smashed beams, spilled stone and lumbering
paraphernalia of heavy infantry

programmed for the intensive industry
of siege warfare in winter.
Steel tracks rage over pulverised streets
as enemy armour-piercing, self-propelled artillery
lashes pointblank at our newborn organism scuttling,
limbs entangled, heads devoutly flattened to earth,
huddling together under the barrage.
Each man clasps his blood brother
on that ancient rock of community
till every autonomous fibre is willed
into one prostrate, protesting entity
as the ponderous imperatives of shellfire

Signal that the position has been outflanked.
We, the living, hitch at weapons and scrabble
under cover of counter-battery fire
over mud-greased heaps of masonry
crusting the wrecked street and congealed
in frozen, formless landscapes against jammed
doorways and bomb-avalanched walls to the next
instalment of death shown the Via Casalina.
The dying wane with the expected stoic calm
Toward their silent territory;
They are already cast out.

Stay with the mob, you can't go wrong.
Now that soldier in the rubble
flinches, and instantly I feel
the thump of shrapnel pillaging
my temporary brother's flesh:
he cries out for help, and grips me
in a child-like hold;
I break his arms from their embrace,
and unbuckle his web gear,
open coat and tunic
and look where his blood
soaks into the dusty stones.
Kaput, the stretcher bearers say,
Don't waste time on him: but I have to trace
the random processes of his death
I draw my knife and hack away the sodden cloth.
The carcase does not stir.

Flora of battlefields, discarded junk of casualties
strews the ground like trampled weeds:
I spread a dead paratrooper's camouflaged jacket
to cover both his stiff body
and the homelier shape sprawled underfoot . . .
The Spandau fire from close range!
A sharp, bone-snapping shock
splinters the smoked-clogged air:
we run,
while I formulate the usual lies,
the righteous words to ease guilt
and sanctify the ritual death
of the man whose abandoned body
has been an expendable shield,
a viable husk in the ruthless cycle
of the omnipotent organism.
We run,
And awkwardly, gun at the ready,
I try to wipe from my shivery hands
The salutary, scab-like clots
Of the necessary victim's blood.

Spring

Demolition: Liri Valley

The Allied Military Government
will pay damages, I said
and swung the axe.
It was good swinging that axe;
the six-foot lengths of oak
split clean at every smack.
Stop! yelled the priest,
barbarians make war on churches!
'The flock are cold
and your bloody old church is kaput'.
Antichrist! moaned the priest.
'*Scapare via*', I said,
'no priest tells us what to do'.

Bandits! he shouted
and went to look for the CO.
But first he cursed us
in medieval Latin doggerel
that crackled like dry bones
around our arrogant ears.

Before we left for the line
we chopped up every stick
in the mortuary, coffins first
then beams from the roof.
Pregnant Maria and family
had warm fires and food
while we caroused in their kitchen.
It was a good spring.

LES CLEVELAND

(New Zealand) *2 New Zealand Expeditionary Force, Pacific, Egypt and Italy, where wounded. Reader in Political Science at Victoria University, New Zealand.*

Christmas in Italy, 1944

History will tell that here the battle swayed
Through pastel towns into beleaguered Lombardy,
How for a week and a day they held the river
And patrols went out while the shells flocked and sighed
Like express trains through the frightened air:
When resistance broke, they gave us up a town
Of ghosts and stones, and the blankly heartbreak stare
Of the voiceless houses there. History will tell
This tale of liberation, but be mute
Concerning the private dream, and the small despair,
All kindness gone, the near known faces fading
And courage, the loneliest virtue, for only friend
(Whose voice is silence). History will transmute
Into a cipher the General's brilliant raiding
Party that lies so quietly under the snow.

And in this desert of tanks and guns and men
Christmas has left its faint-as-feather print:
A small irony of yesterday's fairy lights.
Of tinselled trees, and children, and glowing fires
Pierces a moment's sombreness. And then
We forget again – it was such a long time ago.
Behind the iron and passionate headline years
And the national, sovereign grief (too deep for tears!)
The dupe of time at the iron frontier
Leaves his world of regret with a passport of grinning bone
. . . within the holy silence of the snow.
'To sleep, perchance to dream!' as the Prince said.
But, waiting, I am not frightened of the silence.

Do not think then that I seek to assert:
These are impressions of a festive season
Conceived in a better time. No word of mine
Can change the mystery. So many have seen
The teacher dumbfounded, the lesson gone awry.
In dogma is danger: that I know, having been
Last night in the garden, under the darkened trees
When the bombs came; with the wounded child in my arms.

Morning After Battle

As if for a first time I have seen
The breathless outburst of this winter morning
And never before knew sun so tender in bare trees.
Nor, under the naked branches, green so green
As the silent fields. And the silence is
The calm of the late reprieve. We cannot bear
This silence speaking: so, as if ashamed
To show our joy, are wordless as we turn
Away from that country of fear no one has named.
There are birds singing in the crystal air.
We forget the fear that like a spider's web
Brushed at our faces through the lonely night;
Forget the pall of guns forever spreading
On cities, lights and perfumes, and release
The small history clenched in the fist of fear.

Mutter: 'They copped old Tom (or Dick, or Joe)
Sleeping – just there, look – under the wild hedgerow.
Wouldn't it make you . . .' Yes, when Death nudges,
'Old Flatnose', they are always ready to go,
With a brief sigh, like children woken from dream:
With simple words like these for epitaph
Masking the bright deep fury without a name.

Before these nameless faces what can be said
For a courage that braves the eternally private hell?
Yet it seemed like the promise wrought, the miracle sign
When a girl smiled, drawing water at the well.

Italy, Winter 1944

ERIK DE MAUNY

1940–45 served with NZ Expeditionary Force in Pacific, Middle East and Italy. BBC Foreign Correspondent for seventeen years. Novelist. Lives in Lancaster.

Poem XI

Splendours and miseries: these are the lot of all martial endeavour
(So we are told by the leading authorities.) Shall we recount them,
Therefore, as they appear to a private's or subaltern's eye-view,
Taking the miseries first? Already they slip through our fingers –
Bark of the corporal, bite of the north wind, drill in a snow-storm,
Greasy stew in a greasier bowl, the convict's hair-cut,
Webbing and brass, the machine-gun's stony inanimate malice,
Tea from a bucket, the arm to be swung from the shoulder, and so
    on –
(Odd too how from a private's life all privacy's lacking.)
Later you learn that even a subaltern's life has its drawbacks:
Orderly officer's chores, old rude red regular majors,
Knowledge that other men's lives lie in your untrained, unfit
    hands,
And that the store of a mind, the gain of a lifetime's learning,
Treasures of feeling and sense, so carefully, consciously chosen,
Objects of art and virtù, on the mind's shelves neatly assembled,

All must be instantly tumbled and broken and ruthlessly swept out,
Out to make room for the graceless terms of the art of destruction:
Mines and mortars and beaten zones and fire and manoeuvre,
Brens and Stens and maps and morale and chemical warfare.
Slaughter of course is the aim, but we never, never say so.
Learn your stuff, and muffle your mind, and we'll have a good *party*.

Here then are miseries, sampled. How trivial in recollection! –
Told in twenty-one lines, worth hardly the trouble of telling,
Bruising our self-conceit, and undermining our comfort,
Giving us horrible frights, and doing no permanent damage,
Futile, laughable, almost enjoyable once you've survived them.
Once you've survived. There is now no certainty that we shall do so,
Only the thought that in mean little trials and dismal amusements
All that is left of our lives will run out like the suds from a
    wash-bowl.

Poem XIV

Officers feed upon maps as their intellectual forage.
Spread out a map on a table, to us it's as hay in a manger,
Rumps in a row as we bend and browse, heads swaying, perpendent,
Pondering where we were, are now, and (God willing) shall be.
Here is our frontier, reached. We are up to the point of collision.
This is the critical hour when words must be bodied in action.
'Here' says the major, and points 'is the road running north from
    Naples,
Through Cassino, to Rome. It's called Via National Sixty.
Here we are, at this cluster of spots –' and, brisk and essential,
Puts us (he says) in the picture. We silently hope we shall stay
    there.
Our small part is explained, our orders are given and taken.
Thoughtful, resolved, we withdraw, to assemble our men for the
    battle.
    Lord, let it not be in vain: as we cannot escape, give us courage.
    Lord, let it not be in vain: distinguish the dog from the rabbit.
Now it is almost dark, day fades and a drizzle of rain falls,
Hangs and falls, and veils our valley with night and its curtain.
So much the better; if we can't see, then nobody else can:
Setting the stage for the play we shall act, we have need of
    concealment,

Lights down, safety curtain in place, till the overture's ended.
Orderly, knowingly, calmly the men and the vehicles form up.
Everyone knows his part, we have come to the end of rehearsal.
What will the notices say, when we read them at breakfast
   tomorrow?
Shall we be famous, or dead, or ridiculous? Twitter the first-night
Nerves, twitch under the skin. Our leader presses his starter.
Over the river the enemy waits, in stalls and circle.
Fall night, fall mild rain, envelop us, be our protectors.

Who would believe that it could be so dark? The rain and the
   darkness
Fit on the face like a mask, would seal up sight at its sources
If we allow. But we will not. The tiniest target of vision
Eye must locate and retain. We must hold our place in the
   column,
Tracked on a half-seen glimmer of white on the axle's casing
Under the Bedford in front of us; ear must strain its taut wire
Ready to ring to the stutter and bark of the BSA, weaving,
Jolting, and working its way through the puddles and ruts of the
   hill road,
Link-man in our procession, but lightless. Senses compounded
Ears do duty for eyes, and eyes grow sharper as ears prick.
Davis is stopping his wipers, there's nothing to wipe, no rain now
Muffles the sound of our engine's pulse and the gearbox crooning.
How can they fail to have heard us? They give no sign of it.
   Raindrops
Tremble and fall from boughs: sharp, sweet is the scent of the
   chestnuts.
Slowly and carefully climbing, we round each spur and re-entrant,
Counting them all on the map, and hoping it's accurate. Seven,
Eight – and somewhere ahead, at last, the sound of the gunfire,
Whistle and thump and crash of a shell, ahead of us, somewhere,
But on our route, unmistakeably. Are they raking the road? Well,
If I were them I'd do just that. The next will be nearer.
Breathing short, and damp at the palms, we await its arrival,
Quite without power to escape or avert it; it's ours, or it isn't.
Here it is. Stop! Out! Down in the ditch! Christ, that was a near
   one!
Anyone hurt hurt, no? Wait for the next, it should be behind us,
With any luck – and lucky we are, it's slap on San Carlo
(Also on Val, we are later to learn, to our grief) and behind us.

Let us proceed – we're still on time, praise the Lord – and for
     God's sake
Don't miss the RV sign: eight-one, on a lamp, by the road-side.

Eight-one. Here by the road is the goblin gleam of the signal.
Here we stop and get out of our packing-case, out of our tunnel
Into the wide night air, calm, still down here, but above us
Winds rise, cross and contend, disturbing the sky's dark cloud-roof
Glimmering now with the dim veiled light of the moon late-risen,
And through a tear in its tent, the edges alight with pale flame,
Who was the bastard who called this a path? It's a bleeding
     torrente—
These aren't steps, it's a waterfall – look at the rocks and the
     boulders—
Meant for the stream to go down and not, repeat not, to be
     climbed up,
Though (the good Lord being merciful) presently lacking in water
Save for enough to run over our boots and get in through the
     lace-holes.
But in the deep steep gulley we're safe, and the enemy, anxious,
Knows that we're moving but doesn't know where.
Hard and heavy and cold on our shoulder the mortar's barrel,
Stonier, steeper the way, each yard, and again fine rain falls
Filling the air and the dark; hands slither and slip on the metal.
Quietly out of the dark comes the challenge, the halt and the pass-
     word.
George is waiting to guide us. We follow him under the archway,
Under the vaults, up silent streets, our mission accomplished.
Here are your mortars, David, and bombs for them, too, in the
     boxes.

Up the valley and over the hill there's a battle in progress.
Men who are hunters trained or bred, pursuing their calling
Grapple and shoot or are shot, strike down or, failing, are struck
     down,
Hand against hand, hot-breathed. We are not admitted to join
     them.
That is a place for the few, the elect, in battle-dress vested,
We are the acolytes only, the server, the verger, the sidesman.
There to the inmost shrine, to the altar of ritual murder,
There we do not penetrate. (*Procul o procul este profani*).
There they must enter and slay, or die at the hand of the victim.

Priest or sacrifice? Nobody knows, till the slaughter's
    accomplished.

Is this all? Have we drilled, marched, trained, to be stopped at the
    doorway?

R.H. ELLIS

*Enlisted British forces on St Crispin's Day 1939. Served as a subaltern
during the Second World War.*

Cassino

A million tons of wreckage piled high
Upon the streets and pathways of the town,
Which only yesterday was teeming with
A multitude of people in their home.
A flock of happy children played their games
In alleyways which now are merely dust
And heaps of rubble left there by
The passing of the Allies' powered host
Of aircraft, blotting out the sky
Till all of it seemed overcast
With shadows of their wings in great array.
A day or so ago, the chickens ran
Squawking when motor-cars approached,
Dogs barked, and women stood around
And gossiped, or they merely watched
Their offspring playing on the ground.
And now, what is there left to tell the tale
Of all these centuries of rural lore?
A mass of ruins, left there in the trail
Of total war.

January 1944

C.P.S. DENHOLM-YOUNG

OBE, FCIS *Commanded the Signal Regt of the 51st Highland Division.*

War Dead

With grey arm twisted over a green face
The dust of passing trucks swirls over him,
Lying by the roadside in his proper place,
For he has crossed the ultimate far rim
That hides from us the valley of the dead.
He lies like used equipment thrown aside,
Of which our swift advance can take no heed,
Roses, triumphal cars – but this one died.

Once war memorials, pitiful attempt
In some vague way regretfully to atone
For those lost futures that the dead had dreamt,
Covered the land with their lamenting stone –
But in our hearts we bear a heavier load:
The bodies of the dead beside the road.

Near La Spezia, April 1945

GAVIN EWART

Officer RA, North Africa, Italy. Poet and critic.

Kriegy[1] Ballad

NOTE: This is somewhat nearer to being a definitive edition than previous
definitive editions have been. In fact, it is the definitive edition to end
    definitive editions in the meantime, under the circumstances.

CHORUS:
Toorally Oorally addy etc.
Here's hoping we're not here to stay.

Yes, this is the place we were took, sir,
And landed right into the bag,
Right outside the town of Tobruk, sir,
So now for some bloody stalag.

There was plenty of water in Derna,
But that camp was not very well kept,
For either you slept in the piss-hole,
Or pissed in the place where you slept.

And then we went on to Benghazi,
We had plenty of room, what a treat!
But I wish that the guard was a Nazi,
He might find us something to eat.

We sailed on the good ship Revalo,
She carried us over the sea,
You climbed up a forty-foot ladder
Whenever you wanted a pee.

And then we went on to Brindisi
With free melons in fields on the way,
Parades there were quite free and easy,
Except that they went on all day.

In transit-camp at Benevento
We stayed a long time, truth to tell,
It was there that we all got the shivers
And were all bloody lousy as well.

The sun it grew hotter and hotter,
The shit-trench was streaked red and brown,
The stew it was like maiden's water
With gnatspiss to wash it all down.

With hunger we're nearly demented,
You can see it at once by our looks,
The only ones really contented
Are the greasy fat bastards of cooks.

And then we went on to Capua,
On hard ground we mostly did snooze,
The bedboards got fewer and fewer
As we smashed them up to make brews.

It was there that we got Red Cross parcels
With bully and packets of tea
Would you swop it for . . .
For want of some brew-wood? Not me!

And now it was late in the Autumn
And our clothes they were only a farce,
For torn K.D.[2] shorts with no bottom
Send a helluva draught up your arse.

In Musso's fine box-cars we're riding,
All fitted with wheels that are square,
They park us all night in a siding,
But somehow we bloody get there.

At Musso's show-camp at Vetralla
They gave us beds, blankets and sheets,
They'd even got chains in the shit-house,
But still they had no bloody seats.

We were promised a treat for our Christmas
Of thick pasta-shoota, all hot,
But somehow the cooks got a transfer
And shot out of sight with the lot.

So somewhere they wish us good wishes
That we're not all feeling too queer,
And while they are guzzling our pasta
They wish us a happy New Year.

1 German slang for P.O.W.
2 Khaki Drill

The Presoner's Dream

In Italie, in strang presoun,
on Christmas nicht I beddit suin
    on my wee sack of strae.
Cauld gained on me: I couried doun
and happit me my greatcoat roun,
    wi puirshous blankets twae.
Thon day in special we had dined
on pastashoota biled wi rind
    of kebbuck, I daursay.
I'd hained a supper of a kind,
a big raw ingan, as I mind,
    or wes it Hogmanay?
It's queer hou memory gaes dim;
I ken ma stammick wesnae tuim:
    it wes some special day.
But, fir aa that, the Christmas cauld

nippit me, fir ma bluid wes thin,
    altho I wesnae auld.
Thaim that hauf-stairve their presoners
are no exactly murderers;
    whan the taen sodger dees
they scrieve wi sooth in registers
    some orthodox disease.
There arenae monie sophisters
    wad prieve sic truths are lees.
Our sentry, sloungin at his post,
kechlit outbye wi Christmas hoast.
his rusty rifle white wi frost
    frae whilk reid fire micht flee.
Aye frae the village campanell'
I never saw, I hear'd the bell
cancel ma hours . . . eleeven . . . twal . . .
    sleep wadnae come to me.
The New Guaird cam, het frae their fire;
I hear'd his fuit outbye the wire,
I hear'd his kechlan mate retire,
    I hear'd his Moorie sang,
a belly-sang of luvers' stour
like Baudrons in the midnicht hour.
The kindly cauld brocht me succour:
    he didnae sing owre lang.
The presoner's friens are sleep and time;
I cuidnae sleep, I hear'd the chime,
fu lang I lay, forspent wi care;
the saft seduction of despair
forset me till I gied-up, syne
intill her slouch I sank faur hyne
    and fand some easement thair.
I dream'd as I wes waukan yet
in Edinbrugh, in Canogait,
    aye heidin wast, uphill.
I saw the dial of the Tron
and read the time: hauf efter ane,
    the swevyn seemed that real.
I luikit owre the Nor Brig,
I saw the Auld Toun on its rig,
    and, in the tither airt,

Lord Nelson on the Calton Hill
raxt for the Embro Muin, but still
    she keepit weill apairt.
The Embro ambience curled roun,
    like haar, about ma hairt.
The bite of inwit shairpt on sin
nirlt me like the east wind.
Whit I had duin I didnae ken,
    binna that it wes wrang,
wi glowran wemen and sour men
    the causey wes that thrang.
Fechtin ma life's ain pressure, chokin,
I hear'd a sang, and I wes waukan
    intill yon presoun strang.
It wes our sentry's Moorie sang
whilk in ma lugs like music rang;
    wi joy I hear'd him singing.
But whitna bogle wes't thon nicht
gied me in dreams sae fell a fricht?
Nou, luikin back, I think I'm richt:
    It maun hae been the ingan.

ROBERT GARIOCH

Served in Middle East, captured when Tobruk fell 1942. Garioch wrote in
Lallans or the 'doric' of Lowland Scots.

The I.G. at War

I'm Captain Blenkinsop. I.G.[1],
Sent by mistake across the sea,
To land upon this dismal shore
And find myself involved in war.
Sad is the tale I have to tell –
For a man like me this war is hell.
For how can anyone expect,
My fall of shot to prove correct,
When everything I tell the guns,
Is interfered with by the Huns?

When bombs are dropping down in rows
How can I make my traverse close.
Or take a bearing on the Pole
While cowering in a muddy hole?
It's plain that the opposing forces,
Have not been on the proper courses.
But, worst of all, the other day,
When I was checking someone's lay,
The Germans rushed the gun position
Without the Commandant's permission.
I had to meet them, man to man,
Armed only with a Tetley fan.
O send me back to Salisbury Plain
And never let me rove again!
Larkhill's the only place for me,
Where I could live at ease and free
And frame, with sharpened pencil stroke
A barrage of predicted smoke.
Worked out for sixteen different breezes,
With extra graphs, in case it freezes,
For non-rigidity corrected,
And on a Merton Grid projected!
O take me to the R.A. Mess,
To dwell in red brick happiness,
Enfold my body, leather chair,
And let me fight the War from there!

1 Inspector of Gunnery

TONY GOLDSMITH

Lieutenant, Royal Artillery, killed at Longstop, North Africa, 22 April 1943. Inspired Spike Milligan, who served in his battery.

This Italy

I had not seen the earth so tender green
For two long dusty years:
Only I knew nostalgia too keen
Where sands of Egypt stretched

In utter desolation to the line
Of merging sand and sky . . .
Until at length with bridled hopes we came
Upon this little land
So like the sea-girt shores of home it seemed
That head and heart and eyes had spanned
The continents between:
Not all a tourist's paradise man made –
Her tired cities knew
Such poverty and want and grim disease
The Nile is heir unto.
And yet there lay the land her soul had tilled
Throughout the stricken years –
The gnarled and roughened hands of peasant folk
Who understood not wars,
But from reluctant sod, with sweat and tears,
Coaxed the sour-wine grape,
And wove a patterned patchwork from the soil.

This, nature's garnering,
The iron rape of war cannot despoil.
The stalwart casas and the ramparts lie
A helpless heap of rubble,
But still the twisted olive drops its fruit
Upon the terraced hill
And calm, deep-barrelled oxen bear the yoke
Of wooden plough and mill.

GWENYTH HAYES

(New Zealand) *Middle East, First New Zealand VADs (Voluntary Aid Detachment) January 1942, private secretary to commanding officers of 2nd New Zealand General Hospital at Kantara on the canal, Egypt; then 2nd New Zealand Div. in Italy. Twice mentioned in despatches.*

Leaflet[1]

The dusty leaflet shows a smiling girl
Holding a basket of grapes.
Open the fold and see a giant skeleton
Rising out of a river, tipping up assault boats
And gloating over drowned men.

This awaits you, soldier,
Not the clean-shaven city gent setting out
For work who smiles up at you
From the mud by your boot.
The calculated words in bold type
Boast of his self-satisfaction bought
With your blood.

So that he can breakfast in peace
Soldiers have to die at the river crossing.
For his wife to go to the bank,
Take the dog for a walk,
Drink coffee or go to the cinema
Your striated body must suffer
The dementia of the guns.

In office-block and sitting-room
You will fall into
A framed portrait of respect;
A milestone in the family history
On the mantelpiece;
An absentee who will no more use
The domesticated chain hanging
By its perfumed seat,
Wash his hands in the basin,
Dab the speck of blood from his chin
Or turn the taps in the scoured bath.

1 Distributed by enemy propaganda.

Dear John

Letter 1
Dear John,
Now don't be put upon
In your new service life.
Every day I'll think of you
And you must think of your wife.

Letter 2
Dear John,
I know it won't be long
Before you come back home
To stay with me for ever more
And never more to roam.

Letter 3
Dear John,
I must tell you I'm four months gone
And it cannot be your child.
We played together at pontoon once
But now the joker's wild.

Letter 4
Dear John,
I'm telling you I've gone
To live with another man.
I thought you were a winner once
But now you're an also-ran.

Off Limits

A chastity belt of iron gates
Bars the entrance to the courtyard
And prevents the battle-stained mob from assaulting
The bastille of naked bodies behind its walls.
Fists are raised, shouts are hurled, and bars gripped
As curses are screamed at the porteress sitting
At a small desk with a bundle of tickets
At the seat of custom.
Every few minutes two clogged harridans
Force the gates open for three determined squaddies
To squeeze their way through.
The gates clang shut to a cheer by supporters as though
The home team had scored a goal.

In a ghetto in a back street redcaps patrol in pairs
To deter intruders from houses under their protection
Patronised only by the bold or the privileged,
But chiefly by themselves with cans of bully
In their trousers sticking up like truncheons.
All over the country, as red signal lights go up
And barrages come down, good luck boys
On leave, or out of the line, are laying hands
On female mine-fields in village or town.

After the masculine roar of guns
And the snarl and whine of coward-provoking shells;
After the resistance of defended strongpoints,
They long to be served by ungrenaded hands;
To hear the swish of skirts after the hiss
Of bullets, feel the grace of curved buttocks,
Touch smooth flesh after the rough shattering
Embrace of torn ground;
To caress motherly breasts, handle tits
Like ripe grapes and grasp the vigorous sunburnt thighs
Of peasant girls, to lay them over sacks in barns,
Or in wide, ornate, flea-ridden, old-fashioned
Family beds smelling of corn husks:
Or outside in fields under shrapnel-studded skies:
In darkened rooms down narrow alleys

Where they kiss the crucified necks of recent virgins
Who stare wide-eyed muttering Ave Marias
As the devil takes possession of their bodies
If not of their souls.
Others, housewives with children,
Sell themselves for bread, as pasty-faced pimps
Lurk at corners touting for custom
And small ragged boys offer their immaculate sisters.
Frowning M.O.s thrust hostile syringes
Into the battle-scarred casualties
Of unsupervised brothels, treating their wounds
As self-inflicted and the weapons
By which they achieved them infected sores.
Far better to stick to your mates – or up your mates –
Your company, your regiment, and follow the Mad Major
Who hates all bitches and spits out daily
From his embittered moustache –
'I can't stand it, even in dogs.'
V.D. is a plague, a camp follower
As repulsive as unwashed Barracks.

ROBIN IVY

Served in Italian campaign. Poet and artist.

Mahoney

Then Mahoney, standing in the surf,
the convoy hanging in the misty sea
and landing forces moving up the beach,
dropped down his arms, and said
I wait, O God, I wait,
and these were his last words of common speech.

Christ in the shallows of the water walked
or in the sweaty hollow of his palm
appeared and spoke to his reluctant bone
or moved about the chambers of his skull,
the scourger of the temple, with a whip;
and in his heart also the lash had been.

So Mahoney stood and let his rifle fall
into the sea, where lug-worms claimed it, and
the servant tide; and heard his captain shout,
but did not move; and felt the weight of wheels
and tracks across the cortex of his brain;
but did not certainly hear the single shot.

Wife, children, parents, weep for him, who now
dead with the grey crabs and the starfish rests
where surges heap on him the slow and secret sand.
Yet even in the valleys of the sea
the dead can feel the libel, and Mahoney
in his stripped skull is tortured by a lie.

SEAN JENNETT

Served Middle East. OUP typographer.

Prisoners of War

Like shabby ghosts down dried-up river beds
The tired procession slowly leaves the field;
Dazed and abandoned, just a count of heads,
They file away, these who have done their last,
To that grey safety where the days are sealed,
Where no word enters, and the urgent past
Is relieved day by day against the clock
Whose hours are meaningless, whose measured rate
Brings nearer nothing, only serves to mock.

It is ended now. There's no more need to choose,
To fend and think and act: no need to hate.
Now all their will is worthless, none will lose
And none will suffer though their courage fail.
The tension in the brain is loosened now,
Its taut decisions slack: no more alone
– How I and each of us has been alone
Like lone trees which the lightnings all assail –
They are herded now and have no more to give.
Even fear is past. And death, so long so near,

Has suddenly receded to its station
In the misty end of life. For these will live,
They are quit of killing and sudden mutilation;
They no longer cower at the sound of a shell in the air,
They are safe. And in the glimmer at time's end
They will return – old, worn maybe, but sure –
And gather their bits of broken lives to mend.

Sicily. August–October 1943

JOHN JARMAIN

Captain 51st Highland Division, anti-tank unit. Chiefly Western Desert, killed in Normandy, 26 June 1944. The night before he worked through the records of his unit, assessing each man. Like Keith Douglas, he foresaw his own end. Against advice he went on a recce into St Honorine la Chardonnerette, to be killed by a German mortar bomb.

Midwinter

Gone are the mountains, gone Il Gran Sasso, every peak, every
    cliff and outcrop, gaunt and black, craggy hard
swallowed by the mist;
and gone the fresh little mole mounds, no sooner heaped up than
    beaded with frost, here in the prison yard
no bigger than my fist.

Gone too the country-roads like rods of ebony that cut these
    fields of snow into strict squares of black and white,
rigid rectangles;
and gone the tiny tracks of snails that looped themselves round a
    clean cobblestone shining as beautiful and bright
as jingling bangles,
spooring the gutter's edge, crisscrossing the mess-kitchen steps,
    sparkling even in this crude half light
with the sheen of spangles.
And from the eaves the long, sharp-pointed icicle – winter's
    dagger with hilt and shaft silver-chased – stabbing the sight
no longer dangles.

We have come to the dead-end of all our days, all our nights:
  these four blank walls a drab red brown by day, pitch black by
  night. There is no turning
backward or forward from this.
This is our life, our death-in-life: this gloom, this ghostly pallor
  above each cot at noon, this cold at day's meridian, as cold as
  ice but burning, burning
even at war's embrace, the blazing battle's bitter kiss.

Through the chinks, the cracks in the wide wooden door, the
  shattered window, the mist seeps. Its wisps cluster, drift and veer
above each wooden bed.
The floor is of cement. There is no stove or fire. In two long
  rows we lie freezing under our blankets. In this grey
  whiteness lingering around us, drooping, drear,
from which all speech, all sound has fled,
no one speaks. All the old battles, desert scraps, dogfights,
  crashes on the desert's deck, swimming around in the cold,
  dark Med before the slow red dawn, all the heroism and
  gallantry, all the cowardice and the horror and the fear,
nothing, nothing has been left unsaid.

We have come to the end of all our small talk, our tether, our
  high hopes, ambitions. We have exhausted even the
  bickerings, the stupid quarrels, the sneer, the snarl. We have
  forgone all that we loved, cherished, held most dear
and all our books are read.

Prisoner of War Camp, No. 78, Italy

The White Road

(Abridged)

The white road winds away from our prison camp
  through the peaceful countryside where men are happy tilling the
    fields
  bending, rising, stretching themselves, then bending again
  coaxing with calloused hands out of the rich black loam
  the crisp brown bread their teeth will crunch in winter

drawing from the damp earth's secret cells
the gem pure essence of the vine that will brim the vats in autumn
splashing their copper with crimson.

The white road winds away from the prison camp
through quiet hamlets, country villages, San Pietro, Tubiano,
and Tuturano with its pink and white streets
redbrick church tower
small sun-washed squares
where fountains tinkle
and children skip and play.

There
men come and go as they please
grey beards pass the time of day with their cronies
around the marble-topped tables of little cafes
reminisce, disagree
fall into an argument over a memory,
then hold their peace again.

There
young men's eyes are quick to appraise
the easy grace and shapely limbs of girls
who trip by
with a merry click of heels
upon the cobble stones.

There
one may buy a paper and even —
between one sip of coffee and the next —
casually read grandiloquent fulminations
by IL DUCE...

★ ★ ★

The white road winding back to the prison camp
is a dagger stabbing the heart.

Only when twilight falls
when the meagre meal is done
and the door closes on the bungalow
where a hundred men must endure the length of night
only when warmth and weariness
steal over their senses

and sleep at last seals up their eyes
is the dagger sheathed.

Tuturano, Prisoner of War Camp, Italy, 16 December 1941

UYS KRIGE

(South Africa) *War correspondent Egypt and Abyssinia. South Africa's
leading Poet Second World War, POW Camp No. 78 Italy.*

Motor Transport Officer

Pyatt had something to do with horses.
No, that's not what I mean,
  wipe that smirk off your face.
I mean that in Civvy Street he had
  something to do with horses.
Not as a Trainer, you know, but in
  the buying and selling line.
A horse-chandler, or something.

We didn't have any horses in The Regiment,
  though we had some mules with us in Greece.
So we made him our Motor Transport Officer,
  as he was a Captain, and none of the other
  companies wanted him, not being a Gent.

He made a damn good transport officer, actually.
'Not afraid to get his head under the bonnet,'
  the Colonel always said.
And he could nurse a three-tonner back on the road,
  like a horse with an injured fetlock.

He didn't like the fighting much, and when shells
  fell, managed to be back with 'B' Echelon;
  and he drank too much.

But I wouldn't have wished his end, on man or beast.
Slewed a 15-hundredweight across the road, into a wall

when he came upon a sudden roadblock.
Trapped in the cab, when the bastard truck caught fire.

Well, they shoot horses, don't they?

COLIN MCINTYRE

Black Watch, Company Commander, Lovat Scouts. BBC.

Com-bloody-parisons

*Butman, founder of Melbourne, is quoted as saying, as he looked at the Yarra
Yarra river: 'This is the place for a village.'*

If you stand beside the Tiber
Where it splashes on the rocks
You can feel the ancient history
Come soaking through your socks
But I'm no man to give a damn
For others' rape and pillage
The bloody muddy Yarra is
The place I'd build my 'village'.

Have you seen the Colosseum
Where the plebs would get a treat
Watching hungry bloody Christians
Being given lions to eat?
But for me the Melbourne Cricket Ground
Is calling calling calling
With all those blokes from Pommieland
Their bloody wickets falling.

The plains of bloody Lombardy
We're led to understand
Are famous for their poplar trees
So tall and straight and grand
That's dinkum for the Ities
The tree for me, old chum,
A dirty great big sticky
Aussie eucalyptus gum.
There's quite a lot of beautiful

Ragazzas here in Rome
Attractive till they start to talk
Just like the birds at home
I dunno what they're saying
And I do not bloody care
I guess a sheila is a sheila
Any bloody where.

KEVIN MCHALE

(Australia)

The Soldiers At Lauro

Young are our dead
Like babies they lie
The wombs they blest once
Not healed dry
And yet – too soon
Into each space
A cold earth falls
On colder face.
Quite still they lie
These fresh-cut reeds
Clutched in earth
Like winter seeds
But they will not bloom
When called by spring
To burst with leaf
And blossoming
They sleep on
In silent dust
As crosses rot
And helmets rust.

Italy, January 1943

SPIKE MILLIGAN

Bombardier, Royal Artillery, North Africa and Italy. Wrote Monty, His
Part in my Victory *and sequels.*

Imprint of War (Italy 1943)

(Prose Poem)

Land desolate as a lone sheep lost from flock
in snow storm's hazing; olive trees walk as
grey ghosts hand in hand denuded as sparse
rock strata'd land; land winter clutching at
its throat, manacled by invading armies' steel
encircled moat.

A daub in artist's dingy scene child figure
tends a twig-fire green, sketchy garments
rent in every seam cling dejectedly to a body
honed to starvation's rampant paw;
misery oozes from his every being crouched
on feet ridged and raw, his legs as pea-sticks
after you had plucked pods – and left sticks
to weather's unruly nods; child body pregnant
in its import of need – all about war's greed.
Wise eyes that stare apathetically through
an alien in narrow soul destroying life
he always knew; across a curl of coiling
smoky haze a pleading cretin looks with
soul-filled gaze, hope tinged in thrust of a
wizened chin, an old man mask creased in
merest grin; embittered tread of war's rough
shod chariot, firmly imprinted on features
lineated in certain death.

WILLIAM E. MORRIS

*(New Zealand) NZEF in Western Desert and Italy. NCO on railway
lines to run military stock in Desert Construction Unit, June 1940 (12th
Railway Survey Company).*

Sicilian Town: August 1943

What was your crime, you little mountain town?
Why is that mother picking through those stones?

The entrails of the church stare to the sky;
The Military Police say: 'Out of Bounds,'

'No halting on the Road': the people stare
Blank-eyed and vacant, hollow-eyed and numb.
You do not seem to hate us: we are they
Who blew your town to dust with shell and bomb.

'Water not drinkable': 'One Way Street';
The road machine runts rubble from the track.
Was this a house, home of two lovers' joys,
Reduced by chemists' blast to pristine rock?

The moody mountain frowns, aloof, detached.
What was your crime, you little mountain town?
Just that you lay upon the Armies' route;
Two tracks met here by whim in ancient time.

N.T. MORRIS

Enlisted September 1940, 50th Royal Tank Regt., Western Desert, Sicily, Italy and Greece.

Being Bombed in the Open

We are as people that are seen
Waiting in Harley Street front rooms
With paper-gripping dread of who
Shall next be called through the opening door.

Each plane above is a dentist's room,
Unseen through walls of night,
The opening of whose bomb-rack door
Is a butler's call to doom.

Who wouldn't grip now a seat's side-arms
And face the whirring drill
When his fingers dig in the sliding sand
As the line of the 'stick' crumps near
And not the slightest hope we'll hear

Some soothing voice declare –
'Now rinse away your fear'.

North Africa

On the Bombing of Monte Cassino

They did not choose to wash in blood
The lintels of this valley's door,
Who had to die in hell below
To save the hill-top shrine from war.

There is no sense in killing, nor
In war's unplanned destruction:
Nor was it sense that men should die
For heavenly obstruction.

Who shattered centuries in short time
No pride could find in perfect aim:
They only saw below that hill
Was man now crucified again.

WILLIAM G.R. OATES

*Territorials, August 1939. CO in Royal Welsh Fusiliers for two years.
Staff of 1st, 5th and 8th armies and Allied Commission, North Africa and
Italy.*

Italian Road

Down the road they came,
The women of Italy.
The children, and the old,
Old men of memories.
Stumbling with their torn feet
On this broken road;
And we watched in silence
From the high turrets
Of our brutal armour.

Slowly they passed
Weary with children,
And the faltering footsteps of age.
Burdened with shock
And their pitiful bundles.
Treasured salvaged hopes
Of the home-makers.
These women of Italy
Powdered with dust,
Heavy with fear and fatigue
Trail past.
Only their eyes raised briefly
To the sun – and us,
From out of the sweat, mud and pain
Speak mutely, of the beauty,
The gentleness that must have been.
In them is no hate
Yet must we avert our gaze
Lest our pride be dry in our mouths
And the sweetness of our dreams
Be bloodied by their wounded feet.
And as they pass in the bitter dust
Of trucks and noise of distant guns
Our column moves
As the advance grinds on.
We leave them
These weary women of Italy
Lost in the harsh world of men
And our hearts grow a little tired
A little old.

R.M. ROBERTS

Western Desert and Italy.

L.C.A.

(Landing Craft Assault. Written on landing in Italy in the year 1944)

Waiting,
Squatting beneath the gunwales contemplating
   What lay ahead unknown –
   Three rows of helmets –
And over all the moon looked down,
   Condescending, cold;
And, but for the engine's gentle throb –
   Inevitable, pulsing throb,
Quiet reigned, told
Of lessons remembered – (Sound,
They told us, carries far at sea by night) –
And so we suffered the cold
   And occasional spray, phosphorescent, white,
In silence the more profound,
   Waiting.

Was it smile or sneer on the moon's face?
The moon whose very presence had been sought
To aid us in our task, and grace
With light the blunderings of those who fought,
And why the fear? –
   The strange uneasiness the athlete feels and durst
   Not show; the fear of what? –
Our task was clear,
Co-ordinated, planned, rehearsed,
Every jot
   Thought out; and yet it lurked there hidden,
   Unbidden.

On the hard wet seats we crouched, cramped,
   Legs tucked under us, and damped
   With spray. The soft,
Relentless, throbbing engine driving
Us nearer the shore, depriving
Us of precious minutes, long minutes,
Dragging, lagging minutes. Oft
Our thoughts would stray,
Eager to be away

From the cold and chill of the present,
  To the pleasant
  Warmth and friendliness of home,
Of those who slept
Of those who kept
  Their love for us till we should come.
We thought of them as we sat there,
We fought with time as we sat there
  Waiting.

'Get ready' –
A whisper down the craft –
We tried to gather our thoughts and steady
Our hammering hearts, and concentrate.
In stark reality we stood and almost laughed
As we stretched our cold wet limbs. No hate
  We bore for those we must overrun –
No fear now, as the purring engine ceased,
But relief that our hardest fight was won,
Relief that can only come from pain released
  Or Waiting.

MALCOLM N. SHARLAND

*Commissioned Royal Engineers N. Africa, Italy. Wounded while bridge
constructing over Rapido River, Cassino. Died 1946.*

Cassino Revisited

This place did catch a vast pox from off the Moon;
Crater and wrinkle all are here,
And we are travellers from another Time;
This place still keeps its own infected counsel;
The most thin atmospheres of loneliness and fear
Still make a heavy labour for the heart;
Yet tribes, I know, lived here, those loved and clumsy tribes
That men call regiments; one tribe would start
The day with telling of its beads; the men of one
Would talk of killings with the knives, and rum;
Yet others talked of the clean unchronicled Antipodes,

Of pasture and a blue haze of trees;
Some had left their private silken skies behind,
Folded neatly with the storemen, out of mind;
And all read letters smelling of the mules,
And talked of two myth-planets, Rome and Home;
For battle cries they used shy word – 'Perhaps' or 'Fairly soon'.

DOUGLAS STREET

Commissioned 1/7 Middlesex, MMG (Medium Machine Gun) TA British
Expeditionary Force, 3rd Division Dunkirk. Chief instructor Intelligence
Staff Course. Liaison with General Leclerc, Free French, GSO 1 Intelli-
gence 8th Army. SOE Yugoslavia and Greece, liaison in Trieste. Com-
manded Allied Information Services under the then General Sir John
Harding.

Vineyard Reverie

A lemon-coloured house, lying
    Cross-wise upon the rising slopes;
Vine-green, wine-red, always
    A column of sweet smoke
Rising, rising, and the broad
    Blue water of the Southern sea.

Who came here, and why, and when?
    Whose voice calling in the vineyard?
Where are those who lived here?
    What memory have they carried
Into the dim land whence
    They are departed?

The Germans were here, grey-faced,
    Grim-helmeted, their guns
Remain behind the balustrade, round
    The corner of the road.
A thick, black-barrelled tube
    Lurks in the alley-way.

The beach is attractive, opalescent water,
    And the cold, clear virility

Of the mountain stream,
  Piles of 'S' mines, plates
And tapes – the strange silence
  Of deserted fortifications – unused.

Blood has sunk into soil,
  This year the new wine
Stamped under boot, is richer.
  Children gaze with saucer eyes,
'Sicilia bara' – jump and run
  Playing dive-bombers in the glittering sun.

Yes now, look now!
  There is a house standing.
Yes, this was Messina,
  Stone on stone –
They say it was
  A large and prosperous city.

Sicily, 1943

JOHN STRICK

London Irish Rifles, i/c Battle Patrol, twice wounded. Killed by shell at Anzio, 1944.

Infantry Coming out of the Line: Anzio

So must the ancient dead
Have climbed from Acheron
Or Aeneas' ditch of blood,
Their ineffectual substance
Still spangled with fine dust
Like phosphor that reflects
And holds the wistful light
A little longer, a little
Longer – Brittle the tension now
Between the real and the dream
Dewed with the bloom of death
Still, these drained faces,
(Embrasures of the eyes

Frame the long bore of guns)
And every feature bleak,
The nerves withdrawn and hiding,
Blind walls of a beleaguered city
That has not realised
The siege is raised, the invaders
Gone with the sly night.
They do not look. They walk
Like blind men, boots shuffling.
Maybe one shouts a greeting
But the sound is detached, wild,
Has another meaning than ours
Like a gull's cry.
                    Inside
The skull their riot begins,
The mob of memory straining
Against the cordon of pride.
Rest will be no rest
But a fear of falling, till
Sleep softly supervenes
And slips the knot of will,
Horror with laughter mingling,
And the frontier melt
Between despair and longing
And felt things be but things
Divested of emotion

RANDALL SWINGLER

To F.D.S.S.M.

Together, my friend,
We smiled at death in the evening,
Recalling the goodness of gray stones and laughter;
Knowing how little either of us mattered,
We found a kind of happiness, if not peace.

You went, my friend,
To spread your wings on the morning;
I to the gun's cold elegance; and one

– Did you feel too the passing of a shadow
Between the glasses? – one will not return.

9 December 1939

Requiescat in Pace

Silenced by well-hid sniper
he spreadeagled the slit-trench bottom.

Shed no tears for him, for
he has a resting-place of panoramic view
carefully sited
tactically sound
with excellent field of fire.

For him
no quick-tossed clods of earth
to press him into nothingness.

He shall be exposed
to all the changing seasons
and the gentle soothing rain
and he shall lie at peace – forever.

Or at least, until
the War Graves people
bag him up
move him on.

FRANK THOMPSON

*Volunteered although under-age. Commissioned Royal Artillery 1940.
GHQ liaison regiment, Libya, Persia, Iran and Sicilian landings.
Dropped in Yugoslavia; ambushed in May 1944 with a group of Bulgarian
partisans near Sofia. Notwithstanding wearing the King's uniform, treated
as a rebel. 'Tried' at Litakovo defending himself in fluent Bulgarian
condemning Fascism. Shot 10 June 1944. Had working knowledge of nine
European languages. Poetry compares with the best of the First World
War.*

Overseas

Here is the airgraph's destination,
nucleus of the guardian thoughts
from those at home who think of us.
This is the country which we might so easily
have visited as tourists,
but with a camera rather than a pistol,
rubbing on the thigh.
Here is where we must forget
the numb bewilderment of separation,
and begin to learn
appreciation of new things,
such as the elegant ellipse
of Spitfire wings,
tilting and glinting in the sun.
Here the ties of tenderness
are stronger and delve back
into a precious past.
Here upon the battlefield,
the pawn on war's gigantic chessboard
can become a queen.
But with each coming night
a simpler thought prevails,
when soldiers make their bivouacs
into a fragile, private shell
tuned in across the waves
to England and their vivid home.

Monastery Hill (Cassino)

Away from the temptation of the town,
in disapproval of the valley's vice,
the monastery crowns the hill,
austere and celibate,
its isolation only pierced
by a deterrent, winding road.

Now its tranquil vespers are supplanted
by the wailing agony of *nebelwerfers*[1],
and its inmates are the paratrooper
and the panzergrenadier,
who finger bandoliers of ball and tracer,
the rosaries of their fanaticism.

Even in mountain mist, night gloom
or fog of smoke-shells
still the monastery persists,
an outline lit occasionally by flares.
Below there sprawls Cassino,
hiding its rubble carcase
underneath a winding sheet of smoke,
and in among the ruined maze
the infantry play hide-and-seek.

Hidden in the olive-grove
and on the forward slope of our own sector,
we observe . . .
and are observed ourselves.
In our student minds we strive to find
a means to break this deadlock
in a difficult campaign,
to burst the lock-gates
that will lead to Rome.

We wonder too if monks will ever
resurrect the spirit of the monastery,
or if it will be forbidden them,
forever branded as an evil monument,
a bastion, fêted by historians,
and once a valuable accomplice
in the art of war.

1 Smoke-shell mortar

ALAN WHITE

Lieutenant in Royal Artillery. Killed at age of 24 at Cassino, 12 May 1944. Poems collected in Garlands and Ash.

Ballad of the D-Day Dodgers

*A rumour started in Italy that Lady Astor had referred to the boys of the
C.M.F. as D-Day dodgers*

We're the D-Day Dodgers, out in Italy —
Always on the vino, always on the spree.
8th Army scroungers and their tanks
We live in Rome — among the Yanks.
We are the D-Day Dodgers, way out in Italy.

We landed at Salerno, a holiday with pay,
Jerry brought the band down to cheer us on our way
We all sung the songs and the beer was free.
We kissed all the girls in Napoli.
For we are the D-Day Dodgers.

The Volturno and Cassino were taken in our stride
We didn't have to fight there. We just went for the ride.
Anzio and Sangro were all forlorn.
We did not do a thing from dusk to dawn.
For we are the D-Day Dodgers.

On our way to Florence we had a lovely time.
We ran a bus to Rimini through the Gothic line.
All the winter sports amid the snow.
Then we went bathing in the Po.
For we are the D-Day Dodgers.

Once we had a blue light that we were going home
Back to dear old Blighty never more to roam.
Then somebody said in France you'll fight.
We said never mind we'll just sit tight,
The windy D-Day Dodgers in sunny Italy.

Now Lady Astor get a load of this.
Don't stand on a platform and talk a load of piss.
You're the nation's sweetheart, the nation's pride
But your lovely mouth is far too wide
For we are the D-Day Dodgers in sunny Italy.

If you look around the mountains, through the mud and rain
You'll find battered crosses, some which bear no name.
Heart break, toil and suffering gone
The boys beneath just slumber on
For they were the D-Day Dodgers.

So listen all you people, over land and foam
Even though we've parted, our hearts are close to home.
When we return we hope you'll say
'You did your little bit, though far away
All of the D-Day Dodgers out in Italy.'

The last verse to be sung with vino on your lips and tears in your eyes.

ANONYMOUS

Footnote to the Ballad of the D-Day Dodgers

From the many versions of this popular ballad by some anonymous cynic we have chosen the above – guided by Hamish Henderson who was responsible for *Ballads of WW2* (Caledonian Press, Glasgow 1948).

Common to all versions is the core verse about Lady Astor. Hamish Henderson believes that this gibe quite possibly originated as a 'think-up' of 'Axis Sally', the female Lord Haw-Haw of the Italian Campaign. If so, it well and truly boomeranged, becoming one of the most popular soldiers' songs of the Second World War. Before printing the poem in a previous anthology, I read the Lady Astor documents in the Reading University archive. The Lady in an appeal to FM Montgomery at the end of the War protested her innocence – such a remark would not be made by her. I worked through Hansard of the war years. None of her speeches alleged the soldiers in Italy were 'D-Day Dodgers'. However, her speeches showed the Lady to be somewhat hostile to the troops – very hostile. Including her proposal in December 1943 to halve the troops' pay overseas to combat VD. She spoke of coins jingling in soldiers' pockets. Aside from pay being in occupation paper money, the Mediterranean allowance was a magnificent 1/6d (7½p) a day. The poem goes in.

Victor Selwyn

AIR

Night Out

Tonight I'd have been with Suzy,
A kiss and a cuddle for sure.
Back seat at the Ritz, she's not choosy;
But tonight I'm over the Ruhr.
At the Ritz I'm her Errol Flynn
Though at first she'd play coy and pure;
But now I've soared to a bigger sin,
In a turret over the Ruhr.
Suzy is soft and warm to hold,
Sighing love that's a cert to endure;
Back of this Lanc I'm alone and cold
In the mad sky over the Ruhr.
And strangely, I hear my Suzy say,
'The boy I loved, he just flew away'.

ROY BAUME

*Joined RAF in 1941, Bomber Command, sergeant air-gunner, stationed in
England until 'demob' in 1945. Operations over the 'roaring Ruhr' – came
through 'fairly unscathed'. Published poetry post-war.*

Bomber Pilot

It was a quiet evening as we left.
I can remember along the curve of lane
the briar carving the air and the blackthorn
unlucky even at May festivals,
standing as still and dark as statuary.

Above the horizon line
only small clouds were stirring
and in the west the first star
stood over the park benches,
and I could see the evening lovers
stroll over the grass
and in the twilight turn face to face.

Others have found grace in a machine
pinned on a dark sky
carded like a butterfly
by a searchlight cone.

Such dreams are cured
when flying alone.
We do not call a plane
burning, a meteor,
firework or falling star.

Above the aerodrome
out on the uneven track
over the cloud-wrack
uncharted wind currents reach
take us and trick
sick heart and memory.

Moving due east, we were
over the sea; the land
distant and darkening. Coast
had caught at us as we passed
and the known river cast
silver rays at us.

Over light flak we rode
lurched up and lifted
– on over town and wall
scrawled river, straight canal,
Up as our bombs let fall,
hell breaking round us.
Death's intricate design
is often spoilt and soft
earth or split second
may cheat the best aim,
and the spread rose of fire
reach up like red fur,
wrap its creator . . .

As we returned, the moon
hung between barred cloud
the sea lay with teeth bared.
Only three engines
spanned the great distances.

As held in God's fist
driving through belts of mist
with seven silent men
swung in star balances.

Over a friendly coast
to west we saw fires burn,
flaring like summer flowers
– our own had flared brighter
now left far behind.

Here came the storm-wind
late in October, rising to gale force.
we like a tired gull
circling a lighthouse,
finding no light there
battling, the ground a blur,
blown like torn shuttlecock
ragged about the air.

Then a new engine cut
– no time for words, the curt
scream of tired metal.
We tried to crash-land, failed,
ploughed down a grey field.
Others were ashes, I
live with this memory.

JOHN BAYLISS

Flight Lieutenant in R.A.F. Co-editor of New Road, 1943–44, *with*
Alex Comfort.

Parachute Descent

Snap back the canopy,
Pull out the oxygen tube,
Flick the harness pin
And slap out into the air
Clear of the machine.

Did you ever dream when you were young
Of floating through the air, hung
Between the clouds and the gay
Be-blossomed land?
Did you ever stand and say,
'To sit and think and be alone
In the middle of the sky
Is my one most perfect wish'?

That was a fore-knowing;
You knew that some day
To satiate an inward crave
You must play with the wave
Of a cloud. And shout aloud
In the clean air,
The untouched-by-worldly-things-and-mean air,
With exhilarated living.

You knew that you must float
From the sun above the clouds
To the gloom beneath, from a world
Of rarefied splendour to one
Of cheapened dirt, close-knit
In its effort to encompass man
In death.

DAVID BOURNE

Pilot Officer, Royal Air Force Volunteer Reserve. Shot down 5 September, 1994. Left 140 poems.

Query

I find it hard to understand the latest German plea
That four-and-sixty rescue ships may cruise about the sea
For picking up of pilots who have found to their regret
That England's still an island and the English Channel wet.

For surely Doctor Goebbels says – and he is always right –
A couple's all they ever lose in any running fight.

If one ship rescues both of these please tell me, Doctor G.,
Whatever are you wanting with the other sixty-three?

O.C. CHAVE

Flight Lieutenant. Shot down 1943.

Casualty

'Easy boys; leave it to the doc . . .'
'Afraid he's pretty bad, doc; we've not heard
A word from him since just before we bombed . . .'
Hands under his arms and knees
Lift him down gently; unplug his intercomm.
And disconnect his oxygen.
Now guide his shoulders and dislodge his feet
From the wrecked turret;
So lay him down, and look at him.

'Much you can do?'

               'No – I'm afraid he's dead,
Has been for hours – 'Oh. Well, I'm sorry –
                     'Yes,
Probably never knew what hit him.'
But in the torchlight you can see
His face is frozen:
Cannon shells pumped into his side
From neck to knee. Skin white like rigid lard,
Eyes glazed, with frosted lashes,
Flying suit crusted with red chalk
That was his blood . . .
                   Such is the cold
In a smashed turret open to the wind
Torn at that height and speed through icy darkness.

DAVID STAFFORD-CLARK

*War service 1939–45 RAFVR. Medical parachutist. Twice mentioned
in despatches.*

The 31st Operation . . .

We might have known
That there would be a catch . . .
To match the occasion . . .
Thirty ops they said
Completes a 'tour' . . .
Sounds like a picnic . . .
Or a leisurely perambulation
Around the scenic margins of the coast . . .
Where teas with Hovis
Are the major hazard . . .
And rural deans preside
To serve the host in splendid isolation . . .

'Sorry, chaps,' the Flight Commander droned . . .
'But Group stress maximum effort . . .
Every kite to go . . .
It should be quite a show . . .'
He spoke his awkward lines
Without conviction . . .
His words struck like a shower of ice . . .
To freeze our hearts
And add a weight of doom to inner thoughts . . .

'You have my word . . .'
His twitching eye-lid froze
For just an instant . . .
'Your passes will be waiting on my desk . . .
Signed for your sure return . . .
First thing . . . tomorrow . . .'

There was nothing more to say . . .
Tomorrow was a night of fear away . . .
And sure returns
Were not the order of the day . . .

'Good show, chaps . . .'

'Good show, chaps . . .' the Wingco drawled . . .
He fumbled for the score . . .

A heavy silence drowned his words . . .
He was a very charming man . . .
The very essence of elan . . .
True blue to the core . . .
He never took an easy trip . . .
He did his share, and more . . .

'I thought I ought to say a word
About the ops last night . . .'
Dawn grey faces met his gaze . . .
He stumbled on without support,
Longing to be gone . . .

'Our casualties last night were grim . . .
But war is war . . . I won't say more . . .
My thanks to everyone . . .'
And glancing quickly at his watch,
He made his getaway . . .
'Good show, chaps . . .' an Aussie mimed,
To raise a weary laugh . . .
We grimly thought of trips to come . . .
Of more good shows to match this one . . .
And lumbered out to meet the day . . .
Red eyed and sleepless from the fray . . .

With Tommy lying in the morgue . . .
All but cut in two . . .
As though a scythe had done its work,
To slice him cleanly through . . .
While standing by the pilot's seat
To watch the grand attack . . .
He fell a victim to Fate's whim . . .
A shell of heavy flak
Cut through his taut spare youthful frame . . .
And in a trice snuffed out his flame . . .
To leave the plane a wreck . . .
The wonder is they nursed it home . . .
To pancake on a bed of foam . . .

The second victim of the night
Lay like a crumpled bird . . .
The evidence of shot and shell
For all to see, and some to tell,

Of a brief encounter that went well
For an intruding '88'[1] . . .
He stalked them coming from the coast . . .
Had them on a piece of toast . . .
Raked them from below . . .
The first they knew that he was there,
Was when his burst hit fair and square . . .
And almost laid them low . . .
The Kiwi, Mac, shared in the fun,
With three nine-millies in the bum . . .
Which caused no end of mirth . . .
As standing on his blood stained legs,
He tucked into his breakfast eggs . . .
Before they carted him away . . .
To live and die another day . . .

1 Junkers plane.

GEORGE E. COCKER

Flight Lieutenant, Air Gunnery Officer. Enlisted December 1939. 31 operations with 218 Wellington Squadron 1941. Took part in 1000 Bomber Raids, 1942. Air Gunnery Instructor, Middle East.

. . . Ad Astra

I took my leave of the earth and men,
And soared aloft to the lonely sky,
Thro' the gathering dark, to the silent stars,
And the whisper of Angels passing by.

I heard the beat of the Angels' wings,
In the silent watch of the starlit night.
I felt His touch, and I heard His Voice.
I, Man, communed with the Infinite.

Far below lies a burnt-out wreck,
Soft, the strains of the bugles sound.
The Ensign flutters a last salute
As another pilot is laid to ground.

Men are sighing, and women weep.
Ah! foolish friends, do not grieve for me,

> For I heard God call in the silent night,
> And flew on, into Eternity.

MOLLY CORBALLY

SRN Territorial Army Nursing Service: Called up January 1940. Egypt, four years' service at 19th General Field Hospital, Bitter Lakes, nursing battle casualties (ours, allies' and enemy's) — and working with the eminent surgeon Lieutenant-Colonel Professor Ian Aird.

Reprisal

> They worked all night with cardboard and with wood
> to make those dummy planes to hoodwink the foe,
> and in the chilly morning solitude
> wheeled out the dummies to places they should go
> on the dispersal fields, and went away;
> the hours passed uneventfully, and even
> no reconnaissance planes were overhead that day.
> They evacuated in the twilight, just after seven,
> and when they'd gone the Germans flew above the drome
> and by each plane they dropped a wooden bomb.

Armament Instructor

> Drysouled, he mumbles names of working parts,
>   watching the clock and book, scared lest he vary
> system laid down. Never gay or merry,
>   his words, like cherries, each have solid hearts,
> and he spits them to the airmen, deft by habit,
>   circumscribed by fear of losing tapes.
> If any fidgets, or if another gapes,
>   he pops with frightened temper like a rabbit.
> Museumpiece himself, he grabs and snatches
>   at information twisted, vague, uncommon,
> and doles it at the men like mud, in patches.
>   Sometimes, despite his fear, he's almost human,
> and leaving guns, to human things he looks,
>   and natters of glory and honour, both from books.

Missing

They told me, when they cut the ready wheat
the hares are suddenly homeless and afraid,
and aimlessly circle the stubble with scared feet
finding no homes in sunlight or in shade.
– It's morning, and the Hampdens have returned,
the crews are home, have stretched and laughed and gone:
whence the planes came and the bright neon burned,
the sun has ridden the sky and made the dawn.
He walks distraught, circling the landing ground,
waiting the last one in that won't come back,
and like those hares he wanders round and round
bereft and desolate on the close-cropped track.

HERBERT CORBY

RAF Armourer in a bomber squadron. Foreign Service post-war.

What I Never Saw

I was ready for death
Ready to give my all in one expansive gesture
For a cause that was worthy of death
I wanted to fear, to watch blood and torture,
To draw my last breath
Amidst a chaos of dramatic thunder.
I dreamt of aeroplanes sweeping the sky,
Gave war her ghastly lure,
Came, ready to fight and to die.

I thought in my mufti
Of brave men marching to battle
And came here to join them,
To share the machine guns' rattle

What I never saw,
Were the weary hours of waiting while the sun rose and set,
The everlasting eye turned upwards to the sky
Watching the weather which said,
'Thou shalt not fly.'

We sat together as we sat at peace
Bound by no ideal of service
But by a common–interest in pornography and a desire to outdrink
   one another.
War was remote:
There was a little trouble in Abyssinia;
Some of us came from Kenya and said,
'Why I was on the spot all the while
And the Italians sprayed the roadsides with mustard gas.'
Theirs were the stories of war.

Then came the queuing, the recurrent line of pungent men
The collar that is cleaner than the shirt
And the inevitable adjectives.

The papers ran out early today,
There was no butter for the bread at breakfast,
Nobody calls us at dawn,
We never strain or sweat,
Nor do they notice when we come in late.

When I was a civilian I hoped high,
Dreamt my future cartwheels in the sky,
Almost forgot to arm myself
Against the boredom and the inefficiency
The petty injustice and the everlasting grudges,
The sacrifice is greater than I ever expected.

TIMOTHY CORSELLIS

In ARP during London Blitz. 2nd Officer in the Air Transport Auxiliary.

Zum Waffen Garten

To sail my boat, to fly my kite,
To fill my jar with fish,
To laze away the livelong day,
What more could any boy wish.

'Bandits, Skipper, starboard high,
Coming fast in a dive,

Turn right, turn right, turn – now
If we want to stay alive.'

I remember those summer days,
Without a worry or care,
The afternoon on the sinking raft,
The excitement and the scare.

'How long to the target now?'
'Fifteen minutes will see us there.'
'Look out for the flak and searchlights,
And watch for the marker flare.'

White flannels and a sunlit pitch,
The crack of bat against ball,
The golden days of eternal youth,
Gone, alas, beyond recall.

'There's the marker and the flak!
Oh target, bright and clear,
Left, steady – bombs away,
Get the hell out of here.'

To sail my boat; Christ, we're hit!
Searing flames, curses and screams,
A blazing torch across the sky,
Turns to ashes, all my dreams.

Somewhere in the night, 1943

JOHN DURNFORD

Commissioned Royal Artillery; India, North Malaya, POW 1942–45 in Siam. Post-war Regular Commission, Royal Artillery. Holder Army Flying Brevet.

My Hands[1]

Do you know what it is like to have death in your hands
when you haven't a murderer's mind?
Do you know how it feels when you could be the cause
of a child being blind?

How many people have died through me
From the skill in my finger tips?
For I fashion the clay and portray the landscape
As the fliers are briefed for their trips

Do those young men in blue feel as I do
The destruction
The pain.
Let me cover my eyes as you cover the skies
Let me pray it can't happen again.
Don't show me the pictures you take as you fly,
They're ruins and scape – little more.

Is all this part
Of the madness we choose to call War?
If there is a God up above who listens at all
Does he know why this has to be.
Did he give me my hands just to fashion the plans
That my own land may always be free?

1 Mary E. Harrison, topographical model maker in the WAAF making
models to brief air crews for bombing raids, wrote the poem after being
shown the photographs following a raid and then remembering the photo-
graphs from which she had worked.

MARY E. HARRISON

*WAAF as Special Duties Clerk Operations Room HQ 12 Group
Fighter Command. Watnall, Notts. Trained as Model Maker RAF
Nuneham Courteney, Oxon. Posted to Allied Central Interpretation Unit
(Photographic Intelligence) RAF Medmenham, Bucks with team making
models for dam raids, Ploesti oil fields. Peenemude flying bomb sites and
Cologne, which inspired the poem.*

12.8.40

If I never live again,
This day will always be,
A rapture of my soul.
A treasured memory.

If I go down ere night,

At least this day I knew,
With all its combat wild,
In skies of azure hue.
Old Time, with cruel scythe,
Sends all memories to decay:
Yet, neither Death, nor Time,
Can ever steal this day.
If I never live again . . .

SGT PILOT E. LINMAR

RAF, posted missing 13 August 1940.

Heil Hamburg, Forty One

Height is just ten thousand feet. The night
Lit dimly by stars, is solemn, quiet, still.
My sergeant in the nose, his target map a sorry, crumpled mess,
His bombsight checked, his figures proved and double proved,
I sniff. The smell of fear is in this craft, it clings.
We wait the tracking guns below to find us.

Now into the glare – ahead the searchlights probe, then group,
And in their mingling hold a victim, their moth,
The guns are on him now: we watch the killing
In that bright slaughterhouse where we shall be
Two minutes hence. I check the time and wait.
And there he goes! He burns, he falls, he spins,
And still he drops, and still we look and pray for 'chutes –
But none, he's gone. There will be no prisoners to feed.
God rest them all. And now . . . it's us in the crucible:
We start survival drill. I turn full five to starboard,
Two hundred up, then port for ten. Down again, five more,
No constant course to aid the murd'rous guns below,
No rest, no peace, no hiding place, naught our human skill our
    aid.
And then the last of it – and us? – the straight run in on target.
The hoarse non-actor's voice from nose and lung and heart –

'Bombs gone'. Lightened, the aircraft leaps, I turn then,
Diving to port, a vertical steep turn. We enter cloud, glad shelter,
A thundrous crack, blue flames along the wing-edge, we drop,
    rise.
The static deafens: my cockney aimer drives away my terror
'Cumulus, skipper, currents vertical, course two seventy for home'
Home . . . happy word, land we left three hours since.

While in Hamburg they rake the cinders of the dead from one
    small plane.

In a Bristol Blenheim, Autumn 1941

To Germany, Three Nights A Week

The little airbus jogs us round the rim
Of 'drome, to bombers radially aligned.
Its faint blue lights illumine aircrew eyes,
Strained, old beyond their years:
No talking now, no boasting.
We have, if we survive this night,
Two days of peace, of boozing, lethe and love.
I sign
The Blenheim is maintained and fuel fed.
We clamber in, we strap, I switch.
The batteries connect, the engines hum.
Off/on magnetos, all is well, the chocks
Are slid away, and we await the start.

Near Maastricht now: my gunner shouts
'Fighter with lights on, Skip, the starboard bow'.
A tyro he; I turn to look but see
No enemy with 'lights on'. Then he fires
A hundred rounds at Venus, low ensconced.
I muse. If stared at, stars *do* seem to move . . .

I think back. At home, the ground crews waiting,
Thaw cold, skilled hands on tiny spirit stoves.
No glamour here, those fitters, riggers, all
Who keep the planes aloft, who light with joy

When their own plane, own crew are back with them,
Anxious, stricken, when theirs is overdue.

We bomb, come home and end
In the debriefing room, all smiles and mugs of tea.
The stories mount to epics, lies abound,
Are checked, debunked. We count the missing dead.
The eyes are young now, thankfully, we know
We have, each of us, two more days of life.
To Germany, three nights a week.

REDMOND MACDONOGH

Commissioned 1937. Served as pilot in Nos. 21 and 101 Squadrons.

Dead Air Gunner – 1943

I tried to remember the wind's formula
for sleep – the way to listen
when the wind closes a window
or opens a door

At 3 AM they brought
a Tail Arse Charlie back

The wind doesn't care –
bullets went clean through
the summer nightsky
ignorant even of themselves

Robert's life ended
I was not there

The others were too tired to listen
to the white clothes
taking themselves off
to feel the blood in his pockets

too tired to hear a blackbird
whistle his breakfast up

He is locked into a season
which goes on hurting itself

I don't know where they put him
I don't know where they put any of them.

JOHN MILLETT

(Australia) *Air gunner attached to RAF.*

For Johnny[1]

Do not despair
For Johnny-head-in-air;
He sleeps as sound
As Johnny underground.

Fetch out no shroud
For Johnny-in-the-cloud;
And keep your tears
For him in after years.

Better by far
For Johnny-the-bright-star,
To keep your head,
And see his children fed.

1 Written on the back of an envelope in the London Blitz.

Air Gunner

The eye behind this gun made peace
With a boy's eye which doubted, trembled,
Guileless in the mocking light
Of frontiers where death assembled.

Peace was as single as the dawn,
Flew straight as the birds migrating,
Timelessly in tune with time,
Purposeful, uncalculating.

So boyish doubt was put away;
The man's eye and the boy's were one.

Mockery and death retreat
Before the eye behind this gun.

Security

Empty your pockets, Tom, Dick and Harry,
Strip your identity, leave it behind.
Lawyer, garage-hand, grocer, don't tarry
With your own country, with your own kind.

Leave all your letters, suburb and township,
Green fen and grocery, slip-way and bay,
Hot spring and prairie, smoke stack and coal tip,
Leave in our keeping while you're away.

Tom, Dick and Harry, plain names and numbers,
Pilot, Observer and Gunner depart.
Their personal litter only encumbers
Somebody's head, somebody's heart.

Combat Report

'Just then I saw the bloody Hun'
You saw the Hun? You, light and easy,
Carving the soundless daylight. 'I was breezy
When I saw that Hun.' Oh wonder
Pattern of stress, of nerve poise, flyer,
Overtaking time. 'He came out under
Nine-tenths cloud, but I was higher.'
Did Michelangelo aspire,
Painting the laughing cumulus, to ride
The majesty of air. 'He was a trier
I'll give him that, the Hun.' So you convert
Ultimate sky to air speed, drift and cover;
Sure with the tricky tools of God and lover.
'I let him have a sharp four-second squirt,
Closing to fifty yards. He went on fire.'
Your deadly petals painted, you exert

A simple stature. Man-high, without pride,
You pick your way through heaven and the dirt.
'He burnt out in the air; that's how the poor sod died.'

JOHN PUDNEY

RAF Squadron Leader, 1940–5. RAF Poet of the War.

It Will Never Happen to Me

'I'll always come back' said air-gunner Jack,
'That's one thing that I'll put my shirt on.
I feel quite safe sitting alone at the back,
Its not I who'll go for a burton.'
But the Messerschmitt pilot had not heard this said
As he lined up his sights on the 'Lanc'.
And Jack felt his parachute canopy spread,
As down into darkness he sank.

'They'll never get me' said the young WOP/AG,[1]
To the rest of the boys in the flight.
'Twenty Ops – don't you see – Lady Luck flies with me,
She's with me by day and by night.
My Mickey-Mouse charm keeps me clear of all harm,
Friendly fortune takes care of our Bill'
But his luck went awry one night in the sky,
Through the shells of an eighty-eight mil.

'Of course I feel fear when the flak's very near,'
Said Sam who had guns at the front.
'When the moonshine is brighter, the heavens are lighter
And fighters are out on the hunt.
But my totem-pin wards me, my talisman guards me,
I trust and believe I'll come through.'
But the flak came the wrong way and blew up the bomb-bay,
And Sam's gone to stay with his crew.

'I do not see why it just seems they all buy it'
Bert said to me up in the bar.
They're efficient and plucky – I guess we've been lucky,
We've each got a good guiding star.

Now we're walking the wire – with less of our fire,
Together still – inside the bag!

1 Wireless Operator Air Gunner

BILL RAINFORD

MBE *Wartime Air Gunner, ex 38 'Wimpy' Squadron POW, Member
RAF Escaping Society, the Caterpillar Club and Air Gunners Association.*

Poem

Beside his aircraft,
Twisted lies my love,
Charred are the limbs that once lay close to me

No doubt some German woman weeps
For him that you shot down.

For all of Woman
War is agony.

MOLLY REPARD

Radar Operator WAAF.

Kit and Effects

'Reported missing . . .' So they closed his room,
Packed up his kit, according to 'King's Regs.'
His batman grumbled at the extra work,
Being a new chap, one of those square pegs
In a round hole. (He'd been a grocer once
In civvy street and owned a little joint
On the first corner.) . . .

                              The officer in charge
Made out the inventories, point by point –
Four shirts, six collars and nine pairs of socks,
Two uniforms complete, some flying kit,
Brushes and comb, shaving gear and shoes –
(He tried a jumper on, which didn't fit!)

There was dirty washing, too, which was a bore,
Being certain to get lost in the delay,
A squash racket with two strings gone, and a cap
That, like himself, had seen a better day.
Then there were letters, beginning 'Darling Dick',
Photos and snapshots all of the same girl,
With a pale eager face and fluffy hair . . .
This business put your brain-box in a whirl,
Sorting each item out. And then Main Stores
Hadn't sufficient packing cases left
To hold the residue . . .
                    Oh! Hell!

'Such odd impersonal things now . . . Darling, do you remember?
Oh! do you remember that day when we shopped together?
And you laughed, because I said I was proud to have a pilot husband!
Laughing . . . can you remember? Why did we laugh?

Can you hear me, now . . . Can anyone hear me? . . .'

                              The chest of drawers
Was empty at last and then the wardrobe cleared,
And the washing stand made tidy. So the place
Was fit for a newcomer. That job was done –
And satisfaction on the batman's face.
The Adjutant rang up and said: 'Good show!
Thanks for taking Dick's effects in hand.
He was a cracking type. Oh! by the by,
His wife's been on the blower, I understand,
She wants his wings – the ones on his best blue.
Just cut them off and post them. That's the trick.'

With everything nailed down and locked and strapped!
The batman said: 'Unpack! That's pretty thick!'

'I wouldn't have troubled you . . . but to wait so long . . .
Something that was his . . . so personal . . . he wore it just above his
    heart . . .
For memory's sake, you see . . . and it's all so difficult being so alone . . .'

The Equipment Officer issued them a set
Of brand-new pilot's wings. They picked and rolled
Stitches and cloth, rubbed in a little dirt
To give the thing a look being old.

'I can't thank you enough . . . and you have so much to do . . .
I shall always think of your great kindness. When I think of him . . .
Thinking of him . . . always and always . . .'

And, conscientious to the last degree,
The batman posted them immediately.

Address to the Mother of a Dead Observer

Madam, this war is scarcely of my making –
Why pick on me? I'm sorry about Jack.
There was a gunner and a pilot, too,
Who won't come back . . .

I had to bring the news. It's just a part
Of an Adjutant's work. It breaks your heart?
Madam, I have no heart, I have none left –
So much bereft!

And can't you stop your wretched husband crying?
It's really rather trying.

That's right, sir. Pull yourself together, that's the 'gen' –
At least amongst men.
'Poor bloody men . . .' My wife said that,
When war broke out.

Madam, I frankly cannot see the use
Of treating me to your abuse.
I didn't kill your son. I gave no order
Posting him across the final border.
I'm only here to see if I can help . . .

Help? Stranger, what help could you give?
Can you make the dead live?

Once he grew within myself and lay
Wrapped in my body. Every night and day
He grew within me in that fast embrace,
Until at last I saw him, face to face,
And he was in my likeness and I, aflame,
Cried out to God: 'I glorify Thy Name.'
And now God snaps his fingers . . .

Madam, I loved him too . . .

                      You owe me yet
Two shillings for the wire I sent his wife,
But that, alone, I'm willing to forget.

ANTHONY RICHARDSON

Flight Lieutenant, RAFVR.

Empty Tent

The tent next door is empty
The flap so tightly laced
Protecting scattered clothing
In that littered living space.

The shaving kit
The fresh–darned socks
The knick–knacks on
The upturned box

And there amidst the photographs
A letter ready, to be sent
Should this just be
An empty tent.

DONALD E. VINCENT

Served with 142 and 104 Squadrons CMF September 1944 until March 1945. Flight-Sergeant Bomb-aimer, on Wellingtons.

Frayed End

'Frayed End' remembers a funeral. It was the only one I attended. The curious thing was that although losses in Bomber Command were so high, one's friends normally just disappeared. It was strange on this occasion to be standing at a grave.

'. . . till he hath put all enemies under his feet . . .'

What a strange, awkward ritual is this –

The sullen, leaden grey
Of a winter sky drooped low with unshed snow,
And here below
The rough-dug clay,
The wind-frisked play
Of a Padre's flapping surplice.

'. . . Death is swallowed up in victory. O death, where is thy sting? . . .'

Death, where is thy sting?
A row of us here with our minds astray . . .
Off to the right a little way
Are the riflemen,
With three rounds each.

'. . . Man that is born of a woman hath but a short time to live,
      and is full of misery . . .'

I can't connect that rigid shape
Under the flag's flat drape
With someone quite so full of life as Mike.
The loping walk and the sideways grin
And a car that was hell to travel in,
Mike . . .

'. . . We therefore commit his body to the ground; earth to earth,
      ashes to ashes, dust to dust . . .'

When did I last see Mike alive?
Briefing before the Hamburg trip –
No, later on – that bumpy drive
Along the uneven perimeter track
In the rattling, jolting Flight Dispersal Van.
We stood together in the back
And clung, with the usual desperate grip,
To the things that brace the tarpaulin top.
That was how Mike's last trip began –
Just as on any other night . . .
After a while he peered outside
And muttered, 'Hell! He's passed our kite,'
And shouted, 'Stop!'
But nothing happened – it never does –
The drivers are always half asleep

'. . . the miseries of this sinful world . . .'

The sun was low and watery;
Wan blue sky;
Hangars and trees a sharpened silhouette
In the translucent moment before night.
Frost was a flashing dance of tinsel light,
Sputtering white,
Leaping until the sun slipped down and set.
With the last slanting rays of it
Burning across the tarmac underfoot.
Mike was standing there,
Muffled to the ears in flying kit –
Brown leather jacket, sweater, spotted scarf,
Parachute harness – legs set rather wide,
With a curl of frost along each flying boot.
He gave a sudden laugh,
Stepped to the van and reached inside –
'Hey – shift your arse!' he said. 'You're on my parachute.'

'. . . that we, with all those that are departed . . .'

It was bitter cold that night,
Over the bleak North Sea to the German shore,
Doped in the drumming engine-roar
Of long, straight, level flight . . .
Then the weaving climb –
The sudden plunging swerves –
Seconds when the flow of time
Was dammed by tautened nerves
And stopped, to hold us there eternally . . .
A jerk which shook us free
Out of the Flak and searchlights' clinging hold –
And then again the dark, unbroken sea,
The bitter cold . . .

. . .

At last the warm caress of England's coast
Sighted across the water, far ahead –
Some beacon flashing red,
And a thin white whisp of surf like a fading ghost!

'. . . prepared for you from the beginning of the world . . .'

A little after one we taxied in,
Motors kicked a last time round
And stuck . . .
A strange, unearthly sound
Replaced their steady eight-hour din –
Silence . . .
Then, in the stillness, just as Tony's hand
Fingered the switch, the earphones' hissing crack
Was broken, for the last of many times,
By Mike's voice cutting in, asking his turn to land.
I looked at Tony – 'S-for-SUGAR's back!'

'. . . and Redeemer. Amen . . .'

Strange how completely unaware,
How casual and easy in our mind
Were we who listened, in the stillness there,
Listened to that brief message down the air.
It meant for their crew, as it had for ours,
Dark laboured miles of flying put behind,
Bringing an end to seeming-endless hours –
That message – 'May we land?'

'. . . evermore. Amen . . .'

Why was that night's performance of the fantasy,
Which Mike had played before,
Given so poor a tragic epilogue?
There was a time somewhere among the roar
Of steady barrage, and the lash and flog
Of vicious tracer flailing up the sky –
There was a time for climax, for the stroke
Which severs all the close-knit earthly ties
Of earthly folk,
And hurls us,
Into the vast unknown.
But to be home – to see the winking lights –
The good, firm, solid earth
Spread comfortingly out on either hand –
To hear the order telling you to land,
And know the nearness of a blazing hearth,

Of food and drink, and common daily sights . . .
And then –

'. . . Load . . . Pre-sent . . . Fire! . . .'

They found S-SUGAR strewn across three fields
A mile or two from here.
Some farmer heard the rumble as they hit,
Or saw the glare,
And guided by the lurid flare of it
He hurried there –
To find a pair of wheels,
An engine and a section of the wings
Littered about the molten fuselage.
. . . thin-drawn brazen notes shiver on the wind . . .

Last Post, Reveille, die away . . .
Rifles and bugles, voices, all are mute.
One after one we face the fresh-turned clay,
Pause and salute.
The snow has turned to rain,
Whipping in clammy fingers, full of hate.
We pass out slowly to the lane
Beyond the wicket gate.
To-morrow night there will be Ops again.

RAF Raid Heard From a Prison Camp Near Berlin

Tonight, in the cool peace of my sleep,
Comes a sound, tugging, tugging at my brain.

Fully awake, I listen and I wait . . .
Down the long wire the floodlights disappear,
Leaving the swirling dark, alive with fear,
Ebbing in waves of half-reluctant hate . . .
From the small bunk below
A whisper sharply cutting in –
'The boys are on Berlin!'
I wait and listen. It is often so.

Out there to west of us the sky is clear . . .

Bombs will be falling now . . . (their muffled sound
Is flowing over rolling miles of ground
And after seven minutes will be here).
I picture the great city underneath
The droning aircraft; in the void between –
Crossing on downward, upward paths, unseen –
The mutual interchange of bursting death . . .

There . . . Listen now . . . 'Yes – those are bombs all right!'
There is a tremor wooden walls receive –
Reverberations gather in the night . . .
Mind flashes back – September '40 – Leave –
Mother and Father in the shelter – cake
And China tea – London beneath the Blitz . . .
Here are my ears, still listening, half awake,
And now it is Berlin that flies to bits.

What of those German guards, the listening ones
Along the wire. When faintly, far away
They hear the ruin of their homes; do they
Caress the tempting triggers of their guns?
Or do they curse the folly – not the men
Whom folly caught as chaff upon the blast;
Just as we, watching the dead years slip past,
Are wholly drained of feeling towards them?

Beyond you, Hans, withers my joyous life
From which you ward me off with gun and wire,
And over there my kin are raining fire
And death upon your own beloved wife.
Dear God! What men are they can piece it out
Into such tidy, pigeon-holed ideals?
Rather admit what the appalled heart feels –
We are insane; our duty is to doubt.

Stalag Luft 1944

PETER ROBERTS

Navigator, 10 Squadron. Bomber Command, Leeming. April 1942 shot down at Trondheim during attack on Tirpitz. *1942–45 Stalag Luft 3, Silesia. 1945–46 Air Ministry;*

SEA

The Troopship

Through the tropics once again,
with a stinking cargo of two thousand men,
each one sweating in his hammock; –
hip to buttock . . .
Bear us quickly to our journey's end,
we have our freedom to defend.

She carried prisoners before
to the Antipodes; we go to war:
But here they pack us as they packed the foe,
eighty in this foul-aired space below.
Bear us quickly to our journey's end,
we have our freedom to defend.

At sea, December 1940

HARRY BEARD

Commissioned 1941, Egypt and 8th Army in Italy. Fluent Italian,
interrogation of prisoners of war; Intelligence.

Leaving the Med

We came this way before
In different ships
Which knew no casual watch.
The hills rose crimson from the brooding coast
As at the guns we watched the light's last span
Shrink with the fatal sun
To night, and eyes the night concealed
Peering from black waters.

Historical islands
Familiar as midday bombers
Pass, known by their battle names,
Islands with the dead we once had watched
When dawn was shell plunged
Dragged by gaunt islanders down jagged graves
Or buried in torn groves.

Now leaves are green and ruins are arranged
To soothe the tourist on the languid cruise;
Bored elegance can gaze,
Admire the luscious view, the beach,
And ask, when guides are hired in hills,
Which bones are which.

We have raced periscopes
Slanting for murder
From neat waves, seen water lap blood's blue serge
From gun decks when ships screamed,
And when night's bombs had ceased,
The sick convoy, limbs floating in loose scarves,
And bobbing aimless caps.

Soon even the love we learnt will be lost,
Blotted from memory like the ports of Egypt,
Buried in obscure images of distant poetry.

This was our way.
We know faith's private history
Alone defines a way.

December 1945

MICHAEL CROFT

OBE *Royal Air Force 1940–1, Royal Navy 1942–6. Founder, National Youth Theatre.*

Air Sea Rescue

Twenty-three hundred – and Skerries light is steady
Coming through the rain and the night:
MLs[1] are in harbour lined and silent lying ready
And Sparks is dozing in the light.

Telephone . . . Duty Officer? . . . Telephone: Warning
Plane believed down in sea.
Broadcast. IMMEDIATE. Operator yawning
Switches on and reaches for the key.

'All British ships in area quoted
Keep a good lookout for plane . . .

Keep a good lookout for plane . . .
All British ships . . . position to be noted . . .
Sending message through again . . .'

Enter Commander, magnificent and swearing,
Gentleman, vague to the hair.
Clutching the warm British sack[2] he's wearing
Over crimson Gent's Night Wear.

'Send this to SOUTHERN SPRAY — IMMEDIATE. No, cancel,
Send what I gave you before.'
The Duty Officer, distractedly wielding her pencil
Scribbles and smiles to the floor.

'Message coming in, Sir. Object sighted,
Believed rubber dinghy.' 'Go ahead —
Phone through to Valley and get some flares lighted —'
'One picked up, believed dead.'

Feet on the stairs, to the SDO and back again.
Telephone . . . 'Anything new?'
Drifting Commander in his warm British sack again . . .
Messages . . . the long watch through.

O Five Double O — and Skerries light is steady
Coming through the rain once more.
MLs are in harbour lined and silent lying ready
And Sparks is scrubbing the floor.

1 Motor Launches, used as part of the coastal forces for patrols and for
air-sea rescue.
2 Since I had never seen a duffel coat before, I described it as it seemed to
me, a cross between a sack and a British Warm.

Sunday Watch (Extract)

Man is not lightly shaken from the ways
Formed in a thousand lifetimes — he outstays
One generation's battles, hates and haste.

Recall to mind the sometime treasured taste
Of native Sundays — forenoon interlaced
With lights and incense, evening half asleep
With Garth-air in the head and boots unbraced.

And though it is legitimate to kill
For seven days a week, we have our fill
By Saturday. The business on the air
On Sunday is approximately nil.

Cast off your stockings then and take a chair
Sunday's not far away for those who care
To smell the rosbif at the Ward Room door
And note the tiddlys the ratings wear.

And when the time arrives to go ashore
Put on again the rain-wet shoes you wore
And crystallizing random globes of praise
Go up to church as you have gone before.

LISBETH DAVID

*WRNS 1942, W/T Operator – commissioned Third Officer WRNS
1943, Cypher Office on staff of NCSO Belfast, C-in-C Portsmouth (Fort
Southwick) and C-in-C East Indies (Colombo).*

Fleet Fighter

'Good show!' he said, leaned his head back and laughed.
'They're wizard types!' he said, and held his beer
Steadily, looked at it and gulped it down
Out of its jamjar, took a cigarette
And blew a neat smoke-ring into the air.
'After this morning's prang I've got the twitch;
I thought I'd had it in that teased-out kite.'
His eyes were blue and older than his face,
His single stripe had known a lonely war,
But all his talk and movements showed his age,
His jargon was of aircraft and of beer.
'And what will you do afterwards?' I said.
Then saw his puzzled face and caught my breath.
There was no afterwards for him but death.

When He Is Flying

When I was young I thought that if Death came
He would come suddenly, and with a swift hand kill,
Taking all feeling;
Want, laughter and fear;

Leaving a cold and soulless shell on earth
While the small winged soul
Flew on,
At peace.
I used to think those things when I was young,
But now I know.
I know
Death stands beside me, never very far,
An unseen shadow, just beyond my view
And if I hear an engine throb and fade
Or see a neat formation pass
Or a lone fighter soar, hover and dart,
He takes another step more near
And lays his cold unhurried hand on my heart.

OLIVIA FITZROY

Worked in library of London store at beginning of war. First book Orders to
Peach *published by Collins 1942. WRNS fighter direction officer Yeovilton,
later Ceylon, 1944. Her pilot boyfriend killed near Singapore early 1945: a
WRNS girlfriend killed in a car smash. These two events affected her
deeply.*

Royal Naval Air Station

The piano, hollow and sentimental, plays,
And outside, falling in a moonlit haze,
The rain is endless as the empty days.

Here in the mess, on beds, on benches, fall
The blue serge limbs in shapes fantastical:
The photographs of girls are on the wall.

And the songs of the minute walk into our ears;
Behind the easy words are difficult tears:

The pain which stabs is dragged out over years.

A ghost has made uneasy every bed.
You are not you without me and *The dead
Only are pleased to be alone* it said.

And hearing it silently the living cry
To be again themselves, or sleeping try
To dream it is impossible to die.

ROY FULLER

*Ordinary Seaman 1941. 'Service discipline made my verse more precise'.
1942 East Africa. 1943 Fleet Air Arm. Professor of Poetry 1968–73,
Oxford University. Governor of the BBC 1973/80. Awarded Queen's Gold
Medal for poetry.*

To a German Airman

Who flew slowly through the British Fleet

Perhaps you knew not what you did,
That what you did was good;
Perhaps the head I saw was dead,
Or blind with its own blood.

Perhaps the wings you thought you ruled,
With sky and sea beneath,
Beat once with love for God above –
And flew you to your death.

Perhaps: but I prefer to think
That something in you, friend,
No inch would give to land and live,
But conscious chose the end.

That something in you, like a bird,
Knowing no cage's bars,
Courage supreme – an instant dream
Of mind beneath the stars:

Misguided, arrogant, or proud,
But – beyond telling – great,
Made you defy our fire and fly

Straight on, to meet your fate.
Steel-capped, we cowered as you went,
Defiant and alone;
A noble thing, we watched you wing
Your way to the unknown.

You passed us, still a mile from death,
Rocked by the wind of shell;
We held our breath, until to death
Magnificent you fell.

Whatever comet lit your track –
Contempt, belief, or hate –
You let us see an enemy
Deliberately great.

BRIAN GALLIE

DSC, Captain, Royal Navy, served in Mediterranean.

Assault Convoy

How quietly they push the flat sea from them,
Shadows against the night, that grow to meet us
And fade back slowly to our zig-zag rhythm –
The silent pattern dim destroyers weave.
The first light greets them friendly; pasteboard ships
Erect in lineless mists of sky and sea.
A low sun lingers on the well-known outlines
That take new beauty from this sombre war-paint;
Familiar names trail childish memories
Of peace-time ports and waving, gay departures.

Only at intervals the truth breaks on us
Like catspaws, ruffling these quiet waters.
Our future is unreal, a thing to read of
Later; a chapter in a history book.
We cannot see the beaches where the dead
Must fall before this waxing moon is full;
The tracer-vaulted sky, the gun's confusion,
Searchlights and shouted orders, sweating fumbling
As landing craft are lowered; the holocaust

Grenade and bayonet will build upon these beaches.
We are dead, numbed, atrophied, sunk in the swamps of war.
Each of those thousands is a life entire.
No skilful simile can hide their sheer humanity.
Across the narrowing seas our enemies wait,
Each man the centre of his darkening world;
Bound, as we are, by humanity's traces of sorrow
To anxious women, alone in the menacing night,
Where the rhythm of Europe is lost in their private fear
And El Dorado cannot staunch their grief.

NORMAN HAMPSON

Ordinary seaman in HMS Carnation, *Sub-Lieutenant in HMS* Easton *in Eastern Med., escorting convoys. Liaison with Free French on landing in South of France. Professor at York University.*

Naval Base

Waiting in the bar for the war to end –
Those who for the second time saw it begin
And, charting the future, watched death crawling
Like a lizard over the lidless eyes of the sun
And the leprous face of the coast being eaten
Away by the sea – the glass shows them now
The face and features that they find appalling.
Reflections of launches move across the mirror,
Destroyers and corvettes swinging round buoys, sweepers
At anchor – but here the voyages begin and end,
Gin-time stories which they hear, like keepers
Of lightships, as they wait for news of friends –
The same routine, continuing the war until it ends.

Survivors

With the ship burning in their eyes
The white faces float like refuse

In the darkness – the water screwing
Oily circles where the hot steel lies.

They clutch with fingers frozen into claws
The lifebelts thrown from a destroyer,
And see, between the future's doors,
The gasping entrance of the sea.

Taken on board as many as lived, who
Had a mind left for living and the ocean,
They open eyes running with surf,
Heavy with the grey ghosts of explosion.

The meaning is not yet clear,
Where daybreak died in the smile –
And the mouth remained stiff
And grinning, stupid for a little while.

But soon they joke, easy and warm,
As men will who have died once
Yet somehow were able to find their way –
Muttering this was not included in their pay.

Later, sleepless at night, the brain spinning
With cracked images, they won't forget
The confusion and the oily dead,
Nor yet the casual knack of living.

Destroyers in the Arctic

Camouflaged, they detach lengths of sea and sky
When they move; offset, speed and direction are a lie.

Everything is grey anyway; ships, water, snow, faces.
Flanking the convoy, we rarely go through our paces:

But sometimes on tightening waves at night they wheel
Drawing white moons on strings from dripping keel.

Cold cases them, like ships in glass; they are formal,
Not real, except in adversity. Then, too, have to seem normal.

At dusk they intensify, strung out, non-committal:
Waves spill from our wake, crêpe paper magnetized by gun metal.

They breathe silence, less solid than ghosts, ruminative
As the Arctic breaks up on their sides and they sieve

Moisture into mess-decks. Heat is cold-lined there,
Where we wait for a torpedo and lack air.

Repetitive of each other, imitating the sea's lift and fall,
On the wings of the convoy they indicate rehearsal.

Merchantmen move sideways, with the gait of crustaceans,
Round whom like eels escorts take up their stations.

Landfall, Murmansk; but starboard now a lead-coloured
Island, Jan Mayen. Days identical, hoisted like sails, blurred.

Counters moved on an Admiralty map, snow like confetti
Covers the real us. We dream we are counterfeits tied to our jetty.

But cannot dream long; the sea curdles and sprawls,
Liverishly real, and merciless all else away from us falls.

ALAN ROSS

*Royal Navy, Arctic and North Seas. Intelligence Officer with destroyer flo-
tillas. Naval Staff, Western Germany, 1945–6. Editor,* London Magazine.

Coming into the Clyde

Part of me for ever is the January morning
Coming into the Clyde in the frosty moonlight
And the land under snow and the snow under moonlight,
Fall upon fall, a soundless ecstasy.

I alone on the bridge, below me the helmsman
Whistling softly to the listening voicepipe,
And no sound else but the washing of the bow-wave
As the buoys go by like marching pylons.

I gaze from the glory of the bared universe
To the guarded secret of the winter world
Rapt, and the helmsman now is silent,
And I wait for the time to alter course.

To port lift the magic scenario mountains
White above the shoulders of Holy Island,
And nearer, clear as a square-lined coverlet,
All the fields and hedges on the slopes of Arran.

But further and smaller, away to starboard,
The plaited hills of Ayrshire gleam,
And I in thought am over them all
Away to my darling and my little son.

Beyond the moonlit hills that morning
My darling lay, and my little son;
But she in her cold bed lone and waking,
And he in the frozen ground asleep.

The Jervis Bay (Abridged by the poet)

The Jervis Bay, a passenger liner plying between Australia and Britain, converted to an armed merchant cruiser on the outbreak of war, was the sole escort of Convoy HX 84 when it was attacked in mid-Atlantic by the German pocket battleship Admiral Scheer, on 5 November 1940. Sunk with three-quarters of her company, including her Captain, Fogarty Fegen, she enabled 32 of the 37 ships in her charge to escape under cover of darkness

On either side the *Jervis Bay* the convoy was dipping,
And the Captain as he paced the bridge paused, one hand gripping
A stanchion, to study them against the amber rim
Of sky – the ships whose safety was entrusted to him.
And now his pulse is racing hard, but his eye is steady and clear,
And the smudge on the horizon shimmers into shape, and is the
  Admiral Scheer,

And Captain Fegen had that day a second, or maybe two,
As he stood on the bridge of the *Jervis Bay*, to choose what he
  would do.
Astern of him the convoy, labouring heavily in flight,
And one long hour till they could win to cover of the night.
To port the Nazi battleship, with six eleven-inch guns
Secure in triple turrets ranged to hurl their angry tons
Of blasting steel across the miles his guns could never span,
With twice his speed, with a Naval crew, trained, expert to a man,

With armour-plated sides and a deck, a warship through and
   through,
The pride of the German builders' craft. All this Fegen knew,
Knew his foeman as he came in overmastering might,
Knew well there was no hope at all in such unequal fight,
Knew his own unarmoured sides, his few old six-inch guns,
His fourteen meagre knots, his men, their country's sturdy sons,
But hasty-trained and still untried in the shock and din of action.
To starboard were the merchantmen, and he was their protection.

Rarely it comes, and unforeseen,
In the life of a man, a community, a nation,
The moment that knits up struggling diversity
In one, the changing transverse lights
Focused to a pin-point's burning intensity
Rarely and unforeseen.
In that stark flash the unregarding universe
Is a hushed agony. The suns and planets
Stay: the dewdrop dares not tremble:
The dead leaf in the electric air
Waits: and the waterfall still as a photograph
Hangs in that intolerable minute.

But what does he know, he at the focus,
The man or the nation? Joy and terror knows,
But chiefly a blessed sweet release,
The complex equation at a stroke resolved
To simple terms, a single choice,
Rarely and unforeseen.
So Fegen stood, and Time dissolved,
And Cradock with his ships steamed out
From Coronel, and in the pass
Of Roncesvalles a horn was sounding,
And Oates went stumbling out alone
Into that Antarctic night,
And Socrates the hemlock drank
And paid his debts and laid him down,
And through the fifty-three, Revenge
Ran on as in Thermopylæ
The cool-eyed Spartans looked about,
Childe Roland, trembling, took and blew,
The *Jervis Bay* went hard-a-port.

'Hard-a-port' and 'Hard-a-port, sir.' The white spray flying,
She heeled and turned and steadied her course for where the foe
   was lying
'Salvoes, fire.' Her guns speak, but they are old and worn,
The shots fall in the water, short. The raider as in scorn
Keeps his fire on the convoy still, now veiled in smoke, now clear,
But the *Jervis Bay* is closing fast and her shots are creeping near.
And now he swings on her his turrets, as a thief surprised might
   turn.
His anger thunders near, ahead. She trembles from stem to stern.
A flash, and she staggers, as through her egg-shell plates
Tear the eleven-inch projectiles, malevolent as the Fates,
And smoke pouring and wreckage flying as the shells fall like rain,
But she fights, and the convoy are scattering fast, and every minute
   is gain.
'Am closing the enemy' Fegen signals. She heaves, and is hit again.

Now the wolf is among the flock,
The sheep are leaping to ledge and rock
Like scattered clouds. To left and right
The wolf is at work and his teeth are white,
His teeth are white and quick is he.
Soon the flock will cease to be
That grazed along so peaceably.

But suddenly the sheepdog comes
With growling as a roll of drums,
Stiff and heavy, eyes a-blear,
But he knows the wolf is near
And within the agèd brain
One thought only may remain
Headlong as he hurls himself
At the grey throat of the wolf
Where his old teeth sink and stay.

But he, with fury and dismay,
Drops his kill and turns to tear
The creature that affronts him there.
This way and that he rends and claws
But cannot break those ancient jaws
That never while they live relax,

While flanks are torn and sinew cracks
And haunch a mangled tatter lies
And the blood runs in his eyes
And hanging so, he dies.

And it is cold and it is night
Before the finish of the fight
When the panting wolf shakes free
From the bloody corpse, and he
Lies like a sack, defaced and dead,
And the sheep into the hills are fled
And the wolf slinks to his bed.

Now the *Jervis Bay* is ablaze. The fo'c'sle is blown away.
Splinters rive her decks to ribbons and bury her under spray,
And her burning hull as she plunged on was a bright torch that
    day.
She shudders. With the clearing smoke her main bridge is gone,
And Fegen's arm is a shredded stump, and he fights on.
He staggers aft to the docking bridge. Another blinding blast.
The Ensign down. 'Another Ensign! Nail it to the mast.'
A seaman climbs and nails it there, where the House Flag used to
    fly,
And there it speaks defiance to the shaker of the sky.
He strives to climb to the after bridge, but it is unavailing,
One arm and half the shoulder gone, and strength fast failing.
But there is still the after gun that he can bring to bear.
'Independent fire!' he cries, as heaves into the air
The after bridge. He lives, and staggers forrard again, before
The rolling smoke envelops him, and he is seen no more.
Now her engines had ceased to turn, but still the shells came
    pouring,
Till with a roar her boilers burst, and the white steam went soaring
Away to the sky. Her back was broken, and she was settling fast,
And the fire blazed, and the smoke-pall brooded like a banyan
    vast,
But still the torn Ensign flew from the black stump mast,
And the after gun was firing still and asking no quarter
When the hot barrel hissed into the wild grey water.

So ended the fight of the *Scheer* and the *Jervis Bay*
That for twenty vital minutes drew the raider's fire that day,
When of the convoy's thirty-seven, thirty-two went safe away
And home at last to England came, without the *Jervis Bay*.

But now thick night was over the sea, and a wind from the west
    blew keen,
And the hopeless waters tossed their heads where the *Jervis Bay* had
    been,
And the raider was lost in the rain and the night, and low clouds
    hid the seas,
But high above sea and storm and cloud appeared the galaxies,
The Bear, Orion, myriad stars that timeless vigil keep,
A glimmering host the stars came out across the heaving deep,
And they shone bright over the good shepherd of sheep.

MICHAEL THWAITES

(Australia) *Royal Naval Volunteer Reserve 1939–45. Trawlers and
Corvettes. Atlantic and North Sea. Commanded corvette.*

Convoy

We were three weeks
in a small ship on the North Atlantic –
forty seasick Cwacs
lurching through
military footdrill on a heaving deck
with the wind whipping up our skirts
and those RAF officers
watching.

Nothing but
slowly rolling ships
as far as anyone can see
with grey corvettes
heeling dangerously
darting at the convoy's edges
whooping horns
lamps blinking wildly from mast tops
to signal reassurance – warning –
how are we to know which?

especially when the ship behind
goes suddenly mad with signals
still unexplained
when we
go below to the bar
to fraternize with the RAF –
boyfriends by mid-Atlantic.
Coming down the Channel
(where excited middle-aged Colonels,
getting into the war at last,
man anti-aircraft guns)
we all have RAF fiancés.

Those signals from the ship astern –
are from their wives.

November 1944

PATIENCE WHEATLEY
(Canada) *Served in the Canadian Women's Army Corps from June 1943
to June 1946, at the Canadian forces' record office in Acton, London.*

Atlantic Convoy

Written in HMS Bideford, August, 1941

Zig . . .
                Zag . . .
        Zig . . .
            Zag . . .
Zig to port;
            Zag to starboard;
Follow the wake of the ship ahead.
            Zig . . .
All peaceful men should be in bed.
            Zig . . . Zag . . .
Phosphorus gleams upon the water,
A ghostly light inviting slaughter.
        Zig . . .
                Zag . . .

Pin–n–n–n–n–g. Pin–n–n–n–n–g.
No echo from the Asdic dome
within the arc it has to roam.
Pin–n–n–n–n–g. Pin–n–n–n–n–g.
Thrump! Thrump! Thrump! Thrump!
The twisting, churning of the screw
drowning the talk from 'B' gun's crew.
Thrump! Thrump! Thrump! Thrump!
The watch has two more hours to go.
     Zig . . .
Zag . . .
The time crawls on, so slow, so slow.
Pin–n–n–n–n–g. Pin–n–n–n–n–g.
Tired eyes straining without hope
of ever sighting a periscope.
Two more hours, then to my bunk –
Providing we have not been sunk!
       Thrump! Thrump!
       Pin–n–n–n–g. Pin–n–n–n–n–g.
       Zig . . .
            Zag . . .
Nothing yet to be seen
upon the moving radar screen.
Thrump! Thrump!
The night is cold with sings of snow.
Smells permeate from the decks below.

PING! PING! PING! PING!

Contact . . . contact . . .
Range and bearing . . .

ACTION STATIONS!

Men tumble from their hammocks swearing.
Short sharp rings on the alarm bell.

'A' GUN LOAD WITH STAR SHELL.

A tiny dot on the radar screen:
a U–boat on the surface?
  Crash-dived . . . now no longer seen.

INCREASE SPEED TO TWENTY KNOTS.

Thrump! Thrump! Thrump! Thrump!
Ping! Ping! Ping! Ping!
Range closing.
Bows nosing.
Closing fast.
Shadowy vessels streaming past.

Ping! Ping! Ping! Ping!
SET THE CHARGES!
   The pinging stops . . .
Target right below.
Press hard the knob.
Depth-charges go . . .
   Boom-m-m-m-m
      Boom-m-m-m-m
         Boom-m-m-m-m
            Boom-m-m-m-m
Dropped astern, thrown to each quarter;
brilliant flashes on the water;
flashes making night like day,
decks awash with falling spray.

Turn through an arc of one-eight-o
over the spot where down below
men are dying.

Silence.

Then crunch . . . crunch . . . crunch upon the hydrophone.
She's breaking up down there alone.
The reek of oil invades the night.

STOP ENGINES! BURN A SEARCHLIGHT!

Some tangled wreckage, a leg or two:
of oily corpses there's a few;
enough evidence of a kill.
So this night's score is now one-nil!

Thrump! Thrump! Thrump! Thrump!

Back on station.

SLOW AHEAD!

And in Greenhow they're still abed.

Pin-n-n-n-g. Pin-n-n-n-g.
Zig . . .
        Zag . . .
Leave the bloated bodies torn.

It's lighter now, here comes the dawn,
morning for us, who have come through,
but never again for the U-boat's crew.
Yet in killing I find no delight;
perhaps I'll be dead before tonight.
                Zig . . .
    Zag . . .
            Zig . . .
        Zag . . .

KENNETH WILSON

*Joined Royal Navy as a boy, 1932. Petty Officer Telegraphist, Malta and
Atlantic convoys in destroyers. Dunkirk, Narvik, Salerno and Far East.*

Drifting at Sea

Look! my beloved, the sea-waves are rocking,
softly the eddies hurry past the boat;
here are no moments, we are not caught
in the dance of hours, and are excused
the sounding of the chimes.

For there to be time there must be sense
and consequence; the perception that rotates
in the changing of the symbol;
the opening and closing of the flower,
the scent of honeysuckle drifting in the wind,
the swoop of predatory birds
and the interminable agonizing instant
drained of precision, when the ferret
comes slinking towards the rabbit.

Such is the time of landsmen; but here
is only the continuous indifference of the sea
and the inconsequential rocking
while the cold, tireless moon
reiterates her journey in the sky.

DARRELL WILKINSON

*Surgeon-Lieutenant, RNVR, 1942–6 mostly with SOE Forces and NE
(Greece and Crete). Trust Founder.*

In Answer to a Sonnet from a Wren Hall Porter at Machrihanish

(Prose Poem)

Darling – To me you write in verse; that I cannot do,
I never could, a curse, but still perhaps I'll try another
line, and write in prose that rhyme; as Rupert Brooke or Keats
or Shelley; and so display emotion whil'st I eats, and fills
with starch my patient uncomplaining belly.
Beloved – You came to me just now, and with your eyes, your
lips, completely spoilt my taste for fish and chips.

What is the use of trying to hide my wish, my thoughts are
not for charm of any culinary dish, but of you in your office
still, at case, your body slack, relaxed by effort that must
will your brain to do its utmost, even if in vain, to keep
appeased the stream of deadly queries flowing through the
narrow entry of the hatch that is your only contact with that wild
unruly bath of men that stand and wait, and wait, and wait, for
transport that is always bloody late.

God what a station – what a place, what rain, can you wonder that
    a man must steel himself to keep his brain from slipping into
    thoughts
removed from cold and mist, to lips that look as though they must
    be kissed.

Do not pride yourself beloved that 'tis only you and all your
    charm
that makes me be so rash and lose my head; you are but the field
    within
the farm to which the bull must dash to get his normal instincts
    fed.

God what a farm! But Darling what a field!!

ANONYMOUS

NORMANDY TO BERLIN

Poor Dead Panzer

Poor dead Panzer!
It must have cost you some
to crawl through this wheat
setting it alight,
into this ditch
where swollen flies
buzz round the stiff upturned legs
of a Uccello cart-horse:
And you must have hated the stench
of which you now stink too.

Dragging your torn shoulder
through the corn, an oily smudge
on your tunic sizzling, and clutching
to your chest this evil-looking
Schmeisser machine pistol I covet,
and which sure you must have treasured
to spin round it a frothy cocoon
of brain tissues and dried blood
oozing from that hole in your forehead?

Poor old Panzer!
You sought to protect it so,
did you not? And you felt less vulnerable
with it in your hand.
Now here I am – half jew
and victorious invader –
dispossessing you.

And as I take the butt
into my plough-hands
seeking the point of balance,
I catch a whiff of Bavarian
harvest fields and temporarily
drop it back beside you.

Epron Cross Roads, D-Day Plus 20

A Man of Few Words

Black eyed Corporal Farrell
was a man of few words other
than the usual anglo-saxons
sprinkled around barrackrooms
and camps. He had no words
for the ragged shrapnel slicing
through his knee-caps but
used his morphia and that was that.

We sat side by side in the sun,
for 'lightning never strikes twice
in the same place' I had said.
Side by side wishing the frank
sharp crack and slap of shrapnel
would cease and leave us be.

He might have dreamt of England
and some soft hospital bed. I don't
know, and we just waited. And then
a sniper's bullet holed his head.
He looked at me reproachfully and barked
        'Fuck!'

Touffreville, D-Day Plus 41

MELVILLE HARDIMENT

*Regular Army Sergeant with 2nd East Yorks Regiment, landing in
Normandy on D-Day to be wounded at Toufreville, east of Caen, 41 days
later.*

Christian Soldiers

*'This is the Lord's doing; it is marvellous in our eyes.' From a Commander-in-
Chief's Order of the Day*

The Lord is with us, saith the General,
Behold His doing; war is nearly done.
He will bring the Hun to book,

With one last Divine Left Hook;
Fill your soul with Christian courage.
   Clean your gun.

Was it the Lord, then, made things happen thus?
I often wonder – I'm a simple soul.
He, then, who killed my mate outside Falaise?
And brewed that tank up, just beyond St Paul?
   Was that the Lord?

We saw a stiffened hand in khaki sleeve
Protruding from the earth at Templemars.
What did he think, thought I, how did he feel,
Alone and finished, spirit riding far
   To meet his Lord.

I praised the Lord the day He shelled those trees:
A mortar there was making life too hot.
The Lord, He missed, and maimed a dozen kids.
Almighty God, Thou art a rotten shot:
   Wrong bearing, Lord.

We often hear Thee, Lord, about Thy work,
Screaming above us while we wake at night,
We bow before Thy Shrapnel Incarnation,
Thy love sears through the clouds
   And heals our fright.

And yet, oh Lord, perhaps our General has his lesson wrong,
Unless Thy tone has changed since we last met.
I hate to think that Thou wouldst thus unsay
Thy sweet unmartial thoughts
   On Olivet.

Antwerp, September 1944

Waiting

  'We move at first dark –'

   As soon as half-light turns
   The fairy spring-time trees to sentry ghosts,

Proud in imitative glory
At their ineffective posts;
And the wicked eighty-eight they cloak
(Breathing all day its casual puffs of smoke
At rocketing Typhoons) shall drop its spiteful sight
And scatter arbitrary death
Among the sons of night.

At night we move –

As shadows veil the tell-tale litter
Left behind in bygone camps,
Men of guts and men of letters,
Side by side, eclectic tramps,
Creep from holes once gravely hated,
Empirically loved like home,
Venture to the open darkness
From the safe familiar loam.
And the hedgerow that this morning
Represented all we dared,
Hour to dream of sun-blessed heather,
Ribboned hills, horizon's spires,
Hour to dream of mortal vacuum,
Where the breath of love suspires.
Hour to dream of idle cities,
In their Sunday pall of smoke,
Where the men of weekday patterns
Live and love and drink and joke,
Rush in trains to seek the woodlands
And the lakes where air is free,
Where the lily of the valley
Nods just now in dusty scree.

No lilies here,
An hour of waking,
Seizing daydreams learned by rote,
Where the smoke of distant cannon
Speaks distress for souls remote;
Dream of tanks that scour the brushwood,
Other fields we once held dear,
Where the apprehensive tree-tops

Quiver with infectious fear.

Dark trembles near –

Hamminkeln, March, 1944

JOHN BUXTON HILTON

Beds & Herts and Royal Norfolk, 1941–2. Royal Artillery 1943 (Gunner). I Corps, 1943–6 (Sergeant – despatches).

Rhine Jump, 1944

They dropped us on the guns, left us in a flaring
lurch of slipstream kicking like sprayed flies, –
till canopies shook sudden heads, inhaled, held a breath, –
alive again we slanted down,
too many, into their doomed sights.

One scrambled moment it was red, green,
dragging to the door of the Douglas then
falling through a monstrous aviary roof
on Guy Fawkes Night (only this was day)
into shrill scarifying glory . . .

then Germany, the Fatherland, a zooming field –
banged down on it, stood up among the chaos, with
fingers flopped like rubber gloves trying
to slap one's box, slough the afterbirth of chute,
make somehow that snatch of wood.

There were chutes already in those trees, caught:
battalion boys who'd dropped too late or drifted . . .
harness-ravelled, cocooned there –
like silkworms, moveless, wet . . .
so easy, against all that white.

But not so many resistive earthworms –
the early birds had seen to that.
Soon, it was rendezvous: a stodgy farm.
The war was folding: fight-thin.
Prisoners happened; columned, toneless.

Next day it was hearing tales again,
having a kip in a pigsty, scouting the dropping-zone
to get silk (knickers for sweethearts, wives);
maybe a green envelope, speculation
about leave, Japan.

Oh and a gun-pit by the way, an 88:
bodiless, nothing special, –
only the pro's interest in other's kit:
grey slacks for the use of, old, ersatz;
with a brown inside stripe: non-ersatz.

GEOFFREY HOLLOWAY

Royal Army Medical Corps, 225 Parachute Field Ambulance, 6 Airborne Div., N.W. Europe.

German Prisoners of War – Antwerp, 1944

In a courtyard of the shelled farm they stand,
The dusty mirrors of defeated eyes
Obscuring those proud days of fierce 'Sieg Heils!'
They droop, dispirited, parched of all hope,
Their faces black with battered Europe's dust,
Dark with prophecy of hearts' forebodings.
Against the crumbling walls their arms are stacked,
Neat mounds, packages of surrendered death.
Our guns, now mute, mime articulation,
Persuasive signposts to captivity.
'Où est le Bosche?' is chalked upon our truck,
Releasing Belgian shouts and plausive hands.
We sway our victor's way through the faint light:
They say we'll be in Antwerp for tonight.

W. G. HOLLOWAY

64th Medium Regt RA: Eritrea, Western Desert, Alamein to Tunis, Normandy to the Baltic.

In a Ruined Country

Flesh-and-blood but, nonetheless, spectral
the grey, defeated columns,
flanked by their indifferent guards,
march precisely away from the battle.

Some of these wan figures once would have paraded
at the vainglorious rallies with emblazoned banners,
burnished spades, blazing torches,
while wives, daughters, shining-eyed, fervent,
tossed blossoms joyfully before sleek limousines
in the ominous processions.

Others, unconcerned with ideologies,
went resignedly when their time came,
burned under blood-red suns,
froze mutely in Russian winters,
routinely cursed officers and NCOs,
longed only to return to old, safe routines.

Now, ghost-like, relics, merely, of distant, heady days,
the long lines of crazed fanatics, sober patriots
and reluctant conscripts snake along the dusty roads
of their ruined country.

With HQ 33 Armoured Brigade on the banks of the Rhine, 1945

JIM HOVELL

Air Ministry for two years before joining 61st Training Regiment, Royal Armoured Corps in March, 1942. Commissioned 155 RAC and Yorkshire Hussars, North-west Europe 1944, Liaison Officer with HQ33 Independent Armoured Brigade.

Crash Dive

Shortly before D Day, our Part Two orders read,
'Get used to the Assault Boats or you're gonna wind up dead'
You know, those six man doughnut things; they're known as
    Spin or Sink
So we had to get familiar or we'd wind up in the drink.

They took us to a river just about a mile away
The Colonel called 'Battalion swimming team here. No delay.
Strip off and if some twit falls in, it's certain he can't swim.
Dive in and save his rifle and if possible, save him.'

Since I was in the swimming team, I said to my mate Dai,
'I could do with a dip, eh Taff?' and Taffy murmurs "Aye."
'You topple out the War Canoe and I'll dive in to save.
We'll have a dip and p'r'haps I'll get a gong for being brave.'

Halfway across, dramatic like, Dai gives a mighty yell.
Which of us hit the water first was difficult to tell
But like most other rivers this was only deep in flood
And half a foot of water covered two foot six of mud.

The pack that Dai was wearing saved him much of the distaste
But I hit water headfirst and went in down to my waist
And as I gained my feet and had a monumental swear,·
The Colonel asked, 'What's happening? Speak up you. That man
    there!'

I said, 'I'm up to there in shit. I'm covered in this goo!'
Then heard the bastard Adjutant say, 'Tell us something new.'
While Taffy cried, 'There goes your chance to get yourself a gong.
The King would not come near you when you're covered with
    that pong.'

I didn't get a medal, nor I didn't get a swim
But all praise to our Colonel and I must say this for him,
He gave me a huge tot of rum and said, 'Well done my friend!'
And then gave Taff a bollocking, which cheered me up no end.

PETER HOPKINSON

RAF 1941–42. Army 1943–46.

The Weeping Beeches of Sonnenberg

Ankle deep in old dead leafs
I strode among the stately beech trees
of this old battlefield,
Anguish in my heart.

I wept for long dead comrades,
I wept for the peace and silence
In these dark woods where trees,
like my soul, are scarred and pitted with old wounds.

The melancholy anguish I have carried these many years
Those boys I killed (shall I ever be forgiven?)
I see these boys every waking day,
the grey green uniforms,
their white marble, dead faces.
People say 'why do you grieve, they would have killed first'
Would that I had been killed first,
than bequeathed with a life of guilt.

Those questions I put to the trees,
they answer, 'Why do you grieve so?'
Did you not leave us shattered, torn and broken,
swathes of destruction left through us?
But look at us now, Look well my friend
for we are regrown and reborn,
Look closer, see we still carry scars.

Mute and silent I ponder this.
Closer I looked and noticed the trees too were weeping,
but not with my anguished weeping.
They wept for joy
Small nodules each with a tear duct I noticed everywhere,
Each nodule a piece of shrapnel ejected and rejected.
As they rejected they wept for joy, reaching up to the sky
and joyfully rejecting the iron from the soul.

And so the trees have repaired, regrown,
Deep and lovely are the groves of weeping beeches of Sonnenberg.

P.A. HYATT

*Military Medal, 4th Ind. Parachute Squadron RE, 1st Airborne Division,
North-West Europe, Arnhem/Oosterbruck 1944.*

The Question

Perhaps I killed a man to-day,
I cannot tell: I do not know,

But bare three hundred yards away,
   Where weeping willows grow,
Fell sudden silence on the heels
   Of my last shot, whose echoes rang
Along the Rhine. A silence steals
   Across the river, save the bang
Of distant, screaming shell;
   The tapping of the Spandau
Comes no more; brief quiet fell
   Where weeping willows grow.

Perhaps I killed a man to-day,
   The secret's hid, forever laid
Among those willows o'er the way;
   Here, beneath the quiet shade
Of a heeled, abandoned tank,
   I fired across the river,
   Made water ripples shiver,
    And perhaps I killed a man
Upon that distant bank.

Who am I to play at fate,
To aim, and fire, and arbitrate
'Tween life and death; not knowing hate,
   To send with sad, departing whine
   Irrevocable death across the Rhine.
The willows answer not. The scent
Of clover lingered while I went
   Between the fields where ruins stand;
   Dead horses lie along the land,
   Who died, and did not understand
Why this should be; no more may I
Explain why any man should die.
And still I fired; and wonder why.

Nijmegen, April 1945

ALEXANDER MCKEE

OBE, FRGS. Served with London Scottish and the Gordon Highlanders; Normandy July 1944 with HQ of 1st Canadian Army. Discoverer of the Mary Rose. Writer and producer of radio documentary programmes.

The Padre[1]

Greenjackets
Eleventh Armoured Division
Charging black bull, badge of Mithras
Bridgehead breakout, Orne and Odon
Hill 112.
Out of battle for a refit
In a field at Bretteville l'Orgueilleuse
Service in few minutes, Communion after
Disperse on air attack.

Coming, brother?
Me? In Civvy Street I'm a dustman
Quipped the sergeant – childhood echo –
Jesus wants you for a sunbeam
Clouds they parted and a voice said:
In no wise will I cast him out.

Unwashed, unshaven
All hands soiled, including padre's
Oil and petrol
Blood, earth and sweat, et cet.
Surplice dirty, torn and crumpled
Sleepless eyes and slurring speech
Military Cross and death hid future
Pulpit bonnet, altar bumper
Wine long finished
Wafers halved, then quartered, crumbled . . .
Carry on to the Amen.

Time and water – wash and shave
Take a pickaxe and a spade
Unto God's most gracious mercy
Go bury now our youthful dead.

1 The padre is identified as the Rev. H.J. (Jeff) L. Taylor, M.C. CF. He was awarded the MC for saving the lives of two severely wounded men during intense enemy action.

F.E. MACÉ

(Dual English–French nationality.) TA 1939, 2nd London Rifle Brigade (8th Rifle Brigade – 11th Armoured Div.). L/Cpl, Normandy 1944.

In Memoriam

(For the fifty escaped officers who were shot by the Gestapo in March/April 1944)

We dared to hope against the spoken word,
And even when their names were there to see
We couldn't quite believe what we had heard;
That men we'd known in days when we were free
And men who'd shared our prison lives, were dead.
It seems a little thing, 'midst blood and war
To cry against the Fates, but these had bled,
Had suffered, looked at death, and heard the roar
Of white eternity, but still had lived.
For years they'd passed the waiting days
In frenzied striving. Not submissive,
They had fought the loaded odds against delays,
Confinement, revelation; every card
Was in the other hand, and yet they won.
By day and night, with disregard
For every danger they had walked and run
In freedom; just a glorious hour was theirs,
For soon the human dragnet wide was set
And very few escaped the outspread snares;
Like glinting salmon threshing in a net
They nearly all returned; but not to us.
Returned to die, defenceless and untried,
To satisfy a hate as ravenous
As ever was before. Oh, they have died
In war, but theirs is death that ever calls
For retribution. Ere the curtain falls
Their sacred lives, so callously betrayed,
Will be avenged, atonement will be made.

DENIS MACKARNESS

(POW)

Defensive Position

Cupping her chin and lying there, the Bren
Watches us make her bed the way a queen
Might watch her slaves. The eyes of a machine,
Like those of certain women, now and then

Put an unsettling influence on men,
Making them suddenly feel how they are seen:
Full of too many purposes, hung between
Impulse and impulse like a child of ten.

The careless challenge, issued so offhanded,
Seems like to go unanswered by default –
A strong position, small but not commanded
By other heights, compels direct assault.

The gunner twitches, and unreprimanded
Eases two tensions, running home the bolt.

JOHN MANIFOLD

(Australia) *British Army U.K., 1940–6, West Africa, Normandy, NW Europe. Short stories, radio scripts and poetry translations.*

'Evrecy', July 1944

Men of the 'Black Flash', 'Sospan' and 'Dragon',
Wading through 'bayonet' wheat, knee-high and wet,
Mortars and 'eighty-eights' playing their 'overtures'
Spandaus and Schmeissers are waiting and 'set' . . .

Up to that hill enshrouded in mortar smoke,
Tellermines, 'S' mines, a'mushroom the slope,
'Tiger' tanks, 'panzerfausts' blasting our 'carriers' . . .
'Air burst' exploding like 'bubbles of soap' . . .

Now cross the singing Guighe into the alder wood,
Remnants of companies merged to platoon,
Screams for the stretchers with 'Mother' and 'Jesus!!',
'Steady old son . . . we'll have you out soon'!!

Men of the 'Black Flash', 'Sospan' and 'Dragon'
Limping it back . . . all haggard and pale,
Two hundred dead for a handful of prisoners,
Just one consolation . . . 'They've brought up the Mail'!!!

JOHN A. OTTEWELL

*Home Guard 1941–3. Joined Royal Welsh Fusiliers 1943. Normandy
June 1944; France, Belgium, Holland – 53 (Welsh) Infantry Div., 7th
Bn. RWF.*

Divertimento

One still feels cause to rage
against the errors made by war
remembering conversations
that sparked the winter evenings,
for at that time we honestly believed
that God was on our side,
longed then for some recognition
of actions that were made –
which seldom came
or came too late.
while the earth turned
and changes arrived
oh, far too swift,
sometimes like lightning,
until one could not comprehend
amidst the plenitudes of anger
such reasons for indifference,
and this unbroken blaze
of disillusionment
rose from the ashes
of our own consistent failures
making it seem that we alone
betrayed humanity.

LARRY ROWDON

*(Canada) Served with Royal Regiment of Canada, 2nd Division Cana-
dian Army. Landed at Normandy beach and wounded near Caen.*

Eichstatt, 1943

Well, Riviere's dead. Muffle a smallish drum,
Beat it in a small way, let us be apt and just.
Small stir kept step with him and can see him home
Very well. The firing party? Simplest
To brief some children for a pop-gun squad.
Art (though he wrote some poems) seems none the worse.
He was in one battle, but unfortunately on the side
That lost. Once managed to ride round a steeple-chase course
(Unplaced). Riviere is dead. Look moderate solemn,
Walk moderate slow behind his seven-foot corpse
Who was a half-cock, pull-punch, moderate fellow,
And symbol of so much and vain expense
For years carried pints and gallons of blood about
To manure this casual, stone-sprouting plot.

Oflag Night Piece, Colditz

'The poor man's wealth, the prisoner's release' – *Sir Philip Sidney*

There, where the swifts flicker along the wall
And the last light catches, there in the high schloss
(How the town grows dark) all's made impregnable.
They bless each window with a double cross
Of iron; weave close banks of wire and train
Machine guns down on them; and look – at the first star
Floodlight the startled darkness back again . . .
All for three hundred prisoners of war.
Yet now past them and the watch they keep,
Unheard, invisible, in ones and pairs,
In groups, in companies – alarms are dumb,
A sentry loiters, a blind searchlight stares –
Unchallenged as their memories of home
The vanishing prisoners escape to sleep.

MICHAEL RIVIERE

*Commissioned in the Sherwood Rangers Yeomanry. Taken prisoner in Crete
1 June 1941: After escaping in 1943 with sixty other British Officers from
Eichstatt in Bavaria, sent to Colditz (Oflag IV C). Mentioned in despatches.*

Walking Wounded

A mammoth morning moved grey flanks and groaned.
In the rusty hedges pale rags of mist hung;
The gruel of mud and leaves in the mauled lane
Smelled sweet, like blood. Birds had died or flown,
Their green and silent attics sprouting now
With branches of leafed steel, hiding round eyes
And ripe grenades ready to drop and burst.
In the ditch at the cross-roads the fallen rider lay
Hugging his dead machine and did not stir
At crunch of mortar, tantrum of a Bren
Answering a Spandau's manic jabber.
Then into sight the ambulance came,
Stumbling and churning past the broken farm,
The amputated sign-post and smashed trees,
Slow wagonloads of bandaged cries, square trucks
That rolled on ominous wheels, vehicles
Made mythopoeic by their mortal freight
And crimson crosses on the dirty white.
This grave procession passed, though, for a while,
The grinding of their engines could be heard,
A dark noise on the pallor of the morning,
Dark as dried blood; and then it faded, died.
The road was empty, but it seemed to wait –
Like a stage which knows the cast is in the wings –
Wait for a different traffic to appear.
The mist still hung in snags from dripping thorns;
Absent-minded guns still sighed and thumped.
And then they came, the walking wounded,
Straggling the road like convicts loosely chained,
Dragging at ankles exhaustion and despair.
Their heads were weighted down by last night's lead,
And eyes still drank the dark. They trailed the night
Along the morning road. Some limped on sticks;
Others wore rough dressings, splints and slings;
A few had turbanned heads, the dirty cloth
Brown-badged with blood. A humble brotherhood,
Not one was suffering from a lethal hurt,
They were not magnified by noble wounds,
There was no splendour in that company.

And yet, remembering after eighteen years,
In the heart's throat a sour sadness stirs;
Imagination pauses and returns
To see them walking still, but multiplied
In thousands now. And when heroic corpses
Turn slowly in their decorated sleep
And every ambulance has disappeared
The walking wounded still trudge down that lane,
And when recalled they must bear arms again.

VERNON SCANNELL

*Gordon Highlanders. 51st Highland Division from Alamein to Tunis,
Sicily and Normandy. Poet, novelist and critic.*

Memories

On winter walks I hate
The sound a dead branch makes
When I step upon it.

In wartime, infantrymen
nearly always buried
their own
and enemy dead.
And the dead died hard, frozen
into grotesque shapes,
their stiffened arms
wildly semaphoring
for help that could never come.

Purchase was obtained
standing on the chest
of the dead man, whilst
the limbs were manipulated
rather in the manner
of an old-time railwayman
wrenching the huge levers
in a manually-operated
signal-box

Arms and legs were broken,
brought closer to the trunk;
not from respect
but simply to lessen
the burden of digging.

God! How I hate the sound
A dead branch makes
When stepped upon.

Even
The snapping of a stick of celery
Chills my spine,
Calls up old memories,
Makes the hairs
On the nape of my neck
Erectile.

MARTIN SOUTHALL

Royal Warwickshire Regiment; Commissioned Infantry platoon commander, Queens Royal Regiment, Italy. RWAFF Gold Coast. Poems published under title Behold a Pale Horse, *1987.*

Casualties, Normandy, 1944

One

Clouds are failing in the sunset,
feathers in a quiet sky,
above the khaki and the camouflage
and the sun like brass on the trees
and across the far hills;
slate and steel and brimstone
stretching vermilion
at the edge of the world.

They lie in this pastoral
habitation of evening,
the dead soldiers.
A bearable beauty alights
on the foreign effects,

the last sun-rays
glancing their tangents
off crab-apple and walnut trees.

Up and down the stream goes
a smudge of gnats,
nettle seeds, the skittering
of brilliant insects;
a guilty donkey
with depressed ears,
snapping at passing thistles,
teased by staccato French
and the French flies.

Clouds move and melt
till the delicate cirrus is a kiss
or a word, day gives to darkness
the gaping cottages,
the fluted fields.

Two

Stretched out under canvas
they lie in the shadows,
not smoking nor talking
but getting cool in the rough wool,
their wounds unhealed for ever
and the pain elsewhere.
Slowly their singleness is reaffirmed.

Babies and girls often
look beautiful being dead
and over the old and sick,
clutching their bedclothes closer,
sinks a common expression
almost of gratitude.

Yet which is better: to go down
with these unlucky soldiers,
unnatural heroes, clowns;
or to have once been young
and end in failure, pious attitude,
bent like a question?

Here I drag on behind an army,
no hero nor a likely one for dying,
and yet I hope I too,
with such weapons as I have,
may spend eventual breath
in some such makeshift place
where battle rumbles on.

Day of Liberation, Bergen–Belsen, May 1945

We build our own prison walls
but that day the doors fell open,
it was holiday time
in the death camp.

Lift him with courtesy,
this silent survivor.
Battle-dress doctors,
we took him from the truck
and put him to bed.

The moving skeleton
had crippled hands,
his skinny palms held secrets:
when I undid the joints I found
five wheat grains huddled there.
In the faces of other people
I witness my distress.

I close my eyes:
ten thousand wasted people
still piled in the flesh-pits.
Death of one is the death of all.
It is not the dead I pity.

PHILLIP WHITFIELD

Captain RAMC, with first unit into Belsen. Paediatrician and specialist in community medicine. Council Member, Amnesty International.

Recce in Bocage[1] Country, 1944

Pinned down in the sunken lane we waited
pressed into the hedgerow's shadows
and carefully encoded our location
reporting back to base our sit rep
hull-down in dead ground
in range enemy S P, mortar and machinegun fire
with their O P 2 kilometres distant in church with spire.

For the landscape of war is different
admitting no valleys but re-entrants
no hollows but dead ground
churches neither gothic nor romanesque only with spire or tower;
but not lying there or sitting on our arses
we kept our head down in radio silence
dozing in the drone of bees and flies and scent of grasses.

Until we heard the beat of feet
and the soft lilt of breathy whistling
and saw the laddie with his shepherd's thumbstick
lead his dust-caked platoon snaking up the side of the lane
and halt only long enough for us to explain,
'From here you're out in the open',
and mark his map with the O P in the church with spire
and he never spoke, just nodded,
and walked on out into the searing sun
and the busy stitching of steel needles from the machinegun
with his platoon plodding behind at an easy walk
across the line of the mortar's crunching stalk.

The whistling stopped
branches broke, the lane gave a groan
and the hedgerows returned to their buzzing drone
until there came the jagged detonation of grenades
and a bren gun spoke.
Uncertain, we waited,
as boots rang out coming down the hill.

Seven came back
and threw themselves down in the shade.
'What're ye waitin' for?' one demanded.
'We've cleaned 'em out.'

So we climbed in and drove up the lane
past the laddie with his thumbstick lying under a cloud of flies
and the rest of the platoon sprawled untidily
where they'd been dropped.
'Guts,' I said. 'He must have known.'
And the reply came, flatly, 'Guts, either theirs or our own'.

For the language of war is different
and admits to no words for bravery
courage or victory
in friend or rival –
only survival.

1 The bocage is the rolling and wooded countryside of lower Normandy,
with endless hidden lanes and concealed tracks.

PETER YOUNG

*1941–46 trooper Westminster Dragoons, RAC sergeant Army Education
Corps. Has written over thirty books for schools. Joint Editor of Open
University Children With Special Needs series.*

Code Poem

We listen round the clock
For a code called peacetime
But will it ever come
And shall we know it when it does
And break it once it's here
This code called peacetime.

Or is its message such
That it cannot be absorbed
Unless its text is daubed
In letters made of lives
From an alphabet of death
Each consonant a breath
Expired before its time.

Signalmaster, Signalmaster
Whose Commandments were in clear
Must you speak to us in code
Once peacetime is here?

LEO MARKS

Signalmaster of SOE (Special Operations Europe) who sent coded instructions in verse. This poem was a special code for an agent.

SOUTH-EAST ASIA
AND THE PACIFIC

Chindit

Have you ever seen a column march away,
And you left lying, too damned sick to care?
Have you ever watched the night crawl into day
With red-rimmed eyes that are too tired to stare?
Have you ever bled beside a jungle trace
In thick brown mud like coagulating stew?
Have you ever counted leeches loping back
Along the trail of sweat that leads to you?
Have you ever heard your pals shout 'cheerio',
Knowing that this is no 'Auf wiedersehn'?
Have you ever prayed, alone, for help although
The stench of mules has vanished in the rain?
Have you ever thought 'what a bloody way to die!',
Left in the tree-roots, rotting, there to stay?
God, I remember last poignant 'Goodbye';
I was one of the men that marched away.

K.N. BATLEY
14th Army

Officers and Gentlemen Down Under

We had as our platoon commander one
Lieutenant Teague. Nobody knew for sure,
but someone spread the rumour he had done
a bit of wrestling as an amateur.
In fact he was a funny sort of bloke
we had not rumbled yet. When he read out
the leave arrangements no-one put their spoke
in straight away until this bit about
the red light district being out of bounds
to other ranks till further notice. Then
from all three sections came the muttered sounds
of unmistakable frustration. When,
to ease the situation, 'Sarge' stepped in
and like all bloody NCOs rebuffed
the whole platoon concerning discipline
etcetera, some joker said 'Get stuffed!'

The sergeant yelled 'That man is on a charge!'
(not being certain who the bastard was)
and when somebody said 'Good on yer, Sarge!'
this Teague bloke took command again because
the matter looked like getting out of hand.
He brought us to attention 'Shun!', ordered
the corporals to shoulder arms and stand
behind the sergeant which no doubt deferred
to principles wherein to undermine
the NCOs in front of other ranks
was infra-dig, walked up and down each line
like on inspection, then came round the flanks
and took up a position facing us.
You could have heard a pin drop. First he took
his bush hat off and with punctilious
exactitude according to the book,
he placed it carefully upon the ground,
removed his fancy jacket and Sam Browne
and folded them, and then with a profound
deliberation bent and put them down
beside the hat, stood up erect and faced
the lot of us, and anyone could see
that he was lean and muscular. He paced
once forward then with calm authority
he said 'Forget the regulations for
the moment, where if any soldier strikes
an officer he'll get three years or more;
if any one of you brave bastards likes
to put his courage where his mouth is, just
step forward now and try it on. No names,
no pack-drill either. Nothing. Shit or bust!'
An opportunity for fun and games?
My bloody oath! But silence. No-one moved.
So HE had rumbled US! There was no need
for further comment. Mr Teague had proved
his point. And afterwards we all agreed
he was the sort of bloke a man could fight
the war with AND call sir. Too bloody right!

JOHN BROOKES

Private with 2/5 Bn Australian Infantry Force (AIF). Worked his

*passage from Liverpool to Australia pre-war, landing with 2/6. On
outbreak of war walked from Broken Hill to Melbourne to enlist.*

Lying Awake At Night

When men die here I am afraid –
Death takes no ceremonial leave
With horse and foot, in a parade
Acceptable to those that grieve,
The silver, and the glossy plumes,
The solemn uniforms, slow tread
Of soldiery, the stifled drums
That make one doubt a man were dead;
Here only the owls betray the grave,
Only the yews are evidence
Of what rich marrow ever gave
Their roots strange sustenance.

When men die here I am afraid –
Too much lies buried deep, too deep
The ancient soil is over-laid
With blood, too many armies sleep
In the same ground unaware;
Too many times the hideous priests
Hallowed their sacrifices where
These thickets stand; too many feasts
Were held on these high places, since
Obliterated by the rain;
Too often has a Burman prince
Slaughtered his heroes in this plain.

When men die here I am afraid –
The night is motionless and still,
Each minute afterwards is made
More silent by the cricket's shrill
Interruption. Sleepless lie
The listeners. Wild dogs keen
In the shuttered village, the whole sky
Shakes with the pinions and obscene
Gloating of vultures, and no moon

Discloses to the frightened skies
The obscure agonies so soon
Changed into birth before our eyes. . . .

But I believe each death conceives
And bears new children, and a store
Of great fertility derives
From every grave. For into them
Only untraceable remains
Without reality or name
Are ever lowered. Who maintains
With any certainty indeed
Anything but that a kindly spade
Turns over soil for ever made
More fertile by another seed?

Chungkai, December 1943

The Camp Cobbler

Poem tells of former Oxford Triple Blue, dying of tropical ulcers in the feet,
Chungkai, December 1943

Taking one's hat off savours of a church:
Cooler inside, out of the sun! the flies hang round
Cracked pots and reeking dressings. Quiet in here!
Expecting sadder visitors perhaps.
The long dark ward leads like a narrow nave
To what vile altar and what sacrifice?

The bed is somewhere near the centre post.
Dreaming in all six-foot of him, he lies,
Dreaming of arched foot, set in its separate hole,
Body a bow for stringing, or a hound
In leash for coursing, waiting for the start,
Of how the arrow, and the dog, and all fleet things,
Seed of Pheidippides, all messengers, springing up
To demonstrate their swift perfection with fierce joy.

That slow, relentless stride, like the last throw
Of a piston over rolling crank; being caught
At corners like loose strings in some great hand
And scattered in the straight; meeting the wind;
Seeing like ribbons of print the lines being drawn
Towards one's eager and impossible self . . .

The runners spin like ballet-dancers in the sun,
This dance-motif is older than they know
The first race run was so, by the forgotten slips
That launched their high-prowed, painted, resolute ships!
So raced the Argives for their mortal olive crowns,
And so raced he at Fenners, five years since . . .

How to find conversation? How to take
One's eye from this? 'I'd several friends up there,
You must have known them, what a term that was!'
Yes – war-spring haste of the reluctant years,
When every stroke, shot, sprint had in themselves
A singular quality, being the last. And after all,
What things we did not many years ago,
Coming from old rooms moated by the river,
Where roistered Marlowe and his favourite crew,
And bridges like soft eyebrows hinted where
The empurpled crocus hid the spacious lawns . . .
Only the great bones show the former man,
Or the futility of bringing to him shoes
He does not know he will not want again.

JOHN DURNFORD

Commissioned Royal Artillery; India, North Malaya, POW 1942–45 in Siam. Post-war Regular Commission, Royal Artillery. Holder Army Flying Brevet.

Mandalay

Jumping like shrimps, clusters of thin brown children
Quarter the road, chucking bully tins of water
At every giggling, shrieking son and daughter.
It is the Water Festival. But the older people

Lack laughter and energy to crush these crippling years;
Lassitude more expressive now than tears.

The main road has been cleared but no one
Can hide the houses. For each roof is disaster,
The gimcrack walls grey-scarred in coloured plaster.
Pantheons of whitewashed Buddhas gleam in sunshine,
Stolid among the weeds of a stonemason's garden
Touched brown on thighs where swaying seed-pods harden.

Half of a smashed temple contains the crumbling
Remains of another Buddha. Splintered gewgaws
Of gods and devils among which young whores
Ruled by a sharp dark pimp in a brown trilby
Wait the same custom Japs had provided there,
Too tired to coax to life, drabs with greasy hair.

Sometimes the river or trees break through the streets;
Fleshy dollops of mangoes, light green jade,
Hang among dark laurel-like leaves. In shade,
A yellow pi dog scuttles among the bones
Of a dead bullock, looks out timid and mean
Through a cage of ribs the sun burned clean.

The tinsel petalled waves of bougainvillæa
Lunge purple and scarlet their abandoned heaviness
Over frail bamboo huts. A mincing dancer dances
Bizarre in asters, his face a godlike white,
Blessing the peace of water and the rain's pity
Among the dark cowed people of a ruined city.

Maymyo

There isn't any doubt what went on here
Before the Japs moved into Flagstaff House.
We pitch our mess beside the gold mohar,
A grey smooth tree propped up like an old man,
Elaborately cynical old man
Pernickety with gout and greying hair.

All that bright gaunt sophistication true
Of the entire bowl in the hills that is the town.
Strawberries come in wicker baskets, brambles
Are splodged with rain. A Regent's Park-like lake
Lulls our hot bodies in its fresh clear waters.
Roses, scarlet cannaes grow in the gardens.

Frankie plays poker in the dining-room
With visiting, tough, boyishly curious Yank
Brother generals and two or three old stooges.
(There is a photo of the Maymyo Hunt,
A lot of backbones crowned by solar topees).
Yes, you can recreate the sunny lives
Before the last troops left – their silver buried –
And Nips moved in. Hear all the tennis-balls;
Grousing as rain or phone would ruin a party;
The gooseflesh at the midnight picnic (Phyllis
Nakedly up to all her tricks again);
The cantering ponies in the pinewood rides.

Yet that was just the mannered childishness
Of la jeunesse dorée. The really hard
And bitter smile, the town smiles to itself.
It sees another set of liberators,
The rescuers sent by those who planned the polo,
Planned cocktails in the club, all those young bores
To act as buffers by being buffoons.
And now to see these likeable bland soldiers
Who bought their vivid pleasure in rest and fresh
Salads, loganberries, dances, the pictures
Out of their luck and with their comrades' blood
Tickles the vicious spirit of the town.

Sniper

Moves in the rocks with inching fingers.
We among the feathery banana trees
Imagine for him his aim: the steel helmet
And English face filling the backsight's V.

Again as it was last time, that spurting noise,
Thud, and the writing figure in long grass.
Until we match precision with precision:
We move ten men to one and have him then.

I saw the sniper in the afternoon. The rifle
Lay there beside him neatly like his shooting,
The grass twined all about his cap.
He had killed neatly but we had set
Ten men about him to write death in jags
Cutting and spoiling on his face and broken body.

The Enemy Dead

The dead are always searched.
It's not a man, the blood-soaked
Mess of rice and flesh and bones
Whose pockets you flip open;
And these belongings are only
The counterpart to scattered ball
Or the abandoned rifle.

Yet later the man lives.
His postcard of a light blue
Donkey and sandy minarets
Reveals a man at last.
'Object – the panther mountains!
Two – a tired soldier of Kiku!
Three – my sister the bamboo sigh!'

Then again the man dies.
And only what he has seen
And felt, loved and feared
Stays as a hill, a soldier, a girl:
Are printed in the skeleton
Whose white bones divide and float away
Like nervous birds in the sky.

Namkwin Pul

Each soldier as he passes looks at their breasts
Laced tightly in childlike bodices (in Northern Burma, the full
Breasts of the Indian women are unfashionable),
    And lets his glance run

Over the swaying hips to their hard ugly feet.
They come to our small market with eggs for salt.
Yesterday there was one girl dressed in crimson
    Who lolled with a whore's walk

And plucked a flower with a sharp pull and jerk
So that her breast came free from her clothes –
As she intended – and at the soldiers' whistle
    Pretended to be shy.

But most are prim as they follow their bullock carts
And crossing the Namkwin Pul avert their eyes
For standing in the pink sunset that glides
    Along the kine grass spears

Knee high in the water the soldiers soap their thighs
And crack their bawdy jokes, brown to the waist.
And gleaming white bottoms – a hundred of them –
    Shock the Burmese lasses.

Myitson. The Sentry

This moonlight scans the river to its banks.
But there the gloss is broken into shadows.
Silence consumes the hollow heart of jungle.
    Movement and noise lie there

Folded by sleep and held by sharp nerves still.
Muscles like springs shudder beneath your skin.
These, the ripples, the croak of leaves, the bird,
    Jolt like a burn.

The prayer is: grant us no noise or movement.
Let the moon soothe the slipping water by
And no quick gasp to drum along the veins
    And drown the temples with fear.

Namsaw, The G.O.

I feel the fall of future when these men
Move in their columns through the green paddy.
The evening shade goes slowly on with them
 And swathes about their feet.

Count, count quickly to you all that you can see,
Tokens to ward that future. By this swift
Quiet river bless, acknowledging this,
 Lime-yellow sunset

Blacken an iron tracery of trees
And watch its failing twistings as a velvet brown
Butterfly marked like old brocade or walnut
 Feints at its future, night.

They walk away, those whom you know, those to die
Or live. All are one man. The man yourself,
The man who has gathered like a clutch of sand
 All these unreal things

To share the strange and stubborn loneliness
Among the jungles. Night gathers. The bells
Move awkwardly upon the pale pagodas,
 The graves sink in the trees.

Death is our sorrow; and sorrow is life.
The bodies cast like over-ripened fruit
To burst beside the ford, the striking voices
 That print an emptiness.

To Buddha there can be no question for
There is no answer. The jungle is the soul
Which accepts, and cannot help but to repeat
 Sorrow is for ever life.

Loneliness swells out my heart. I cannot love
Nor hate, cannot accept, cannot deny.
And even cannot pray for peace like trees
 Or these deserted dead.

BERNARD GUTTERIDGE

Hampshire Regiment. Served in Combined Ops and with 36 Div. in Burma (with Alun Lewis), reaching rank of Major.

The Jungle (Extract)

In mole-blue indolence the sun
Plays idly on the stagnant pool
In whose grey bed black swollen leaf
Holds Autumn rotting like an unfrocked priest.
The crocodile slides from the ochre sand
And drives the great translucent fish
Under the boughs across the running gravel.
Windfalls of brittle mast crunch as we come
To quench more than our thirst – our selves –
Beneath this bamboo bridge, this mantled pool
Where sleep exudes a sinister content
As though all strength of mind and limb must pass
And all fidelities and doubts dissolve,
The weighted world a bubble in each head,
The warm pacts of the flesh betrayed
By the nonchalance of a laugh,
The green indifference of this sleep.

Grey monkeys gibber, ignorant and wise.
We are the ghosts, and they the denizens;
We are like them anonymous, unknown,
Avoiding what is human, near,
Skirting the villages, the paddy fields
Where boys sit timelessly to scare the crows
On bamboo platforms raised above their lives.

A trackless wilderness divides
Joy from its cause, the motive from the act:
The killing arm uncurls, strokes the soft moss;
The distant world is an obituary,
We do not hear the tappings of its dread.
The act sustains; there is no consequence.
Only aloneness, swinging slowly
Down the cold orbit of an older world
Than any they predicted in the schools,
Stirs the cold forest with a starry wind,
And sudden as the flashing of a sword
The dream exalts the bowed and golden head
And time is swept with a great turbulence,
The old temptation to remould the world.

The bamboos creak like an uneasy house;
The night is shrill with crickets, cold with space.
And if the mute pads on the sand should lift
Annihilating paws and strike us down
Then would some unimportant death resound
With the imprisoned music of the soul?
And we become the world we could not change?
Or does the will's long struggle end
With the last kindness of a foe or friend?

The Journey

We were the fore-runners of an army,
Going among strangers without sadness,
Danger being as natural as strangeness.

We had no other urge but to compel
Tomorrow in the image of today,
Which was motion and mileage and tinkering
When cylinders misfired and the gasket leaked.
Distance exhausted us each night;
I curled up in the darkness like a dog
And being a romantic stubbed my eyes
Upon the wheeling spokeshave of the stars.

Daylight had girls tawny as gazelles,
Beating their saris clean in pools and singing.
When we stopped they covered up their breasts;
Sometimes their gestures followed us for miles.
Then caravanserais of gipsies
With donkeys grey as mice and mincing camels
Laden with new-born lambs and trinkets,
Tentage and utensils and wicker baskets,
Following the ancient routes of the vast migrations
When history was the flight of a million birds
And poverty had splendid divagations.

Sometimes there were rivers that refused us,
Sweeping away the rafts, the oxen;
Some brown spates we breasted.

The jungle let us through with compass and machetes.
And there were men like fauns, with drenched eyes,
Avoiding us, bearing arrows.

There was also the memory of Death
And the recurrent irritation of our selves.
But the wind so wound its ways about us,
Beyond this living and this loving,
This calculation and provision, this fearing,
That neither of us heard the quiet voice calling us,
Remorse like rain softening and rotting the ground,
We felt no sorrow in the singing bird,
Forgot the sadness we had left behind.
For how could we guess, oh Life, oh suffering and patient Life,
With distance spun for ever in the mind.
We among the camels, the donkeys and the waterfalls,
How could we ever guess,
Not knowing how you pined?

Burma

ALUN LEWIS

Wrote short stories of the war as well as poetry. Entered Army as Sapper in the Royal Engineers, commissioned in the infantry. India 1943. Killed 5 March 1944, on the Arakan front.

The Tomb of Lt John Learmonth, AIF

'*At the end on Crete he took to the hills, and said he'ld fight it out with only a revolver. He was a great soldier . . .' One of his men in a letter.*

This is not sorrow, this is work: I build
A cairn of words over a silent man,
My friend John Learmonth whom the Germans killed.

There was no word of hero in his plan;
Verse should have been his love and peace his trade,
But history turned him to a partisan.

Far from the battle as his bones are laid
Crete will remember him. Remember well,
Mountains of Crete, the Second Field Brigade!

Say Crete, and there is little more to tell
Of muddle tall as treachery, despair
And black defeat resounding like a bell;

But bring the magnifying focus near
And in contempt of muddle and defeat
The old heroic virtues still appear.

Australian blood where hot and icy meet
(James Hogg and Lermontov were of his kin)
Lie still and fertilise the fields of Crete.

Schoolboy, I watched his ballading begin:
Billy and bullocky and billabong,
Our properties of childhood, all were in.

I heard the air though not the undersong,
The fierceness and resolve; but all the same
They're the tradition, and tradition's strong.

Swagman and bushranger die hard, die game,
Die fighting, like that wild colonial boy –
Jack Dowling, says the ballad, was his name.

He also spun his pistol like a toy,
Turned to the hills like wolf or kangaroo,
And faced destruction with a bitter joy.

His freedom gave him nothing else to do
But set his back against his family tree
And fight the better for the fact he knew

He was as good as dead. Because the sea
Was closed and the air dark and the land lost,
'They'll never capture me alive,' said he.

That's courage chemically pure, uncrossed
With sacrifice or duty or career,
Which counts and pays in ready coin the cost

Of holding course. Armies are not its sphere
Where all's contrived to achieve its counterfeit;
It swears with discipline, it's volunteer.

I could as hardly make a moral fit
Around it as around a lightning flash.
There is no moral, that's the point of it.

No moral. But I'm glad of this panache
That sparkles, as from flint, from us and steel,
True to no crown nor presidential sash

Nor flag nor fame. Let others mourn and feel
He died for nothing: nothings have their place.
While thus the kind and civilised conceal

This spring of unsuspected inward grace
And look on death as equals, I am filled
With queer affection for the human race.

The Deserter

Born with all arms, he sought a separate peace.
Responsibilities loomed up like tanks,
And since his manhood marked him of our ranks
He threw it off and scrambled for release.

His power of choice he thrust on the police
As if it burnt his hands; he gave the banks
His power to work; then he bestowed with thanks
His power to think on Viscount Candlegrease.

Claiming the privileges of the dead
Before his time – the heart no blood runs through,
The undelighted hands, the rotting head –

Strong in his impotence he can safely view
The battlefield of men, and shake his head
And say, 'I know. But then what can I do?'

JOHN MANIFOLD

(Australia) *British Army U.K., 1940–6, West Africa, Normandy, NW Europe. Short stories, radio scripts and poetry translations.*

Dead Japanese

Why does your pointing finger accuse,
your black arm, swollen (skin stretched tight
as a surgeon's glove) point, accuse?
Was your cause just
that you accuse me, your enemy?
You the aggressor, I the defender?

Why do you stink so, fouling the air, the grass,
the stagnant pool in the creek?
No other animal stinks so in putrefaction.
Why do you vent your protest against life itself?
Is it seemly for the dead to fight?

Have you not known the sun,
the sweet softness of a woman's breasts,
rest after work?

Then let your arm drop to your side, as in deep sleep;
hasten your decay, sink into the earth,
unloosing your last hold on personality
to know, unknowing, every man's rebirth
in other life; so, when the winds pass, you may be
part of the sweetness of the rippling kunai grass.

New Guinea, 1943

CHARLES MCCAUSLAND

(Australia) *AIF (Australian Infantry Force), Egypt, Lebanon and Libya. Visiting Associate Professor, University of Calgary. Vice-Principal, Bathurst Teachers' College, NSW.*

South of Fort Herz, Burma (Extract)

Fort Herz is Burma's most northerly post. In this extract, prior to Slim's advance back into Burma over the Chindwin, a Frontier Force column (Lt. Col. Hugo commanding) is moving from Imphal through the hill country of the Nagas, to clear out any enemy up to the river.

At last, it comes in sight.
The long file halts. The few advance

And make their swift reconnaissance;
Locate – and chlorinate – the water
Beyond the village; choose a quarter

For one night's stay and site each post;
Then meet their not unwilling host,
The village headman. Soon the rest
Are summoned up and each addressed
To his own task: they dig the trench –
But first, each man makes speed to quench
His raging thirst, his bottle sinks
Into the pool, then lifts and drinks.

They dig the trenches round about,
Cut fire-lanes, put the sentries out,
Prepare, with so much space between
As may be, cookhouse and latrine,
Light fires, draw water, feed the mules
While order in confusion rules,
Then peace in order, aftermath
Of labour long, a standing bath.
Clean socks, a smoke, and last a stroll
A moment to possess one's soul
And view the village.

                In a wood,
Bamboo within bamboo, it stood.
Though perched upon a rising mound
Its huts, too, rose above the ground.
Bamboo huts on bamboo stilts,
Their sole upholstery the quilts –
Red-woven, trimmed perhaps with beads –
Which serve both home and owner's needs:
A bedspread now and now the plaid
In which and which alone is clad
Their lord when, more from love of show
Than fear of shame, bedizened so,
He sallies forth. All else, from thatch
To platform or to doorway-hatch:
Furniture: mat, screen and trestle;
Utensils: calabash, pot, pestle;
Weapons, for chase or war: the pike,

The springe, the bow, the *panji's* spike;
Fuel and gear; the shoulder-pole,
Sunhat, sandals, tinder, coal –
One wood alone this bamboo
Whose very shoots when young and sweet
Serve the Naga for his meat.

    Far otherwise the mule-borne fare
Of those whom war makes sojourn there
And gives to satisfy their hunger
The messes of an Indian *langar*:
Bannocks, baked in earthen stoves
And – spiced with chillies, saffron, cloves,
With onion, mint and cardomum,
And liquored with a tot of rum
Or else a tea-mug's steaming brew –
Pulse and vegetable stew.
Then, having eaten, drunk enough,
They take to *betel*, *pan* or snuff –
More likely, some rank cigarette –
The while each man's mosquito net –
For now the fading of the light
Warns them of their double fight
Their double foes: the Japanese
The deadlier anopheles –
Is rigged and strung. Each coats his skin
With cream, to each his mepacrine
Is doled, until, without ado,
All harken to the low '*Stand to*'
And man each post and soon Grand Rounds
Inspects the small encampment's bounds
And as he moves, now near, now far,
With orderly and jemadar,
Darkling men hear low voices tell
That all is well, that all is well.
Then silence, immobility,
Till, flooding in, a soundless sea,
The night is on them, sentries drown
And low but clear is heard '*Stand down*'.

    Except where watch the sentries keep.
Quickly now all turn to sleep

And much they need it. With the day
They must up and far away –
Kasom Khulen, Kasom Khunou –
Stage by stage still pressing through.
Yet not for them their well-earned rest.
Unnumbered bugs and fleas molest,
Infest their slumbers. Where they doss
On bamboo matting there they toss.
One rises (sign for all to rise)
And to his larded skin applies
Not midge- alone but flea-repeller,
A pungent film of citronella.
The others follow. Down again,
Down they lie, but now new bane
Afflicts them: blocked at every pore
Sweat keeps them restless as before.
Uneasily the long night through
They strive to sleep till dawn's *Stand-to*
Relieves them and incoming day
Laves all the dregs of night away.

MARTIN MOYNIHAN

Indian Army 1940, North West Frontier and Burma. Liberation under Slim and Mountbatten. Post-war, High Commissioner, Lesotho.

The Desolate Market

Sergeant Godwin advancing through the dust
At first light in the desolate market
Placed his men. After some play with mortars
They withdrew,
Leaving the sergeant in an empty shop
(It was the Indian's who dealt in rice).
A Rajput armoured car tried the same trick
As the sun rose, found a mine
Which knocked a corner off Sam Jimmy's stall
(Sam Jimmy père the shoe-maker).
The rest outflanked the place. About noon
The flies got busy, and the market-place

Buzzed with sunlit emptiness.
At dusk the Japs came back; our gunners dropped
The odd round on them all night long,
Added four corpses and one dying man
To the desolate market's customers:
Two dead in the silk shop, and two
In the open square by the broken armoured car:
The dying man shared Sergeant Godwin's room.

At dawn the Japs left for the hills
Across the river, and Sergeant Godwin's men
Through the dust came back again.
Godwin's corporal
Having deloused the place of booby traps,
Buried the Sergeant, burned his bed-fellow,
And set up quarters in the Indian's stall
Saying
'1111789 Godwin, married, two kids both boys
Believed in the advance of Man
Died for political justice, so he thought,
In a rice-dealer's shop, Toungoo.
All such ideals are false and end in this,
The flies' buzz and the maggots' crawl.
A clean-living Jacobin, nothing of him
But doth change, into something rich and strange,
A new decoction of decay, below the hot earth.
The hot earth of this Burmese square
Walled with darkness roofed with brass
Is the earth of all the world
Earth of a market place where life's a coin
Expendable and base,
How many did he kill before he died?
What rate was his exchange?
Blessed are they who do evil and do it not
Their kind shall inherit the earth,
The desolate earth.'

Beyond the river, up in the olive hills,
Six yellow men tugged at a worn-out gun,
Into the soft hillside dug its steel trail
Fired their last rounds, wrecked the piece
And off into the shadow of the trees,

Shambled on rag-bound feet,
Down to the plain came the shells, whining
Over the river, the temples, the town,
At random killing or not.
In the market the rice-dealer's stall
Gaped roofless at sunset.

His Lieutenant said
'2221830 Byron, single, numerous affairs,
But revenu du tout, had ancestors
And a post-war, depressive attitude.
Plus ça change and all that.' Quite right too.
What did *He* fight for though? He didn't
Like the blood and guts, et cetera.
What brought him to the market-place
Who didn't come to trade for the new world,
Always on sale for some?
'Wrong attitude to history' he said
'The Nazis have', or, 'that fellow Wagner!'
And 'I like Chopin'.
He loved his version of the old. It dies with him.
The living left, to cross a bamboo bridge
Crazily tilted on the sliding river.
The market lay deserted in the sun
The unburied stank, the blow-flies bred
A tuktu called from the tamarind tree
By the gate. Towards dark, from the jungle
Out came Joseph, a Eurasian boy.
He had betrayed his sister to a Jap.
Been local Judas to a friend or two
At the well they found him. One wiped his dah
And said 'He chose the winning side, a choice
Hard to make twice, although he tried.'
They went to deal with others such.
Joseph was buried, with his head,
By a Madrasi transport company.
After a month the rains came, suddenly,
And the old market steamed and splashed
Wrecked and deserted. A new square was built
Not far away; and Joseph's friends
Fell out about the winning side again.

Joseph was dead, no use to hate him now.
So the new market will be just the old
Removed some yards in space or time
A temporary structure in Toungoo,
New York, or Moscow, where men sell
New lives for the old prices once again.

W.A. MURRAY

*Tactical HQ Staff of 90th India Division as G3 Intelligence Burma 1944.
Professor of English, Lancaster University.*

Morobe

The sandflies they attack you
And the mossies they ack-ack you,
And sing a little ditty in your ear.
They chuckle with elation
And attack you in formation,
Till you curse and swear and wipe away your tear.

With the comin' of the mornin',
Just another day is dawnin',
The same routine is on again once more,
The 'dengues'[1] buzz around you
And scream 'Ha-Ha' we've found you,
Then dive bomb you from twenty feet or more.

Then you think of dough you've wasted,
And beer that you have tasted,
With steak and eggs and schooners by the score.
When you think of fun you're missin'
Or some sheila you'd be kissin',
Boy, you wish they up and end this bloody war.

Morobe, New Guinea, 1943

1 Mosquitoes that carry dengue fever.

ERIC A. OXLEY

*(Australia) Commissioned 1st Australian Armoured Regiment, Royal
NSW Lancers. Community pharmacist.*

Malayan Malady

Oh! how I hate this tropic land,
Its burning sun, its baking sand,
Its heavy, humid, sticky heat,
With odorous decay replete.
I hate the feathery coconut trees
Languidly drowsing in the breeze,
The frangipani's cloying smell
And all the other smells as well.

The tropic moonlight leaves me cold,
And all the myriad stars untold;
The rubber trees – unlovely whores
With obscene scars and running sores –
The black sumatra's sudden rain;
The tom-tom's maddening refrain;
In none of these, for me at least,
Appears the glamour of the East.

I hate the morning's blinding light,
I hate the suffocating night,
I hate the listless afternoons,
I hate the dark that comes too soon.
The amorous cheechak's[1] plaintive trill,
The cricket's serenading shrill,
The whining mossies round my net
Have failed to fascinate me yet.

I hate the khaki tunic drab,
The stupid spurs, the scarlet tab,
The portly blokes in naval rig
Who execute a stately jig,
The army subs with weak moustache,
The RAF so short of cash,
The colonels' and the captains' wives,
The smug intrigue, the double lives.

The ceaseless quest for quick romance
The shuffling mob at a Raffles' dance,
The curry tiffins, evening pahits,[2]
The blaring bands and shaded lights,
The futile trek from flick to hop,

The floorshows at the Cathay Top,
The shrivelled dames, the men obese,
From all of these I crave release . . .

Yes! how I hate this sunny clime,
The wanton waste of precious time,
The unmarked flight of heedless days.
Faces that vanish in a haze
Of half-forgotten memories dim,
The apathetic boredom grim,
In all its aspects, fair and bland,
By God! I hate this goddam land.

1 Lizard.
2 Drinks.

GEORGE S. RICHARDSON

Joined Royal Air Force 1937. Posted to 36 (Torpedo Bomber) Squadron at RAF Station, Seletar, Singapore in 1938. Shot down and killed while the squadron's elderly 'Wildebeest' torpedo bombers were attacking Japanese troop transporters off Endau, Johore, Malaya on 26 January 1942. Buried in Kranki War Cemetery, Singapore. Mentioned in despatches.

A Prayer For Food

You know, Lord, how one has to strive
At Shamshoipo to keep alive,
And how there isn't much to eat
Save rice and greens at Argyle Street.
It's not much fun, when dinner comes,
To find it's boiled chrysanthemums;
Nor can I stick at any price
Those soft white maggots in my rice
Nor yet the little hard black weevils,
The lumps of grit and other evils.

I know, Lord, that I shouldn't grumble,
And please don't think that I'm not humble
When I most thankfully recall
My luck to be alive at all.

But Lord, I think that even you
Would soon get tired of daicon stew.
So what I really want to say
Is; if we don't soon go away
From Shamshoipo and Argyle Street
Then, please Lord, could we have some meat?
A luscious, fragrant heaped-up plateful.
And also, Lord, we would be grateful
If You could grant a loving boon
And send some Red Cross parcels soon.

Another Prayer For Food

Lord, I have asked you once before
To send more food into the store.
To send us something really nice –
Not just chrysanthemums and rice.
I asked for meat and lard (or ghi)
And parcels from the B.R.C.[1]
But that was several weeks ago
And nothing has been sent, you know.

It may be that you didn't hear
Or else because good food is dear –

Though, if you shopped at our 'canteen',
You'd know what prices really mean.
You know, Lord, that we're on our uppers
With only rice 'bas' for our suppers;
And that many through this process
Have got this avitaminosis
And some pellagra too, and very
Many have got beri-beri,
While others that I have in mind
Have gone stone-deaf and nearly blind.

I tell you, Lord, there's hundreds who
Would sell their souls for Irish Stew.
I'm sure you've done it for the best
To see how we should stand the test;
But don't you think we've stuck it well

Through two years' pretty average hell –
As far as food's concerned at least –
I don't count thiamine or yeast,
For what we need to cure our ills
Is solid food, not drugs and pills.
A Yorkshire ham, a dozen eggs,
Would cure the aching in our legs
And chunks of beef are better far
Than pills of Wakamoto are
To drive our aches and pains away.
So please Lord, send without delay
Some meat and bread and eggs and cheese
And, if You really want to please,
A crate or two of Guinness stout
To fill our scrawny muscles out.

Bowen Road Hospital POW Camp

1 British red Cross

ROGER ROTHWELL

Lieutenant 1st Battalion Middlesex Regiment. POW of the Japanese in Hong Kong from Christmas Day 1941 until August 1945. Poem written in hospital, where admitted with malaria and dysentery January 1944.

Private Mathy's teeth

When I asked for Private Mathy
In his tent, they yelled, 'Not 'ere!
In the cookhouse, or the shithouse,
Or the beer-line gettin' beer!'
So I thanked them all for nothing,
And I hurried off to look
For my quarry, getting nowhere,
Till I found the Sergeant Cook . . .

Said that 'wallah', 'Private Mathy?
No, I think he's seen the light,
And it's on the cards you'll find him
Singing hymns with Padre White.'

So I thanked the Sergeant Cookie,
And I hurried off to find
Any singing or reciting
Of the Bible-banging kind . . .

'Private Alexander Mathy?
No, my son, this is a shock!
How I wish he were among us,
But he's down at Kukum Dock.'
So I thanked the gentle padre,
And away I went once more,
Down the coral road that led me
To the shipping by the shore . . .

Said a Yankee on the 'Wharton',
'Well it's none o' my concern,
But yer buddy's gone up topside,
An' he's fishing off the stern.'
So I thanked the Yank artificer,
And climbed three steps at once,
Up the gangway of the liner,
Almost winded for the nonce . . .

When at last I found the Private,
With a scowl he said to me,
'You can tell the blasted Colonel
That I won't be in to tea!'
But I soon aroused his interest,
When I told him I had come,
To inform him he could broadcast
His own message home to 'Mum' . . .

'Private Alexander Mathy?
Are you sure you've got it right?
Hang on, corporal — just a jiffy,
I could swear I've got a bite!'
So I hung on to a stanchion,
While he nearly flattened me,
With a salvo of three sneezes —
'A — a — choo! A — cha! A — chee!' . . .

'Three for luck!' exclaimed the Private.
'That's the sign a letter's due;

But a fourth one would encourage
Somethin' better into view!'
So I waited, little knowing
Misadventure would result,
And he'd lose his lower denture
From the fourth and final jolt! . . .

Stammered Mathy, gaunt and gummy,
'Now I've lost me bottom pwate,
An' it's somewhere in the bwiny
Wiff the fish I nearwy ate!'
But I had to leave him cursing,
While I hastened to report
To the 'wallah' who recorded
Soldiers' messages in short . . .

Said that tongue-in-cheek lieutenant,
'Lost his artificial plate?
Go and see the unit armourer –
He'll bring him up to date!'
But I wouldn't be a target
For this kind of persiflage,
And I left the young 'two-pipper',
Ere he put me on a charge . . .

'Private Alexander Mathy?
Let the bludger rant and rail!
For I see the dwindling beer-line,
And I'm off to join its tail!'

Next day . . . Same time . . .

Said the Yankee on the 'Wharton',
'Sure the self-same bitch's son
Has just gone aboard this minute,
An' he's fishing, ten to one.'
So I thanked the chewing Yankee,
And I hurried off once more,
With my message of salvation
From the Island's Dental Corps . . .

'Private Mathy,' I informed him,
'Divvy-Sigs. have put them wise –
There's a "stiffy" up in Vella

With a denture just your size!'
But the Private gave no answer,
Or intelligible sign:
He was much too busy watching
The behaviour of his line . . .

Said that eager beaver, Mathy,
'Take it 'teady, boy – a bite!
Yeah, it weally is a nibble,
An' te line is dettin' tight!'
So, expectantly, I watched it
Till it left the sea beneath,
With its catch all hooked securely –
Ruddy Private Mathy's teeth!

Pacific, 1945

JOHN SMITH

(New Zealand) *24th Field Ambulance, New Zealand Forces in the Philippines. Member of the unit concert party Guadalcanal and Green Island where he established a hospital.*

Lines to the Censor

I wonder what it's like to be a Censor,
And daily read what other people write.
Are they always hunting for the latest story
Or for 'purple patches' loving swains indite?
Or do they deftly track the nimble rumour
With blue-black pencil sharpened for the fray
Or hunt for codes elusive and ingenious
With charge-sheets ready placed in grim array?
I can't help feeling life would be much brighter
For them – yes, and for us, I rather think
If one could write exactly what one wished to;
But then it might just drive them all to drink.

I mean, how nice to know just what the Army
Was thinking re allowances and pay
Or whether some new man who'd been appointed

Was quite the sort of bloke to win the day.
To know just what it thinks about its Air Mail
Which takes from three to four months for the trip.
Does the Censor's office keep it quietly pending
Or is it wafted here by sailing ship?

To learn how much we like to read in 'Victory'
That when we send our girl some local wear
She's now to sacrifice her clothing coupons
('more blessed 'tis to give than to receive!')
But then of course the soldier's wife's so wealthy
Compared with any poor civilian's spouse
That she can well be taxed and docked of coupons
When plutocratic husband sends a blouse!
Well – here's to all those bright 'blue-pencilled' censors
And may they never read between my lines
Or I've a sneaking feeling in my marrow
They'd put me where the Sappers put the mines!

India

ANONYMOUS: 'F.H.T.T.'

The Fortress of the East[1]

A MIGHTY ISLAND FORTRESS
THE GUARDIAN OF THE EAST
IMPREGNABLE AS GIBRALTAR A
THOUSAND PLANES AT LEAST
IT SIMPLY CAN'T BE TAKEN
IT'LL STAND A SIEGE FOR YEARS
WE'LL HOLD THE PLACE FOREVER
IT WILL BRING THE JAPS TO TEARS
OUR MEN ARE THERE IN THOUSANDS
DEFENCES ARE UNIQUE
THE JAPS DID NOT BELIEVE IT
AND TOOK IT IN A WEEK

1 Singapore

ANONYMOUS

THE WAR ENDS

May 8 1945: VE Day

First to Westminster
to hear Churchill
see the Royal Family

then wandering the streets for hours
with Lafarge and Smitty
Melzer and O'Reilly.

The hot sun beat down
we hobbled on sore feet
then took off our shoes and jackets
in St. James's Park
paddled in the lake.

Later,
lights blazed everywhere:
dark buildings
suddenly magical
like stage sets,

the National Gallery
piebald with dirt,
the dark lions
smiling under floodlights.

Along the embankment
water reflected
occulting lights
and fireboats hurled up
shimmering fountains.

Big Ben struck twelve:
the clock face
lit up.

We limped back to Addison Road,
talked
about home.

PATIENCE WHEATLEY

(Canada) *Served in the Canadian Women's Army Corps from June 1943
to June 1946, at the Canadian forces' record office in Acton, London.*

The Meadow

Reaching for a book I am reminded –
a spark illuminates a picture.
A meadow like a summer frock,
the sky a blue saucer,
the wind my mother's hand
and the sun
sketching lines of grass
on my outstretched arm.

An arm that gained full strength in Italy,
killed ruthlessly
beneath the shadow of an olive branch.

Now it reaches for a book
and I wonder about the meadow
and what went wrong.

MICHAEL ARMSTRONG

*Served in Army 1942–47. With the KSLI in Italy 44–45. Sergeant,
Education Corps Palestine and Egypt 46–47.*

Budget for Romance

I fell in love with a sergeant
So took a course in domestic virtues
In Bad Oeynhausen.
The girls in the class
Were drawn from different units
But we shared romantic dreams
Of being super wives and mothers.
They taught us to cook, to clean and mend,
They lectured us on health, on sex and children:
They pointed out the problems
Of finding a home and how to equip it
Worst of all was 'The Budget'.
From our future husband's income
We deducted rent, food and heating,

With other essentials.
Only one girl could make it balance.
Her future husband was an electrician
And would earn £5 a week.
We were envious of her good luck.
We thought her life free from care.

JOY CORFIELD

Joined ATS 1944 at Guildford. Special Wireless Operator, then driver in Germany.

Let's Go Back

(This was written in a moment of cynicism shortly after arriving home)

Do you think, if we asked nicely, for a passage back
   To the German prison camps we know so well,
That the Gov'ment would allow it – or would they still insist
   We endure our homeland's 'welcome' from that Hell?

For years in those surroundings, we dreamed of our return,
   And we built our simple castles in the air:
We'd buy a home and furnish, or we'd rent a little flat,
   And we'd find goodwill a-plenty everywhere.

We've heard so many speeches, and read so many plans,
   We're sure our sons are going to be alright:
But it's so draughty reading papers in the street,
   Right now we're more concerned with our own plight.

The Germans gave us shelter, crowded though it was.
   While Australia gives us nothing – 'cept some cheers.
She's very glad to see us, and hopes we'll hang around,
   'We may need you boys again in future years!'

We're coming in our thousands, from the fronts and camps,
   From Jap and German strongholds far away:
And we find you've failed us badly – as you have failed before,
   Seems like you didn't expect us back to stay!

So when you give your welcomes, and when you play your bands,
  Forgive us if we smile a little, please,
You can call us little heroes, and tell us what you've done,
  But we did have huts to live in – overseas.

19 September 1945

NORMAN MAXWELL DUNN

(Australia) *First officer commissioned under Empire Air Training Scheme. 258 Hurricane Fighter Squadron, Isle of Man and Kenley. POW Germany, four years. Flight Lieutenant. Chairman Council, Australian Telecommunications Development Association.*

Rest On Your Arms Reversed

The peace for which your comrades lived, you found:
Found all alone while they were seeking wild,
Tearing up hell for peace; true fortune's child,
You stumbled on your prize of secret ground.
Let them advance – you found your silent goal,
Untroubled by your name, your rank, your birth,
Uncalled on countless rolls; for you the Earth;
Uncried the broken prison of your soul.

Now let them cry you got their peace for them,
Let them take post to trumpet what you won;
Let them retire to live your gain undone –
You shall not tire of what dull days condemn.
When war-dreams fade, and fireside colonels fret,
Yours not to weep when humdrum men forget.

Berlin, Winter 1945

JOHN BUXTON HILTON

Beds & Herts and Royal Norfolk, 1941–2. Royal Artillery 1943 (Gunner). 1 Corps, 1943–6 (Sergeant – despatches).

Italy to Austria

We knew that peace had come
When driving down the steady tree lined road –
No traffic jams of tanks and guns
Or silent men on foot.
No long delays
When urgent jeeps would slip between:
No bridges blown,
No signs to say that dust brings shells
Or maddening roughly-worn diversions –
We knew that peace had come
Because the convoys one by one
Clocked by at leisured speed,
And in the fields
The trucks were parked in squares,
Patiently awaiting their return
After the dust and thunder of the years.

ROBIN IVY

Served in Italian campaign. Poet and artist.

Armistice Day

Supposing God refused at last?
    Supposing that He said,
'Your fields of blood shall still be blood
    Your fields of death stay dead!
And this good patient Earth shall cease
    To bring forth your desires
Until you bring for offering – Peace,
    And the smoke of unwatched fires!
Until your knowledge so has grown
    That ye shall know your power,
And marvel at each morning's light
    And wonder at each flower!'

MICHAEL KELLY

Navy 1940–45. Schoolmaster, writer and broadcaster.

Victory

I saw a nation crumble. It was not
The distance-rounded epic that you watched –
Those flashing, clearcut figures, all the hot
Fierce breath of Nemesis! No – it was blotched,
Mottled and blurred, pathetically streaked
With human frailty; worlds away from you,
And Destinies, and Rights, and Wrongs, there creaked
Unending trails of waggons, stumbling through
The rain, the snow – I caught the leaden gaze
Of passing eyes turned inward, back, to homes
Shattered forever . . .

                After many days
That hour will rest in History's bland tomes;
    When you will read, and reading seem to know –
    But not those eyes, but not those eyes, that snow. . . .

Silesia, January 1945

PETER ROBERTS

*Navigator, 10 Squadron. Bomber Command, Leeming. April 1942 shot
down at Trondheim during attack on* Tirpitz. *1942–45 Stalag Luft 3,
Silesia. 1945–46 Air Ministry.*

The Going Rate

Hardened soldiers eyed a struggling figure,
Thin, unkempt, ill clad against the cold,
Propelling a battered old pram,
Bumping, swaying, over the cobbled road,
Laden with pathetic bundles from a shattered home.
Ribald comment hid their pity,
Low teasing whistles brought a smile
To her strained young face.
'Old' Bob, thought of a daughter safe and sound,
'Young' Fred, a girlish wife,
Tom, a sister far away.

Others reacted to the smile in hope,
Would she?
Would she trade, for chocolate, or soap?

R.W. TUCK

*Sapper – Royal Engineers; Guards Armoured Division, North-West
Europe; 3rd Infantry Division, Egypt, Palestine.*

The Victors

They had talked of nothing else
but the fishing to be had.
At the Turn–Off for Bayreuth,
our Jeep stopped and we stood down
on rubbery legs, grateful for the lift.
We gave them the fish that bomb–happy
Major had taken out the Naab with dynamite.

Belting seven bells out the road to Prague,
Red Ball expresses hurtled towards us,
beflouring all with dust.
          The day advanced our drought.
Max indicated where a neat farmhouse lay back
off the road, '*Hier mann trinkt wasser, bitte*?'[1]
Suspicious, the old farmer motioned us to wait
in large room while his frau brought us milk.
This, the scene of many family feasts and jollity –
now austere as workhouse . . . or a shrine, perhaps.
As we drank, smiling faces of the young watched,
each from simple black frame: '*Geffalen für der Führer*'[2]
all around, all gone those past years of madness.
No children scampered before us, as we left
sadly musing, disconcerted victors, tails between legs.

1 'Can we have some water, please?' (German)
2 'Died for the Fuhrer.' (German)

*The Red Ball Express was a convoy of non-stop lorries bringing petrol, ammunition
and rations to Patton's 3rd Army, halted on its drive to Prague. This we saw on the
military road. It gave me the chance to swap my Luger for 'K' rations (a pre-packed*

carton of food for an American front line soldier, containing instant coffee, a candy bar
and two cigarettes to last the day) to march on. You can't eat a pistol.

VICTOR WEST

Lance Corporal 1st Rangers KRRC, Greece and Crete 1941. POW 4
years, escaped off-line march, 17 April 1945; in débâcle of 3rd Reich took
control of German village, Brunn, Bavaria.

War Graves

White galaxies of war graves chalk the way
From Flanders southwards to the Libyan coast.
Quiet neighbours dwell in the disputed clay
And none of them now cares who won or lost.
Young men who killed each other in the sky
Share narrow churchyards under English yews.
No rhetoric can reach them where they lie,
No commentaries appended to the news.
Yet why should I declare them innocent
And lay the blame upon authority
With eulogies of general extent
Slyly contrived to cover you and me?
We are all guilty. Only, don't forget
That they have paid and we have not – not yet.

JOHN WARRY

Intelligence Corps and Army Educational Corps.

August 10th, 1945 – The Day After

Who will be next to break this terrible silence,
While the doom of war still shivers over these
Unwilling either to die or to be defeated, –
In the agony of death still torn, contorted,
Torn between saving face and body, both
Mutilated almost beyond recognition?

August 10th, 1945 – The Day After[1]

Who will be next to break this terrible silence,
While the doom of war still shivers over these
Unwilling either to die or to be defeated, –
In the agony of death still torn, contorted,
Torn between saving face and body, both
Mutilated almost beyond recognition?
The face fights on long after
The body's overwhelmed and hacked to pieces.
Every scar of it's their fault; yet I am dumb;
In the blind eyes of pity the good and the evil
Are equals when they're gasping in the sand,
Helpless. The reality so blinds
Our senses that it seems less than a dream,
Yet we shall live to say 'Twice in a lifetime
We saw such nakedness that shame
Itself could not look on, and of all the feelings,
Hate, anger, justice, vengeance, violence, –
Horror alone remained, its organ voice
Searching us with a sickening clarity.'
And now the word comes in of those two cities
With all their living burden
Blown to the wind by power
Unused except by God at the creation, –
Atomised in the flash of an eye.
Who else but God or the instrument of God
Has power to pass such sentence?
Here the road forks, to survival or extinction,
And I hold my tongue through the awful silence,
For if God had nothing to do with it,
Extinction is the least price man can pay.

1 Written 10 August 1945, the day after Nagasaki, which followed Hiro-
shima, before the war ended. First published in *Equator*, magazine of the
Mombassa Arts Club, December 1945.

EDWARD LOWBURY

Served RAMC 1943–7. Pathologist, Professor at Aston University.

Polliciti Meliora

As one who, gazing at a vista
    Of beauty, sees the clouds close in,
And turns his back in sorrow, hearing
    The thunderclouds begin,

So we, whose life was all before us,
    Our hearts with sunlight filled,
Left in the hills our books and flowers,
    Descended, and were killed.

Write on the stones no words of sadness –
    Only the gladness due,
That we, who asked the most of living,
    Knew how to give it too.

FRANK THOMPSON

Volunteered although under-age. Commissioned Royal Artillery 1940. GHQ liaison regiment, Libya, Persia, Iran and Sicilian landings. Dropped in Yugoslavia; ambushed in May 1944 with a group of Bulgarian partisans near Sofia. Notwithstanding wearing the King's uniform, treated as a rebel. 'Tried' at Litakovo defending himself in fluent Bulgarian condemning Fascism. Shot 10 June 1944. Had working knowledge of nine European languages. Poetry compares with the best of the First World War.

The flags stayed furled in '39. Men – and women – went to war; no fuss, no bands. Hitler had to be stopped.

It took nearly six years for the flags to fly. VE Day 8 May 1945. Hitler was now dead, the Nazi army beaten. But for us the flags waved not in triumph but relief. The killing had stopped. The destruction of cities ended. The lights turned on. But most of Europe was refugees and rubble. Our poems do not speak of glory, they tell of compassion and pity for the dead.

John Warry says it in 'War Graves'

> Quiet neighbours dwell in the disputed clay
> And none of them now cares who won or lost.
> Young men who killed each other in the sky
> Share narrow Churchyards under English yews.

Cheering can be left to Hollywood.

After the years of war we present its balance sheet. It adds up to millions – millions of people, many taking no part at all except to get killed. No one asked them.

Soviet Union	7,500,000–10,000,000 military deaths plus 10–12,000,000 estimated civilians 14,000,000 wounded
Germany	2,850,000 killed 7,300,000 wounded
Japan	1,510,000 killed 500,000 wounded
China	650,000 killed 1,800,000 wounded
Britain[1]	326,000 killed plus 62,000 civilians 480,000 wounded

1 Of the British killed 112,478 were in the Royal Air Force, including an estimated 80,000 front-line aircrew, Bomber Command & Fighter Command.

USA   293,000 killed
        590,000 wounded

France 211,000 killed
        400,000 wounded

Italy   78,000 killed
        120,000 wounded

Australia 29,437 killed
           23,214 wounded

India   24,338 killed
        64,354 wounded

New Zealand 11,625 killed
             15,749 wounded

South Africa 12,080 killed
              14,363 wounded

Canada 39,319 killed and missing
        53,174 wounded
        9,045 prisoners of war

Merchant Navy killed 30,248
               missing 4,654
               wounded 4,707
               prisoners of war 5,720

The following are estimates:

Yugoslavia 305,000 killed
            425,000 wounded

Poland (military) 320,000 killed
                   530,000 wounded
                   Poland also suffered 6,028,000 civilians killed.
                   This figure includes 3,200,000 Jews (most of
                   whom are incorporated in the figure of
                   6,000,000 Nazi concentration camp Jewish
                   victims).

                                                    V. S.

Acknowledgments

The Salamander Oasis Trust gratefully acknowledges the voluntary help of its Advisers FM Lord Carver and General Sir John Hackett, who have written an Historical Review of the War and a Foreword, together with the editorial contributions from Martin Jarvis and Spike Milligan. So many thanks to Denis Healey, both for his editorial material and for guidance from his book *My Secret Planet* and reproduction of poems in his chapter on War Poetry.

Our thanks to Robin Ivy for the tedious work of reading past anthologies and other volumes of Second World War poetry and for advice from Jon Stallworthy and Clifford Simmons.

Thanks, too, to the staff of the Imperial War Museum, Roderick Suddaby, Nigel Steele and Mike Moody.

The Trust is also deeply indebted to Christopher Frere-Smith for his legal advice over the years in the difficult area of copyright and contracts and general advice on the workings of a Trust operating too often with limited resources.

From our army of helpers, our gratitude to Simon Gough, Geraldine Scott, Tamara Soom, James Young, proofreader and Mark Thomas at London Law, handler of our mail.

Overseas, we acknowledge the help of the Canadian Authors' Association and Poetry Australia.

The Trust acknowledges the extensive coverage given by the BBC to its activities over the years: BBC Radio Four, Michael Green, 'Not for Glory' programme, Harry Schneider and Erik de Mauny; BBC Radio Two, John Dunn; BBC Overseas; BBC TV, 'War Poets of '39'; Peter Lee-Wright. Also coverage by *Today* and *World Tonight* programmes and local radio. We thank also *The Times*, the *Daily Telegraph* and the *Legion* and its editor Bill Kingdom.

In South Africa, the Trust thanks our colleagues Dr Denis Saunders, Professor Guy Butler and Mrs Hannah Botha, University of Stellenbosch, for help on the Uys Krige manuscripts.

We are also indebted to Wing Commander Derek Martin OBE for his research into RAF casualties.

We especially thank the Trust's benefactors: Dulverton Trust; The Esmée Fairbairn Charitable Trust; Paul Getty Jnr, KBE.

Finally, with so many parts of this anthology having to travel between editor and publisher, this would not have been possible without the help, photocopying and fax services of Stuart and Christina Poulter.

Acknowledgments of Poems

The poems published in previous anthologies had their author's permission to reprint acknowledged at the time. For this collection, aside from seeking permissions for poems not previously included, we have contacted again those agents/publishers still operating whose permission we sought in the past. In the process of selection we have also contacted poets who have given permission directly.

The following comprehensive list indicates where permissions have been given by an agent/publisher. Otherwise it is the poet's own permission – or that of his or her family or executor.

We have endeavoured to contact all poets or their agents/publishers. It will be appreciated that after so many years this has not always proved possible, and we regret any omission.

Collins Angus & Robertson, Australia, for permission to reprint 'Beach Burial' by KENNETH SLESSOR; Octopus Publishing Group Library for ROY FULLER, 'Royal Naval Air Station' and 'The End of a Leave'; The Rt. Hon. A. Jessel for 'When He is Flying' and 'Fleet Fighter' by OLIVIA FITZROY; JOCELYN BROOK 'Landscape Near Tobruk' permission from A.M. HEATH; 'Snapshot of Nairobi' and 'Heartbreak Camp' by ROY CAMPBELL permission from AD DONKER (PTY) LTD, SOUTH AFRICA; JOHN PUDNEY 'Landscape: Western Desert', 'For Johnny', 'Air Gunner', 'Security' and 'Combat Report', DAVID HIGHAM ASSOCIATES; ALUN LEWIS 'Autumn 1939', 'All Day It Has Rained', 'The Jungle' (Extract) and 'The Journey', GEORGE ALLEN AND UNWIN; HENRY REED 'Naming of Parts', JONATHAN CAPE LTD; TERENCE TILLER 'Lecturing To Troops', CHATTO & WINDUS; QUENTIN HOGG 'Night Patrol', HODDER & STOUGHTON; VERNON SCANNELL 'Walking Wounded' and 'War Song', ROBSON BOOKS; JOHN WALLER 'The Ghosts', A.M. HEATH; DEORSA CAIMBEUL HAY (GEORGE CAMPBELL HAY) 'Bisearta', PROFESSOR DERICK THOMPSON, UNIVERSITY OF GLASGOW; RICHARD SPENDER 'The Officer Cadet' and 'Weekend Leave' (Extract); DAVID BOURNE 'Parachute Descent', THE BODLEY HEAD; R.N. CURREY 'Unseen Fire', LONGMAN; DRUMMOND ALLISON 'Verity', THE WHITE KNIGHTS PRESS; FRANK THOMPSON 'Days Journey', 'Hospital' 'To F.D.S.S.M.', 'Requiescat in Pace' and 'Polliciti Meliora', E.P. THOMPSON; ROBERT GARIOCH 'Kriegy Ballad' and 'Prisoners Dreams', SOUTHSIDE; MARTIN BELL 'Reason for Refusal', PETER

PORTER; Uys Krige's English translation of his poem 'Hospital Ship' is by kind permission of Eulalie Krige, his daughter, now Mrs Glanville, who gave permission for the other poems by her father in this anthology; MICHAEL KELLY 'Armistice Day', Scarthin Books; R.H. ELLIS 'Poems', 'Enlisting', The Weybrook Press; HERBERT CORBY 'Armanent Instructor', Editions Poetry London; KEITH DOUGLAS 'How To Kill', 'I Think I Am Becoming A God', 'Elegy For An 88 Gunner' and 'On A Return From Egypt', Editions Poetry, London. SIDNEY KEYES 'War Poet' and 'Advice For A Journey', Routledge; F.T. PRINCE 'Soldiers Bathing', Anvil Press and Menard Press; ALAN WHITE 'Overseas' and 'Monastery Hill (Cassino)', Fortune Press; JOHN MANIFOLD 'The Defensive Position', 'The Tomb Of Lt. John Learmouth A.I.F', 'The Deserter' and 'Defensive Position', Dennis Dobson (Australia); DENNIS MACKARNESS 'In Memoriam', Candy MacKarness; BERNARD GUTTERIDGE 'Mandalay', 'Maymyo', 'Sniper', 'The Enemy Dead', 'Namnkwin Pul', 'Myitson The Sentry' and 'Namsaw The C.O', Routledge (Family); PATIENCE WHEATLEY 'Addison Road', 'Convoy', 'Recruit', Goose Lane Editions; DESMOND HAWKINS, Night Raid.

The permission to reprint other poems has been listed in previous Trust anthologies.

Index